Managing Terrorism and Insurgency

This book examines how governments can weaken the regenerative capabilities of terrorist and insurgent groups.

The exploration of this question takes the form of a two-tier examination of three insurgent actors whose capacity to regenerate weakened in the past: the *Front de libération du Québec* (FLQ) of Canada, the *Movimiento de Liberación Nacional – Tupamaros* (MLN-T) of Uruguay, and the Provisional Irish Republican Army (PIRA) of Northern Ireland during the mid-1970s.

At the first level of its examination, the book investigates the extent to which the regenerative capacities of the FLQ, MLN-T, and PIRA weakened because of an increase in attrition and a decrease in recruitment. The primary objectives of this analysis are to uncover whether a declining intake of recruits played a lesser, equal, or greater role than a burgeoning loss of personnel in weakening the capacities to regenerate of the three insurgent actors; and, in turn, to shed greater light on the broader validity of the prevailing view in conflict studies that a decrease in recruitment is more important than an increase in attrition in effecting the corrosion of an insurgent actor's capacity to regenerate.

At the second level of its exploration, the book assesses the effectiveness of five of the most prominent policy prescriptions in the literature and insurgent recruitment and attrition: ameliorating grievances, selective repression, discrediting insurgent ideology, improving intelligence collection, and restricting civil liberties.

This book will be of much interest to students of terrorism and counterterrorism, conflict studies, strategic studies and security studies in general.

Cameron I. Crouch is currently an Analyst at Allen Consulting Group, an Australian economics and public policy consulting firm. He has a PhD from the Strategic and Defence Studies Centre at The Australian National University.

Contemporary terrorism studies

Managing Terrorism and Insurgency

Regeneration, recruitment and attrition

Cameron I. Crouch

Routledge
Taylor & Francis Group

LONDON AND NEW YORK

First published 2010
by Routledge
2 Park Square, Milton Park, Abingdon, Oxon OX14 4RN

Simultaneously published in the USA and Canada
by Routledge
711 Third Ave, New York, NY 10017

Routledge is an imprint of the Taylor & Francis Group, an informa business

First issued in paperback 2012

© 2010 Cameron I. Crouch

Typeset in Times by Wearset Ltd, Boldon, Tyne and Wear

British Library Cataloguing in Publication Data
A catalogue record for this book is available from the British Library

Library of Congress Cataloging in Publication Data
Crouch, Cameron I.
Managing terrorism and insurgency: regeneration, recruitment, and
attrition/Cameron I. Crouch.
p. cm.
Includes bibliographical references.
1. Terrorism. 2. Terrorism–Prevention. I. Title.
HV6431.C77 2009
363.325–dc22

2009008510

ISBN13: 978-0-415-48441-1 (hbk)
ISBN13: 978-0-203-87158-4 (ebk)
ISBN13: 978-0-415-62227-1 (pbk)

To Rebecca

Contents

Illustrations

Figures

Tables

Acknowledgements

I would like to thank:

The Australian Department of Defence for providing the funding for my PhD scholarship. I would also like to pass on my respects to the family of Sir Arthur Tange; after whom my scholarship is named and honoured.

Professor Richard English, Laurence McKeown, and Danny Morrison for taking the time to meet and share their wisdom with me.

Professor Astrid Arraras and David Cámpora for granting me access to their research and wealth of primary information, respectively. Without their invaluable assistance, my understanding of the Tupamaros would never have extended beyond the superficial.

Dr Brendan Taylor, for his advice, interaction, and friendship.

Dr Robert Ayson, Professor William Tow, and Professor Hugh White, for their support, wealth of knowledge, and constructive comments.

My parents, Rolfe and Mary Crouch, for supporting me throughout my time at both school and university, and, most importantly, instilling in me a sense of responsibility, an ethic for hard work, and an appreciation for logic. Without these essential skills, I would have never been able to persist with my studies, nor be able to continue striving as new opportunities emerge.

My beautiful, exceptional, and ever-considerate girlfriend, Dr Rebecca Taylor, for putting up with my foibles, acting as a source of constant wisdom, and enriching my life.

Abbreviations

AFP	Australian Federal Police
ALQ	*Armée de libération du Québec* (Liberation Army of Quebec)
ASUs	Active Service Units
CAT	*Comandos de Apoyo Tupamaro* (Tupamaro Support Commands)
CATS	Combined Anti-Terrorist Squad
CDP	*Caisse de dépôts et de placements du Québec*
CECM	*la Commission des Écoles Catholiques de Montréal* (Catholic School Mission of Montreal)
DHAC	Derry Housing Action Committee
ETA	Euskadi Ta Askatasuna
FA	*Frente Amplio* (Broad Front)
FAU	*Federación Anarquista del Uruguay* (Anarchist Federation of Uruguay)
FFAA	*Fuerzas Armadas* (Armed Forces of Uruguay)
FISA	Foreign Intelligence Security Act
FLN	*Front de Libération nationale* (National Liberation Front)
FLQ	*Front de libération du Québec* (Quebec Liberation Front)
GHQ	General Headquarters Staff
GDP	Gross Domestic Product
IRA	Irish Republican Army
JI	Jemaah Islamiah
LES	*Ley de Seguridad del Estado y el Orden Interno* (Law of the Security of the State and Internal Order)
M-26	*Movimiento 26 de Julio* (26 July Movement)
MAC	*Movimiento de Ayuda al Campesino* (Movement to Help the Farmers)
MACV	Military Assistance Command, Vietnam
MIR	*Movimiento de Izquierda Revolucionaria* (Movement of the Revolutionary Left)
MLN-T	*Movimiento de Liberación Nacional – Tupamaros* (National Liberation Movement – Tupamaros)
MPM	*Movimiento Peronista Montonero* (Montonero Peronist Movement)
MPS	*Medidas Prontas de Seguridad* (Prompt Security Measures)
MRF	Mobile (or Military) Reconnaissance Force

MRLA	Malayan Races' Liberation Army
NICRA	Northern Ireland Civil Rights Association
NIO	Northern Ireland Office
NSA	National Security Agency
OC	Officer In Command
OIRA	Official Irish Republican Army
PBUH	An Islamic term meaning Peace Be Unto Him
PIRA	Provisional Irish Republican Army
PN	*Policía Nacional* (National Police – Uruguay)
PQ	*Parti Québécois*
PSF	Professional Sinn Féin
RAF	*Rote Armee Fraktion* (Red Army Faction)
RCMP	Royal Canadian Mounted Police
RIR	Royal Irish Regiment
RIRA	Real Irish Republican Army
RQ	*Résistance du Québec*
RR	*Reseau de résistance*
RUC	Royal Ulster Constabulary
SAS	Special Air Service
SERPAJ	*Servicio Paz y Justicia* (Peace and Justice Service)
SSNI	Secretary of State for Northern Ireland
UDR	Ulster Defence Regiment
UQAM	*L'Université du Québec à Montréal*
USAID	United States Agency for International Development
USC	Ulster Special Constabulary
UWC	Ulster Workers' Council
WMA	War Measures Act

1 Introduction

> If there were no regeneration there could be no life. If everything regenerated
> there would be no death. All organisms exist between these two extremes.[1]

On 16 October 2003, just over two years after the devastating attacks against the
World Trade Centre and the Pentagon, Donald Rumsfeld, then Secretary of
Defence of the Bush Administration, penned a memo to four of his top aides.[2]
The subject of this missive was the United States' progress in the 'global war on
terror'. Not surprisingly, given the sieve-like nature of Washingtonian politics,
Rumsfeld's memo soon found its way into the hands of the press. What was surprising, however, was the tone of Rumsfeld's musings – candid and introspec-
tive, in contrast with the Secretary's (and broader Administration's) generally
upbeat diagnosis of the fight against jihadist violence.[3] Indeed, where only a
month earlier Rumsfeld had assured United States Air Force personnel that the
'war on terror' was a 'war we're going to win';[4] he was now asking his key lieutenants: 'Are we winning or losing the Global War on Terror?'[5]

The most notable aspect of Rumsfeld's memo, however, was not its candour;
but rather, how the Defence Secretary conceptualised 'success'. To Rumsfeld,
the United States' relative position in the global war on terror was a function of
the ability of al-Qaeda and like-minded entities to replace arrested or killed personnel with new recruits – what in biological terms would be described as their
capacity to regenerate. From this perspective, the United States is winning the
war on terror if the regenerative capacity of violent jihadist actors is weak or
non-existent. Or, in Rumsfeld's words, if 'we are capturing, killing or deterring
and dissuading more terrorists every day than the madrassas and radical clerics
are recruiting, training and deploying against us'.[6] Conversely, the United States
is losing the war on terror if the jihadists are able to attract enough new recruits
to offset their losses, if not expand their membership base.

While the Defence Secretary was relatively clear about how the United States
could determine whether it was winning or losing the global war on terror, he
was less so regarding how the United States could actually engender success.
That is, what actions the United States Government needs to take in order to
influence and ultimately weaken the regenerative capacities of such insurgent

actors as al-Qaeda and Jemaah Islamiah. For the most part, Rumsfeld's concep-
tualisation of this issue was lacking; consisting primarily of vague questions to
his associates about what they thought should be done (e.g. 'Does the US need
to fashion a broad, integrated plan to stop the next generation of terrorists? ...
Do we need a new organization? How do we stop those who are financing the
radical madrassa schools?').[7]

Though a significant period of time has since passed and administrations have
changed, it still appears that the question of how to weaken the regenerative
capacities of the various jihadi groups is one Washington has yet to adequately
answer. As the United States intelligence community acknowledged in April
2006, although 'United States-led counterterrorism efforts have seriously
damaged the leadership of al-Qa'ida and disrupted its operations ... activists
identifying themselves as jihadists ... are increasing in both numbers and geographic dispersion'.[8] Similarly, a National Intelligence Estimate on the 'terrorist
threat to the US homeland' released in July 2007 determined that al-Qaeda 'has
protected or regenerated key elements of its Homeland attack capability, including: a safehaven in the Pakistan Federally Administered Tribal Areas, operational lieutenants, and its top leadership'.[9] Numerous scholars and security
commentators have reached a similar conclusion. For instance, Benjamin and
Simon state in their 2006 book, *The Next Attack*: 'It is no longer possible to
maintain that the United States is winning the War on Terror. The number of terrorists is growing, as is the pool of people who may be moved to violence.'[10]

This book is an attempt to provide scholars and officials with a greater understanding of how governments can favourably affect the regenerative capacities
of such groups as al-Qaeda, Jemaah Islamiah, and Lashkar-e-Taiba. It seeks to
achieve this goal by investigating more broadly the regenerative dynamics of
insurgent actors – the term this book uses to denote non-state entities (like the
aforementioned groups) that engage in politically-motivated violence.

Specifically, this book will explore the question: *why do the regenerative
capacities of insurgent actors weaken?* Before it can outline how it will conduct
this exploration, this book must first undertake three key tasks. Namely: (1) providing more information about the unit of analysis, insurgent actors; (2) locating
and defining *regeneration* as it applies to insurgent actors; and (3) explaining
how this book will determine the strength of an insurgent actor's capacity to
regenerate.

Insurgent actors

This book defines *insurgent actors* as any non-state entity that seeks to transform
the political status quo through the use, and the threat of use, of violence. Two
determinants of this definition require further clarification. First, the *political
status quo* refers to the prevailing structures of governance (such as socio-
economic systems, sovereignty, and trade regulations) that determine the distribution of resources (both within and between nation-states). Second, in

accordance with Bäck's writings on the subject, *violence* denotes acts of aggression (both attempted and successful), which are undertaken with the intention of causing harm (pain or injury) to another human being.[11] It is important to note that, although this book devised the term insurgent actor, it based the above definition of the concept on a wide consensus about what characterises the 'nonruling group' of an 'insurgency'.[12]

Prominent examples of insurgent actors (both historical and current) include: the *Hukbalahap* of the Philippines, *Euskadi Ta Askatasuna* (ETA) of Spain, *Sendero Luminoso* ('Shining Path') of Peru, Hezbollah of Lebanon, and Jemaah Islamiah of Indonesia. As these examples imply, insurgent actors can: (1) assume varying organisational types (ranging from the hierarchical pyramid-structure of the Italian *Brigate Rosse*, to the more nebulous and informal connections of al-Qaeda);[13] (2) operate mono-nationally (i.e. primarily limited to a particular nation-state, such as the Liberation Tigers of Tamil Eelam of Sri Lanka) or transnationally (like the Armenian Secret Army for the Liberation of Armenia, which conducted numerous attacks across Europe and the Middle East); and (3) be motivated by differing ideologies (such as the revolutionary socialism of the Greek *Epanastatiki Organosi 17 Noemvri*, the Kurdish nationalism of the *Partiya Karkerên Kurdistan*, and the Salafism of the Algerian *Groupe Salafiste pour la Prédication et le Combat*).

Groups like the Loyalist paramilitaries in Northern Ireland, the Ku Klux Klan in the United States, and the Argentinean 'death squad', *Alianza Anticomunista Argentina*, are *not* examples of insurgent actors, since they do not seek to reshape the political status quo, but rather, 'to maintain the power of the state ... or to preserve advantages held by particular groups'.[14]

In the broader literature, many commentators label as *terrorist* (or a derivative thereof) the type of group that this book has classified as insurgent actors. This book favours the latter term over the more popular former for two reasons. First, as numerous scholars have highlighted, terrorist is a pejorative term; 'generally applied to one's enemies and opponents, or to those with whom one disagrees and would otherwise prefer to ignore'.[15] Its use thus signifies more the casting of a 'moral judgment', rather than the conveying of a desired impression to facilitate comprehension.[16] Insurgent actor, in contrast, while by no means a value-free term, lacks many of the negative connotations associated with the word terrorist. Second, to paraphrase Weinberg, Pedahzur, and Hirsch-Hoefler, 'terrorist' 'has become an "essentially contested concept", one whose meaning lends itself to endless dispute but no resolution'.[17] Thus, the literature dedicated to the study of conflict would be better served by abandoning the term terrorist and, in its place, concentrate on existing and/or new concepts, such as insurgent actor; the meanings of which will hopefully engender greater acceptance and, in turn, allow for greater comparability between research projects.

Regeneration

While this book developed the designation of insurgent actor, *regeneration* is an established term. A quick perusal of the broader literature soon reveals two general meanings for the expression. The first of these is attitudinal in nature, denoting concepts of rebirth and renewal of one's mental and/or spiritual outlook. Saint Thomas Aquinas provides an example of this use of regeneration when he states: 'Baptism is spiritual regeneration; inasmuch as a man dies to old life, and begins to lead the new life.'[18] The second meaning, meanwhile, is physiological in nature, referring to the 'process by which organisms reconstitute lost parts of the body'.[19] Goss wrote his famous observation that opened this chapter in the context of this second notion of regeneration.

In both policy and academic discussions, both these meanings of regeneration are evident. Abuza, for instance, employs regeneration in the term's attitudinal sense to describe the Abu Sayyaf Group's recent transformation from what was essentially a criminal gang to a 'terrorist organisation' with deep links to al-Qaeda and Jemaah Islamiah.[20] However, the majority of authors who discuss regeneration in the context of insurgent actors do so in accordance with the term's physiological meaning. From this perspective, insurgent actors are 'organisms', and their 'parts of the body' (which are lost and replaced) are individual members. For example, the Foreign Affairs Committee of the British House of Commons stated in 2003 that:

> We welcome the capture of a number of senior al Qaeda figures.... We nonetheless conclude that those that remain at large ... retain the capacity to lead and guide that organisation towards further atrocities. We further conclude that al Qaeda has dangerously large numbers of 'foot soldiers', and has demonstrated an alarming capacity to regenerate itself.[21]

Likewise, the Australian Government, in its White Paper on Transnational Terrorism, observed that: 'Despite the attrition they have suffered, terrorist networks such as Jemaah Islamiyah are flexible and resourceful. They have a capacity to regenerate.'[22] Lastly, in reference to the ongoing war in Iraq, General (Ret.) John Keane declared that: 'One of the insurgency's strength is its capacity to regenerate.... We have killed thousands of them and detained even more, but they are still able to regenerate. They are still coming at us.'[23]

Given this dominant usage of the term in the literature, this book defines *insurgent regeneration* as the process by which insurgent actors replace lost personnel (i.e. those who have been either killed or arrested) with new recruits. As this definition suggests, regeneration is an interplay between two phenomena: *recruitment* (an insurgent actor's intake of recruits) and *attrition* (an insurgent actor's loss of personnel).[24]

Determining regenerative capacity strength

Given that the goal of regeneration, in both organisms and insurgent actors, is to counteract or repair 'damage', this book will ascertain the strength of an insurgent actor's capacity to regenerate by the extent to which the actor's recruitment offsets its attrition.

Thus, an insurgent actor's regenerative capacity is *strong* if its intake of recruits either exceeds or is relatively equal to its loss of personnel. The German *Rote Armee Fraktion* (RAF) during the early- to mid-1970s is an example of an insurgent actor with a strong capacity to regenerate. In May 1972, two years after the group's formation, the RAF (comprising a 'hardcore' of approximately 30 people)[25] launched its first major offensive; bombing police stations, American military bases, and the offices of the Springer Press. The response of the West German authorities was both instant and fervent; entailing a 'nationwide search operation ... on a scale hitherto unknown in the Federal Republic'.[26] By mid-July, the police had arrested virtually the entire RAF membership. As Pluchinsky states: 'The RAF, as a terrorist gang, ceased to exist.'[27] Despite outward appearances, however, the group's heart continued to beat. Under the direction of the RAF's imprisoned leadership, a 'second generation' emerged; the members of which were primarily drawn from the various political groups that had formed since mid-1972 to protest Bonn's alleged torture of the captive RAF members.[28] By April 1975, the second generation had gained sufficient strength to undertake its first major operation: seizing the West German embassy in Stockholm. Despite losing six of its members in this attack,[29] the RAF continued to attract new recruits; reaching an estimated strength of 30 in 1977.[30] Due largely to this fortification, the RAF was able to embark on its most infamous wave of violence: beginning in April 1977 with the assassination of Siegfried Buback, the Federal Prosecutor-General; and culminating six months later with the dramatic events surrounding the kidnapping and eventual murder of Hanns-Martin Schleyer, a leading Berlin industrialist.[31]

Alternatively, this book deems that an insurgent actor's capacity to regenerate is *weak* if its intake of recruits clearly falls short of its loss of personnel. Accordingly, an insurgent actor's regenerative capacity is *weakening* if the relationship between the insurgent actor's recruitment and attrition shifts from the former exceeding or relatively equalling the latter, to the former clearly falling below the latter. The violent Khalistani movement during the 1990s is an example of an insurgent actor that experienced the weakening of its once-robust capacity to regenerate. Beginning in the late-1970s, India witnessed the emergence of a fluid association of groups – initially led by Jarnail Singh Bhindranwale, an orthodox Sikh preacher – that sought the establishment of 'Khalistan' – an independent Sikh nation-state, primarily encompassing the Indian state of Punjab – through the use of both political and violent means.[32] Though this broad movement was increasingly active during the early-1980s, it was not until 1984 that the Khalistani insurgency began to seriously threaten the Indian Government's authority. The catalysts for this growth in intensity were: (1) the Indian Army's bloody and destructive assault against Sikh militants besieged in the Golden Temple (the holiest site in Sikhism) in June 1984; and (2) the anti-Sikh riots that erupted in Delhi following the assassination of Indira Gandhi, the Prime Minister of India, by two of her Sikh bodyguards four months later. Both of these events triggered an increase in Sikh alienation and boosted support for the violent Khalistani movement.[33] By 1986, Punjab's police force estimated that the insurgency comprised of '300 to 500' 'hardcore' militants, with another '3,000 to 4,000 "on the periphery"'.[34] Over the next five years, the Indian Government sought desperately to curtail the insurgency's rise; arresting an annual average of 2,600 'extremists', and killing 560, from 1986 to 1990.[35] Nevertheless, the violent Khalistani movement was largely able to offset these losses with new recruits. As Wallace notes, official estimates of the movement's strength 'remain[ed] relatively constant' over this period i.e. 300 to 400 'hardcore' militants and approximately 2,000 associated members.[36]

The tipping point for the violent Khalistani movement came in autumn 1991. As a result of a change in political and security force leadership, the Punjabi police' adoption of a highly aggressive (and controversial) counterinsurgency approach (as Singh states, '[m]assacres by terrorists were countered by massacres by the security forces'), and a dramatic increase in the number of security personnel in Punjab, the Khalistani movement's loss of personnel doubled.[37] Concurrently, due to the broader Sikh public's growing distaste for the actions of the militants, and a seeming desire for a return to normalcy, the Khalistani movement's intake of recruits dropped.[38] As a consequence, the movement's capacity to regenerate was severely circumscribed and, in turn, its membership strength plummeted. According to Singh, 'by 1993, most of the leading [Khalistani] military organisations had been smashed'.[39]

Engendering regenerative decay

To scholars and officials searching for guidance about why the regenerative capacities of insurgent actors weaken, the conflict studies literature is both a help and a hindrance.

On the one hand, the existing scholarship is insightful; outlining two contrasting explanations for the phenomenon of regenerative capacity deterioration. The first of these is that an insurgent actor's capacity to regenerate is likely to weaken if its *intake of recruits declines*. This notion formed the basis of the British and Malayan Administration's campaign against the Malayan Races' Liberation Army (MRLA) during the Malayan Emergency (1948–60). Through such measures as resettling Malayan-Chinese peasants into fortified New Villages and increasing developmental assistance, the British and Malayan Administration sought to 'separate' the MRLA (both physically and attitudinally) from its sources of recruits.[40] The second explanation is that an insurgent actor's capacity to regenerate is likely to weaken if its *loss of personnel increases*. This concept underlay the Military Assistance Command, Vietnam's (MACV) 'strategy of attrition' against the Viet Cong during the Vietnam War (1959–75). Relying on the superior firepower and mobility of the American military, the MACV sought to inflict a level of casualties on the Viet Cong that would eventually push the insurgent actor over its 'crossover point' – the point at which the Viet Cong's losses would exceed its ability to replace them.[41]

In providing these explanations, however, the literature raises two new questions; its answers to both of which are problematic.

The first question concerns the relative strength of the contending explanations. From a logical perspective, both an increase in attrition and a decrease in recruitment are valid sources of regenerative capacity deterioration. After all, the strength of an insurgent actor's capacity to regenerate is a reflection of its ability to offset its losses with new recruits. Intuitively, this ability would weaken not only if the insurgent actor's intake of recruits *fell below* its loss of personnel, but also if its loss of personnel *rose above* its intake of recruits. From a practical perspective, however, two questions remain: are an increase in attrition and a decrease in recruitment *equal* sources of regenerative deterioration? Or, is one factor *more important* than the other in bringing about the decay of an insurgent actor's ability to replace its losses with new recruits?

The prevailing response in the literature to these questions is to emphasise a decrease in recruitment, and disregard an increase in attrition, as potential sources of regenerative capacity deterioration. Thompson, for instance, states that, in the absence of disrupting an insurgent actor's intake of recruits, the 'mere killing of insurgents ... is a waste of effort because their subversive organization will continue to spread and all casualties will be made good by new recruits'.[42] In a similar vein, Stubbs maintains that, without a concurrent 'hearts and minds' strategy, a 'coercion and enforcement' approach will be of little utility because 'there will always be recruits ready to take the place of those captured, killed, or injured'.[43] Lastly, Biddle contends that to undercut al-Qaeda's ability to 'replenish [its] depleted ranks' with 'new recruits' requires not offensive measures, but 'action to eliminate the wellsprings of terrorist recruitment'.[44]

This favouring of a decrease in recruitment as the factor more likely to weaken an insurgent actor's capacity to regenerate is both intuitive and a seemingly valid explanation of the regenerative experiences of a number of insurgent actors. For instance, the MRLA gradually lost its ability to replace its casualties with new recruits – with the organisation shrinking from an estimated 6,000 members in 1954 to a 'few hundred' in 1960 – primarily because the British and Malayan Administration was generally successful in separating the insurgent actor from its sources of recruitment.[45] In contrast, the Viet Cong, largely due to its substantial manpower pool[46] and ability to retain 'initiative on the battlefield',[47] managed to withstand the MACV's 'strategy of attrition' and 'keep losses within his capability to replace them'.[48]

Notwithstanding its apparent explanatory power in the above examples, however, the broader validity of the notion that a decrease in recruitment is more important than an increase in attrition in weakening an insurgent actor's capacity to regenerate is questionable. Two observations form the basis of this judgement.

The first observation is that it appears from just a cursory examination of a number of insurgent actors that their regenerative capacities weakened at least equally, if not primarily, because of an increase in attrition. The violent Khalistani movement outlined earlier is a good example of such an insurgent actor. Another is the *Movimiento Peronista Montonero* (MPM) of Argentina. Formed during the late-1960s, this revolutionary group grew to an estimated peak strength of 5,000 members in 1975.[49] However, on 24 March 1976, the Argentinean military overthrew the civilian government and launched an unprecedented campaign against the MPM and its perceived supporters. As Gillespie states, the 'broad sweep of [this] repressive drive', which saw the insurgent actor's casualties increase tenfold,[50] 'helped to prevent Montonero recruitment from matching losses. By the end of 1977, the guerrillas were putting their membership at 40 per cent of the 1975-level.'[51]

The second observation is that there is a prominent belief in the literature that insurgent actors operating predominantly in urban environments have 'historically been more susceptible to repression by an effective state' than primarily 'rural' insurgent actors, like the MRLA and the Viet Cong.[52] Beckett, for instance, after highlighting the 'disastrous outcome of urban action' for such groups as the *Front de Libération nationale* (FLN) during the 'Battle of Algiers' in,[53] the *Acçâo Libertadora Nacional* of Brazil during the 1960s, and the *Ejército Revolucionario del Pueblo* and the MPM of Argentina during the 1970s, concludes that '[u]rban insurgency has not proved very successful where government [have been] prepared to abandon restraint'.[54] Likewise, Laqueur, in his recent history of terrorism, contends that '[u]rban terrorism campaigns have seldom lasted longer than three to four years. Once the security forces have mastered counter techniques, terrorist losses usually become unacceptably high.'[55] If this conviction about the vulnerability of urban insurgent actors to security force pressure is accurate, it suggests that an increase in attrition may play a significant, if not leading, role in explaining the regenerative decay of such groups.

The second question that the existing scholarship raises concerns the issue of how governments can influence the regenerative capacities of insurgent actors. Specifically, if a government has decided to weaken an insurgent actor's capacity to regenerate, what are the best methods the government can adopt to achieve this outcome? The literature is replete with answers to this question; with scholars prescribing a variety of measures as ways in which governments can affect the recruitment or attrition levels of an insurgent actor. Foremost amongst these include the notions, advocated by such authors as Steinberg, Leites and Wolf, and Rosenau, respectively, that the most efficient means for a government to reduce an insurgent actor's intake of recruits is through: (1) the amelioration of the grievances that are motivating people to join the insurgent actor; (2) the employment of sufficient and astute repression; and (3) the discrediting of the ideology on which the insurgent actor's campaign is based.[56] With regard to the perceived best way in which a government can increase an insurgent actor's loss of personnel, possibly the most prominent suggestions include: (1) Paget's contention that '[g]ood intelligence is undoubtedly one of the greatest battle-winning factors in counterinsurgency warfare';[57] and (2) Posner's argument that 'civil liberties … *should* be curtailed' so as to allow governments to deal more efficiently with the likes of al-Qaeda.[58]

However, while some of these prescriptions are both instinctive and appealing, their empirical basis is, for the most part, limited. That is, few scholars have sought to test, for instance, the extent to which 'ameliorating grievances' decreases an insurgent actor's intake of recruits, or whether 'restricting civil liberties' does actually provoke an increase in an insurgent actor's loss of personnel. Of course, this is not to deny that scholars have examined such relationships. Cragin and Chalk, for example, have analysed the impact of social and economic development policies on insurgent recruitment in Israel, Northern Ireland, and the Philippines;[59] while Freeman has investigated the efficacy of emergency powers as an instrument of counterterrorism.[60] These examples notwithstanding, the level of testing of the relationships between the prescriptions outlined above and insurgent recruitment and attrition has generally not been sufficient as a cumulative foundation for either academic understanding or the development of policy.

Objective of this book

From the above discussion, it is clear that there are a number of shortcomings in how academics and officials currently conceive the phenomenon of regenerative decay.

This book will conduct its exploration of why the regenerative capacities of insurgent actors weaken by seeking to address these deficiencies. This attempt at scholarly improvement will take the form of a two-tier examination of the regenerative experiences of three insurgent actors whose capacity to regenerate weakened in the past. Namely, the *Front de libération du Québec* (FLQ) of Canada, the *Movimiento de Liberación Nacional – Tupamaros* (MLN-T) of Uruguay, and the Provisional Irish Republican Army (PIRA) of Northern Ireland.

At the first level, this book will seek to shine greater light on the broader validity of the notion that a decrease in recruitment is more important than an increase in attrition in bringing about the deterioration of an insurgent actor's capacity to regenerate. It will achieve this by examining the extent to which the regenerative capacities of the FLQ, MLN-T, and PIRA weakened because of a decrease in recruitment or an increase in attrition. It is important to note that all of the insurgent actors that will form the basis of this investigation operated predominantly in urban environments. This book deliberately chose its cases to share this characteristic because it appears, from a theoretical perspective, that urban insurgent actors will offer the sternest possible test of the broader validity of the notion in question.

At the second level, this book will endeavour to strengthen the empirical foundations of the literature's understanding of the best ways in which a government can increase an insurgent actor's loss of personnel, or decrease its intake of recruits. It will achieve this by examining the relationships between five of the most prominent prescriptions in the literature (highlighted above and discussed in greater detail in the next chapter) and insurgent recruitment and attrition. Specifically, this book will test: (1) if the regenerative capacities of the FLQ, MLN-T, and PIRA weakened because of a decrease in recruitment, whether this shift was the result of the amelioration of grievances, and/or the use of selective government repression, and/or the discrediting of the insurgent actor's ideology; and (2) if the regenerative capacities of the FLQ, MLN-T, and PIRA weakened because of an increase in attrition, whether this shift was the result of the improvement of the government's intelligence collection capabilities, and/or 'the restriction of civil liberties.

Approach and case selection

This book has adopted Lijphart's comparative method to conduct its two-tier examination. Like the 'two other fundamental strategies of research … the *experimental* and the *statistical* methods', the goal of the comparative method is 'scientific explanation, which consists of two basic elements: (1) the establishment of general empirical relationships among two or more variables, while (2) all other variables are controlled, that is, held constant'.[61] While the experimental and statistical methods attempt to minimise variance of the control variables through the use of 'control groups' and the 'conceptual (mathematical) manipulation of empirically observed data', respectively; the comparative method seeks to produce the same effect through the careful selection of cases.[62] Specifically, by selecting cases that are similar with respect to those characteristics which are the desired control variables.

The first of the three cases that this study will examine is the *Front de libération du Québec* ('Quebec Liberation Front', or FLQ). Active from 1963 to 1972, the FLQ killed five people and committed 212 violent acts; the majority of which were located in the Canadian province of Quebec. Though, in comparison with other prominent insurgent actors around the world, the FLQ was not very lethal; it was, nevertheless, responsible for one of the most notable crises in modern Canadian history. Namely, the 'October Crisis' of 1970, which involved the assassination of the Deputy-Premier of Quebec, the deployment of troops to the streets of Montreal and Quebec City, and the invocation of emergency powers. The October Crisis was also notable because it marked the point at which the FLQ's previously robust capacity to regenerate began to irrevocably weaken; leading to the movement's eventual disappearance two years later.

The second case is the *Movimiento de Liberación Nacional – Tupamaros* ('National Liberation Movement – Tupamaros', or MLN-T). Officially emerging in 1965, the Tupamaros pursued a nine-year campaign against the Uruguayan state. Over this period, the MLN-T killed 37 people and carried out 586 violent acts. Despite Uruguay's relative global anonymity, the MLN-T was an influential insurgent actor; with its 'romantic' exploits inspiring revolutionaries as far away as West Germany, and its eventual downfall heartening governments throughout the Western Hemisphere. The MLN-T's defeat engendered such comfort because, for the first seven years of its campaign, the insurgent actor seemed almost impervious to the Uruguayan Government's countermeasures. From April 1972, however, the Uruguayan armed forces began to strip the Tupamaros of their image of invulnerability. Reeling under the weight of a concerted government onslaught, the MLN-T gradually lost its ability to replace its casualties with new recruits, and ultimately disappeared from the Uruguayan scene.

The third insurgent actor is the Provisional Irish Republican Army (PIRA). From the early-1970s until April 1998, the PIRA waged a brutal 'armed struggle' in pursuit of its goal of a sovereign and united Ireland. During this period, the Provisionals killed 1,706 people and wounded countless others. It is important to note that the entire 28 years of the PIRA's campaign is *not* the focus of this book's investigation. Rather, this book will primarily concentrate on the first ten years of the PIRA's existence (1970–79). This period was one of great significance for the PIRA. It witnessed: the initial dramatic growth of the organisation's membership; a succession of secret talks and cease-fires with the British Government; and the ascendancy of Gerry Adams and Martin McGuiness to the summit of the PIRA's leadership. The 1970s were also significant, from this book's perspective, because it was during this decade that the PIRA's capacity to regenerate weakened (roughly from mid-1972 to 1977) before eventually restabilising. This 'see-sawing' of the PIRA's regenerative capacity will likely provide additional insight into the various factors at the heart of this study.

This book selected the above cases because: (1) the three groups had experienced a prolonged and clear deterioration in their once robust capacity for regeneration; and (2) of all the insurgent actors that met the preceding condition, the FLQ, MLN-T, and PIRA exhibited the most similarities with regard to certain characteristics which this book wanted to hold 'constant'.

The first characteristic is the ideological influences of the FLQ, MLN-T, and PIRA. Generally speaking, all three insurgent actors were motivated by a combination of *nationalism* (defined by Gellner as 'a principle which holds that the political and national unit should be congruent'[63]) and *socialism* (loosely defined as a creed which maintains that a community's socio-economic system should be subject to some form of social control[64]). It is important to note, however, that the three insurgent actors were motivated by nationalism and socialism to differing extents. At one extreme, the PIRA was primarily driven by nationalism. Nonetheless, socialism clearly influenced Republican ideology, and the PIRA increasingly adopted overt socialist policies as its campaign progressed.[65] The FLQ, meanwhile, occupies the middle ground. Whilst the actions of its members were undoubtedly influenced by a nationalist desire to create an independent Quebecois nation-state, the FLQ was also heavily inspired (especially from the mid-1960s onwards) by revolutionary socialist ideals. The MLN-T, lastly, represents the other extreme; with the organisation clearly motivated by socialism. As Porzecanski highlights, however, the Tupamaros also framed their struggle in terms of nationalism; defining the Uruguayan 'nation' as the country's working-class, and seeking to make the Uruguayan political system congruent with this national unit.[66]

The second characteristic is the primary theatre in which the FLQ, MLN-T, and PIRA waged their insurgent campaign. For all three insurgent actors, this was an urban setting. Specifically, Montreal and, to a lesser extent, Quebec City for the FLQ; Montevideo for the MLN-T; and Belfast and Derry for the PIRA.

The third characteristic is the domestic nature of the FLQ, MLN-T, and PIRA's campaigns. Specifically, each of the three insurgent actors fought the vast majority of their 'armed struggles' within the confines of a single nation-state (Canada for the FLQ, Uruguay for the MLN-T, and the United Kingdom for the PIRA), and were almost solely confronted by the security forces of those nation-states (rather than foreign troops, such as the MACV during the Vietnam War).

The final characteristic is the primary political environment in which the FLQ, MLN-T, and PIRA operated. By and large, all three insurgent actors emerged and waged their campaigns in the context of a democracy. According to the *Polity IV Project* (a quantitative data series about political regime characteristics and transitions), from 1970 to 1979, the United Kingdom measured an average score of ten out of a possible ten (signifying a 'strong democracy'); from 1963 to 1972, Canada also measured an average score of ten; and, from 1965 to 1970, Uruguay measured an average score of eight.[67] The only significant deviation was Uruguay from 1971to 1973, with the country receiving a score of 'transition' for the first two of these years, before being classified as an autocracy in 1973.[68]

Unfortunately (and unsurprisingly), the FLQ, MLN-T, and PIRA are not perfect comparative cases. Specifically, they exhibit a number of differences with regard to certain characteristics that, ideally, would be analogous. For instance, the three insurgent actors' overall size varied: ranging from the FLQ's estimated 150–170 members; to the MLN-T's estimated 1,700–1,800 members; to the PIRA's estimated 3,000–3,500 members.[69] Likewise, the three insurgent actors were confronted by security forces with different levels of power; ranging from the significant manpower and resources of the British Army to the relatively-small and less-technologically advanced Uruguayan armed forces. This book maintains, however, that while these differences will limit the strength of its research findings, they are generally not significant enough to prevent the comparison of the FLQ, MLN-T, and PIRA for the purposes of its inquiry.

Layout of the book

The remainder of this book is divided into five chapters. The subsequent of these, Chapter 2, will elaborate on how this book will conduct its two-tier examination.

Specifically, the next chapter will: (1) discuss how this book will determine the relative strength of an increase in attrition and a decrease in recruitment as catalysts of regenerative decay; and (2) outline the five prescriptions highlighted above which form the basis of this book's second level examination.

Chapters 3, 4, and 5, meanwhile, are the heart of this book; focusing on the FLQ, MLN-T, and PIRA, respectively. These chapters will: (1) highlight contextual information relevant to the emergence and persistence of each insurgent actor; (2) detail the regenerative histories of the insurgent actors; and (3) analyse the impact of a burgeoning loss of personnel and a declining intake of recruits on the regenerative capacities of each insurgent actor, as well as the factors responsible for these shifts in attrition and recruitment.

Lastly, Chapter 6 will summarise this book's findings; highlighting patterns and variations, as well as drawing implications for academics, policy-makers, and future research.

2 Concepts, relationships and measurement

The objective of this chapter is to provide greater detail about how this book will conduct its two-tier examination. To this end, this chapter is divided into three sections. The first of these will discuss issues of measurement pertaining to the first level. The second and third sections, meanwhile, will elaborate on the five prescriptions, identified in the previous chapter, which comprise the second level.

Recruitment, attrition, and regenerative decay

As outlined in Chapter One, the first task of this book is to investigate the extent to which the regenerative capacities of the FLQ, MLN-T, and PIRA weakened because of an increase in attrition and a decrease in recruitment. If the prevailing view in the conflict studies literature is correct (i.e. if a declining intake of recruits is more important than a burgeoning loss of personnel in effecting the corrosion of an insurgent actor's capacity to regenerate), then this examination should find that a decrease in recruitment was a greater catalyst of regenerative deterioration than an increase in attrition, across the three cases.

Before this book can undertake this analysis, however, it must first outline how it will determine the relative strength of an increase in attrition and a decrease in recruitment as sources of regenerative decay. This book's approach is twofold. First, it will seek to identify whether the deterioration of the insurgent actor's capacity to regenerate coincided with a declining intake of recruits and/or a burgeoning loss of personnel. If only one of these factors is evident, then this book will deem that it played a greater role in weakening the insurgent actor's capacity to regenerate than the other. However, if both factors are evident, then this book will determine their relative strength by attempting to identify: (1) whether the rates at which the actor's attrition *increased* and recruitment *decreased* were comparable, or whether one factor was more pronounced – more intense – than the other; and/or (2) whether the insurgent actor's declining intake of recruits and burgeoning loss of personnel had a similar impact on the insurgent actor's decision-making process, or did one factor generate greater concern, or trigger a larger response, than the other.

A decrease in recruitment

While the first level examination is focused on the relative strength of an increase in attrition and a decrease in recruitment as catalysts of regenerative decay, the second level seeks to test the validity of the five prescriptions that are prominently highlighted in the conflict studies literature as being the most efficient means for a government to either reduce an insurgent actor's intake of recruits, or increase its loss of personnel. This section will seek to provide greater detail about the three prescriptions which are linked to insurgent recruitment. Namely: (1) *the amelioration of grievances*; (2) the use of *selective government repression*; and (3) *the discrediting of the insurgent actor's ideology*.

Before this section discusses these prescriptions, however, it will first outline the concept of a 'collective action frame'. The reason for introducing this notion is twofold. First, this book is using the collective action frame concept to assist its examination of the amelioration of grievances and the discrediting of the insurgent actor's ideology prescriptions. The extent of this assistance will be discussed in greater detail below. Second, and more generally, the collective action frame concept has significant value as an analytical tool. Its use in reference to the FLQ, MLN-T, and PIRA will enhance this book's understanding of each insurgent actor's recruitment process.

Collective action frames

The concept of a 'collective action frame' originates from the study of social movements, a sub-discipline of sociology. According to Tarrow, *social movements* are 'collective challenges by people with common purposes and solidarity in sustained interaction with elites, opponents, and authorities'.[1]

There are two reasons why a concept borrowed from the social movement literature is applicable to the study of insurgent actors. The first of these is that, given Tarrow's definition, insurgent actors are a subtype (albeit violent and extreme) of social movements. The second reason is one of precedent. Specifically, a number of other scholars have utilised ideas and models from the social movement literature as part of their investigations of various insurgent actors. Della Porta's study of terrorist organisations in Italy and West Germany and White's examination of the PIRA are prominent examples in this regard.[2]

Goffman's seminal work on 'frame analysis' provides the intellectual foundations of the collective action frame concept. According to Goffman, *frames* are 'schemata of interpretation' which help individuals to comprehend the world around them, and to render 'what would otherwise be a meaningless aspect of the scene into something that is meaningful'.[3] As Benford and Snow highlight, collective action frames also serve this interpretive function, 'but in ways that are "intended to mobilize potential adherents and constituents, to garner bystander support, and to demobilize antagonists"'.[4] *Collective action frames* thus play an integral role in the insurgent recruitment process – they are the arguments and ideas that insurgent actors employ in order to convince members of the broader public about the necessity and legitimacy of their activities and campaigns.[5]

According to the broader social movement literature, a collective action frame has three characteristic components. First, it offers a 'diagnosis of some event or aspect of social life as problematic and in need of alteration'.[6] In the majority of cases, especially 'across movements advocating some form of political and/or economic change', the identified problem is a perceived injustice.[7] For instance, Dartnell describes how *Action Directe internationale* sought to attract recruits by focusing on housing issues; in particular, the apparent tendency of property owners to 'let rot perfectly habitable older lodgings' so as to force their early demolition and allow the construction of new, more lucrative, developments.[8] As this example highlights, in addition to identifying a problem, diagnoses also typically attribute blame.[9] Such attribution plays an important role in increasing people's receptiveness to an insurgent actor's collective action frame. As Gamson notes, diagnoses that link a perceived injustice to a vague and abstract agent (e.g. Mother Nature) 'diffuse indignation and make [them] seem foolish'.[10] Conversely, diagnoses which attribute culpability to 'clearly identifiable persons or groups' are more likely to be both believable and generate the necessary 'hot cognition' to motivate participation in collective action.[11]

Second, after identifying what is wrong and who is to blame, a collective action frame will outline 'what needs to be done'.[12] Such a prognosis involves the articulation of both a 'proposed solution' – typically, though not exclusively, the reversal of the identified problem – and a 'strateg[y] for carrying out the plan'.[13] The strategies which insurgent actors promote can vary; ranging from versions of Guevara's *foco* theory (which, in essence, emphasises the transformative power of violence as a means of generating 'revolutionary consciousness');[14] to more classic examples of 'psychological attrition' (which advocates the gradual wearing down of an opponent's 'will to resist' through the application of a constant rate of offensive operations). However, this variance notwithstanding, the strategies of insurgent actors all share an essential ingredient: the use of violence as an instrument of change.

The final component of a collective action frame is a 'call to arms or rationale for engaging in ameliorative or collective action'.[15] In other words, after outlining how an actor has chosen to pursue its proposed solution, a collective action frame will provide justificatory arguments for why such means are right and necessary. In his examination of the United States nuclear disarmament movement, Benford posits that social movements generally frame their justificatory arguments in terms of severity, urgency, efficacy, and propriety.[16] However, according to Gurr and O'Boyle, insurgent actors tend to justify their use of violence by using at least one of two types of basic argument.[17] First of all, *normative* (or deontological) arguments seek to highlight the extent to which the use of violence is morally correct. The Biblical saying 'an eye for an eye' is a simple (yet distressingly widespread) example of this type of justificatory argument.[18] *Utilitarian* (or consequentialist) arguments, meanwhile, seek to highlight how the use of violence is the most effective means of achieving stated goals. An example of a utilitarian argument is the statement by Amrozi bin Nurhasyim (one of the convicted perpetrators of the 2002 Bali Bombing) that '[t]here's no other way than violence to get them [Westerners] out of Indonesia. It's impossible to do by diplomacy'.[19]

Osama bin Laden's 1998 'Declaration of the World Islamic Front for Jihad against the Jews and the Crusaders' provides a good illustration of a contemporary insurgent actor's collective action frame. Bin Laden's central diagnosis is that 'Westerners' (or, more specifically, the United States and Israel) have besieged the Islamic World. He seeks to prove this contention by highlighting 'three inconvertible facts'.[20] First, the United States' seven year occupation of 'the land of the Two Holy Places, the Arabian Peninsula'.[21] Second, the United States' continued aggression against the Iraqi people (in the form of both economic sanctions and military action). And third, Washington's unrelenting support for Israel and its occupation of the al-Aqsa mosque in Jerusalem. In order to redress these grievances, bin Laden calls for the liberation of the 'al-Aqsa mosque and the Holy Mosque [Mecca] from their [America and Israel's] grip', and the expulsion of 'their armies from the lands of Islam, defeated and unable to threaten any Muslim'.[22] Bin Laden's strategy for achieving these goals is relatively simple:

> With God's help, we call upon every Muslim who believes in God and wishes to be rewarded to comply with God's order to kill the Americans and plunder their money wherever and whenever they find it. We also call on the Muslim Ulema, leaders, youths, and soldiers to launch raids on Satan's American troops and Satan's supporters allying with them in order to displace their leaders so that they may learn a lesson.[23]

To justify his call to violence, bin Laden primarily relies on a retributive justice, normative argument. According to bin Laden, Islamic scholars throughout history 'have unanimously agreed that *Jihad* (holy war) is an individual duty if an enemy destroys Muslim countries'.[24] Given that the actions of the Americans and the Jews clearly constitute (in bin Laden's mind, at least) a 'declaration of war on God, his messenger (PBUH), and Muslims', every member of the Islamic faith is thus duty-bound to repulse the enemies who are attacking their religion.[25]

The amelioration of grievances

The focus of the first recruitment-related prescription of interest to this book is grievances. These have long played an explanatory role in the study of insurgent violence. To some authors, such as Conteh-Morgan, Crenshaw, and Ross, grievances are one of the leading structural causes of 'terrorism'.[26] To others, like Johnson, Kitson, and O'Neil, grievances are a driving source of active and passive support for insurgent actors.[27] A number of scholars have sought to specify this latter relationship even further; identifying grievances as a causal factor of insurgent recruitment.

The perceived importance of grievances in this regard is threefold. First, grievances are seen to increase a person's susceptibility to 'insurgent blandishments' about the need for political change and 'corrective' action.[28] Gareth Evans, a former Foreign Minister of Australia, provides a contemporary example of this perspective when he states:

> Where poverty and joblessness do become relevant is in creating a larger class of young men, and increasingly women, insecure to the point of hopelessness about their own futures, who become that much more vulnerable to recruitment – by those who play upon that insecurity, fire up the sense of political grievance endemic throughout the Arab-Islamic world, and, critically, offer a religious justification for jihad: making holy war.[29]

Second, grievances are believed to act as sources of motivation for people to join an insurgent actor. Stern, for instance, describes in her interview with Hassan Salameh, an imprisoned member of Hamas, that while his decision to join the insurgent actor was partly influenced by religious factors, '[t]he most important motivation was the Israeli occupation; he saw Palestinians were oppressed and wanted to take action'.[30] Third, grievances are seen to trigger a psychological chain reaction that increases a person's propensity to engage in insurgent violence. The most notable proponent of this conception is Gurr, who argues that *relative deprivation* (in essence, the perceived gap between what people believe they are entitled to have and what they actually get) generates feelings of frustration; which, in turn, predisposes people towards acting aggressively.[31] It is important to note, however, that despite the theory's popularity, repeated empirical testing has failed to establish more than a weak link between relative deprivation and collective violence.[32]

Given these perceived links between grievances and insurgent participation, a number of authors have suggested that the key to reducing an insurgent actor's intake of recruits is to neutralise or ameliorate the grievances which are facilitating (if not driving) the actor's recruitment. This concept is not only evident in general discussions about insurgent violence: Atran, for example, in his article about 'suicide terrorism', declares that '[t]o attract potential recruits away from jihadist martyrdom ... and to dry up its popular support requires addressing basic grievances before a downward spiral sets in'[33]; but it also forms one of the central planks of perhaps the most well-known strategy of counterinsurgency, the 'hearts-and-minds' approach. Formalised by the British and Malayan Administration during its campaign against the MRLA in the mid-twentieth century,[34] the hearts-and-minds approach contends that, through such programmes as '[i]ncreasing political rights of the people, improving standards of living, and reducing corruption and abuse of government power', a government can undercut both the appeal of an insurgent actor and the perceived need for violent political change.[35]

Previous testing of this perceived relationship between the amelioration of grievances and a decrease in recruitment has been relatively infrequent, though generally supportive. For instance, according to Stubbs, the British and Malayan Administration's hearts-and-minds approach (which included the widespread use of developmental assistance, the introduction of elections, and the provision of greater security) was successful in preventing the MRLA from 'rely[ing] on' rural Chinese-Malayans 'for recruits and supplies'.[36] Likewise, in their comparison of the rise and fall of Quebec and New Left 'terrorism' in Canada and the United States, respectively, Ross and Gurr conclude that, in both cases, terrorist recruitment and the use of terrorism subsided because 'there was movement toward resolution of the issues which had given rise to terrorism'.[37] Specifically, Ross and Gurr highlight the emergence of the *Parti Québécois* (a separatist political party) in Canada, and the 'end of the draft and of American involvement in the Vietnam War' in the United States.[38] Lastly, in their examination of the impact of social and economic development policies on the resurgence of 'terrorism' in Israel, Northern Ireland, and the Philippines, Cragin and Chalk contend that, by providing 'economic alternatives', social and economic development can stem 'the tide of potential recruits' to insurgent actors.[39]

In light of its professed strength in the broader literature, this book will examine the correlation between the amelioration of grievances and a decrease in insurgent recruitment. Specifically, this book will investigate, *if the FLQ, MLN-T, and PIRA's capacity to regenerate weakened because of a decrease in recruitment, whether this shift was the result of the amelioration of grievances.*

However, before this book can conduct this examination, it must first provide greater detail about three key issues. The first of these is the definition of 'grievances'. Somewhat surprisingly, given the widespread use of the term in both the academic and popular literatures, 'grievances' is rarely defined. Klandermans, Roefs, and Olivier provide one of the few exceptions, defining grievances as 'feelings of dissatisfaction with important aspects of life, such as housing, living standards, income, employment, health care, human rights, safety, and education'.[40] While this definition is constructive, this book maintains that it would be easier from an analytical perspective to link 'grievances' more directly to *conditions* which generate feelings of dissatisfaction, rather than concentrate on the feelings themselves. Thus, this book defines *grievances* as conditions – 'both actual and perceived, putative and general' – that generate feelings of dissatisfaction among members of a community.[41]

The second issue is how this book will determine which grievances will form the basis of its investigation. This is an important undertaking, since not all identifiable grievances in a conflict situation between an insurgent actor and a government are likely to motivate or cause people to join the insurgent actor. Thus, in order to ensure the validity of its research findings, this book must develop some method of maximising the likelihood that the grievances it chooses to study will have the strongest possible relationship with the recruitment processes of the FLQ, MLN-T, and PIRA.

This book's solution is to focus on the grievances *publicly emphasised* by the three insurgent actors. Underlying this approach are the assumptions that: (1) as

outlined by the collective action frame concept, insurgent actors highlight particular grievances as a means of attracting new recruits; and (2) since insurgent
actors generally have compelling incentives to ensure that their intake of recruits
remains strong (e.g. so they can offset losses, and/or expand their organisation),
they are likely to highlight grievances which will have the greatest possible
resonance with, and act as the greatest possible motivator for, potential recruits.
This book will identify the publicly emphasised grievances of the FLQ, MLN-T,
and PIRA by using its analysis of their collective action frames.

The third issue is how this book will determine if a grievance was ameliorated. Developing a universal rule in this regard is problematic; given that there
is no fixed 'level of change' that a grievance must undergo for it to be considered
as having been ameliorated. As a consequence, this book will ascertain whether
the publicly emphasised grievances of the FLQ, MLN-T, and PIRA were ameliorated on a case-by-case basis; appealing to the available evidence to support
any conclusions that are made. Important factors that this book will take into
account while reaching such judgments include: the extent to which a particular
grievance disappeared, minimised, or changed in some positive manner; and
whether those members of a community who were dissatisfied with the grievance believed it had been ameliorated.

Selective government repression

The second recruitment-related prescription that this section will outline can
trace its origins to the early-1960s. During this period, the United States'
Kennedy Administration adopted a hearts-and-minds approach to counteract the
burgeoning insurgency in South Vietnam. However, as the decade progressed
and the Viet Cong threat continued to mount, disenchantment with the hearts-
and-minds approach steadily grew.[42] Consequently, a number of scholars began
to develop alternative strategies of counterinsurgency. One of the most prominent of these was the 'cost-benefit' model. Devised by two RAND scholars
(Nathan Leites and Charles Wolf) during the late-1960s, the cost-benefit model
sought to apply 'systems analysis and econometric techniques' to the task of
defeating an insurgent actor.[43]

These influences are arguably most evident with regard to the model's prescriptions about how governments can exert control over an insurgent actor's
recruitment. According to Leites and Wolf, a person's decision to join or not
join an insurgent actor is less a function of 'preferences' (i.e. the person's opinions about the insurgent actors, its ideology, and its goals), and more a reflection
of a rational calculation about which option (joining or not joining) is more
favourable in terms of expected costs and benefits.[44] Thus, a government can
seek to reduce an insurgent actor's intake of recruits by manipulating common
perceptions about the costs and benefits associated with joining the insurgent
actor, to the point where the option of joining the insurgent actor is widely (if
not universally) seen as being less favourable than the option of not joining.[45]

Although the cost-benefit model does allow for the use of rewards (including the amelioration of grievances) to achieve this manipulation of common perceptions, it primarily emphasises the transformative power of government repression. As Leites and Wolf state: 'Unfortunately, the contest between R [the insurgent actor] and A [the government] is often as much a contest in the effective management of coercion as a contest for the hearts and minds of the people.'[46] Leites and Wolf, however, do not claim that a linear relationship exists between repression and a decrease in insurgent recruitment. Rather, they paint a more complex picture; highlighting how a government's use of repression can both deter *and* stimulate an insurgent actor's intake of recruits.[47]

The key question guiding Leites and Wolf's study is not 'whether repression has a deterring or radicalising effect, but which effect is to be expected under what conditions'.[48] Thus, the authors outline a number of 'characteristics of damaging behaviour' that they believe are more likely to deter, rather than provoke, insurgent recruitment.[49] The first of these is whether a government's use of repression is perceived as being selective. According to Leites and Wolf (as well as Mason and Hafez and Wiktorowicz), the fear of repression is more likely to influence a person's decision about joining an insurgent actor if s/he believes that they can avoid the threatened repression by *not* joining the insurgent actor.[50] Indiscriminate repression, on the other hand, undercuts this perception, since aspiring recruits are at risk whether they join the insurgent actor or not. The other characteristics that Leites and Wolf highlight include: 'the degree to which the severity of the sanctions ... is understandable'; the level of protection a government can offer a population from the insurgent actor's use of repression; and the extent to which a government's use of repression is predictable.[51]

The broader literature displays a general scepticism about the utility of using repression as a means of controlling an insurgent actor's intake of recruits. Underlying this scepticism, however, it is possible to discern support for Leites and Wolf's notion that selective repression is likely to have a deterring effect on insurgent recruitment. This support manifests itself not directly, but in terms of a widespread belief that indiscriminate repression is a stimulant of insurgent recruitment. Nevin provides an example of this mindset when he contends that 'violent retaliation' is a counterproductive method of combating terrorism, since it 'adds to the overall sum of human misery for innocent civilians who happen to be in the way of a retaliatory attack, thereby creating potential recruits to the terrorists' cause'.[52] Rosendorff and Sandler likewise state that government operations which 'bomb alleged terrorist assets, hold suspects without charging them, assassinate suspected terrorists, curb civil freedoms, or impose retribution on alleged sponsors may have a downside by creating more grievances in reaction to heavy-handed tactics or unintended collateral damage' – grievances that 'may promote recruitment to the terrorist network'.[53]

Previous testing of the relationship between selective government repression and a decrease in insurgent recruitment is both sparse and contradictory. On the one hand, researchers of the 12-year insurgency in El Salvador (1980–92) contend that the government's widespread and arbitrary use of repression against the *Frente Farabundo Marti para la Liberación Nacional* – during which an estimated 75,000 people were killed – boosted the insurgent actor's recruitment.[54] Conversely, Gillespie argues that the Argentinean military's indiscriminate 'dirty war' against the *Movimiento Peronista Montonero* and its perceived supporters and allies – a campaign which was responsible for the death and 'disappearance' of approximately 9,000 people[55] – suppressed the insurgent actor's recruitment.[56]

As part of the second level of its examination, this book will seek to shed greater light on the relationship between the use of selective repression and an insurgent actor's intake of recruits. It will achieve this by examining, *if the FLQ, MLN-T, and PIRA's capacity to regenerate weakened because of a decrease in recruitment, whether this shift was the result of selective government repression.* According to this book, *repression* is 'any action ... which raises the contender's cost of collective action';[57] *government repression* is any repressive act that is 'observable', 'coercive' (in the sense that it 'involves shows and/or uses of force and other forms of standard police and military action'), and is conducted by 'state agents tightly connected with national political elites';[58] and a government's use of repression is *selective* when it only targets those directly and knowingly related to an insurgent actor.[59] Conversely, a government's use of repression is *indiscriminate* when it 'expands to include supporters, sympathizers, and ordinary citizens suspected of involvement' in the insurgent actor.[60]

Discrediting the insurgent actor's ideology

Like selective government repression, the third recruitment-related prescription of interest to this book can trace its antecedents to the Cold War. During this period, United States' policymakers sought to compliment their assorted military, economic, and diplomatic instruments through the use of what others have variously called 'psychological warfare', 'public diplomacy', and 'a war of ideas', but what this book terms *political warfare*.[61] That is, the engagement of 'carefully targeted sections of foreign publics', through both overt and covert methods of communication, in 'such a manner as to support the accomplishment of national aims and objectives'.[62] Though the United States' use of political warfare during this period was far from perfect, it was nevertheless responsible for a number of foreign policy victories (e.g. helping to prevent a Communist Party victory at the 1948 Italian general election)[63] and, according to the likes of Richmond, significantly contributed to the eventual demise of the Soviet Union.[64]

Indeed, it is largely due to the perceived efficacy of United States' political warfare efforts during the Cold War that a growing band of scholars and officials have called on the United States Government to emulate its predecessors' achievements and vigorously engage in political warfare as part of its 'global war on terror'. According to these observers, the goal of such a political warfare campaign should be twofold. First, the United States should seek to address both its 'serious image problem' and growing anti-Americanism around the world –

particularly in Muslim countries.[65] Second, the United States should endeavour to discredit the jihadi ideology on which al-Qaeda and like-minded entities are based.[66] This latter goal is considered to be of particular importance; largely because there is a widespread belief that reducing the jihadist movement's intake of recruits requires 'a campaign to undermine its ideological appeal'.[67] Rama-krishna provides one of the best examples of this contention when he states that:

> enduring success in the war on terror in the region [Southeast Asia] will not be achieved until and unless the ideological basis of the likes of JI is effect-ively undercut. In other words, only when the global jihadi capacity to regen-erate by attracting recruits and sympathizers to its cause is severely weakened, and more crucially, its cause is regarded by Southeast Asian Muslim com-munities as discredited, can one begin to seriously talk about success.[68]

The key assumption underlying this perspective is that people are motivated to join an insurgent actor less because of material inducements and/or physical compulsion, and more because of their acceptance of the insurgent actor's world view about what needs to be done and the necessity of violence. De-legitimising this world view is thus seen as a necessary measure to undertake if a government wants to exert control over an insurgent actor's recruitment potential.

Few scholars have sought to test directly this perceived link between discred-iting an insurgent actor's ideology and a decrease in insurgent recruitment. Broader investigations, however, reveal indirect support for the relationship. For instance, Rosenau contends that al-Qaeda's recruitment potential in Kenya and Tanzania is weak – despite the presence of such recruitment-friendly conditions as endemic poverty, lawlessness, and sizeable Muslim minorities – because of the stagnant appeal of 'radical Islam' in both countries.[69] Indeed, Rosenau con-tends that 'the extremist Wahabbi ideology that was spreading in Kenya during the 1980s and early 1990s appears to be in decline'.[70]

As part of the second level of its examination, this book will seek to provide greater insight into the relationship between discrediting an insurgent actor's ideology and a decrease in recruitment. Thus, this book will examine, *if the FLQ, MLN-T, and PIRA's capacity to regenerate weakened because of a decrease in recruitment, whether this shift was the result of the discrediting of the insurgent actor's ideology.*

However, before this book can conduct this examination, it must first discuss two key issues. The first of these is how this book will determine what consti-tutes the 'ideology' of an insurgent actor. This is a difficult undertaking, since 'ideology' is, to paraphrase Gerring, a 'semantically promiscuous' concept.[71] As Eagleton states:

> the term 'ideology' has a whole range of useful meanings, not all of which are compatible with each other. To try to compress this wealth of meaning into a single comprehensive definition would thus be unhelpful even if it were possible.[72]

This book seeks to bypass the definitional problems associated with the polysemy of 'ideology' by defining the term in a manner that is intended *not* to cover all or most possible meanings of 'ideology'; but rather, to be simply in accordance with how the term is used by those commentators who prescribe discrediting an insurgent actor's 'ideology' as a means of reducing the actor's intake of recruits.

Such authors tend to emphasise two aspects when discussing the ideologies of insurgent actors. The first of these is the *goal* of the insurgent actor – the desired end-state that the actor is striving to effect into reality. For instance, both Baran and Cohen in their descriptions of al-Qaeda's 'ideological foundations' highlight the movement's objective of establishing 'a modern day Caliphate' across the Muslim world.[73] The second aspect is the *method* of the insurgent actor. Specifically, how the insurgent actor seeks to engender its goals, and, more importantly, why its chosen means are necessary and/or superior to other instruments of change. For example, in discussing al-Qaeda's ideology, Rosenau highlights its 'armed doctrine', which contends that engaging in an unrestrained 'holy war' with the United States and its allies is both a moral obligation for Muslims (given the perceived attempts of Western societies to subjugate Islam) and an effective method of weakening 'apostate' regimes in the Muslim world (such as the monarchy of Saudi Arabia).[74]

Given the general emphasis on these two factors, this book (inspired by Mullins and Seliger) defines *ideology* as a set of ideas by which insurgent actors 'posit, explain, and justify' their goals and methods for 'organized social action'.[75] This book will identify the ideologies of the FLQ, MLN-T, and PIRA by using its analysis of their collective action frames – focusing particularly on the prognoses and justificatory arguments of the three insurgent actors.

The second issue is how this book will determine if an insurgent actor's ideology was discredited. There are few obvious or 'standard' measures in this regard. This book's approach is to focus on popular perceptions about the believability of the insurgent actor's ideology. Specifically, this book will deem that the FLQ, MLN-T, and PIRA's ideologies were discredited if the number of people who approved of the goals and methods which comprised their respective ideologies either noticeably or completely declined. The analysis of data sources such as opinion polls, ethnographies, and historical observations will be used to ascertain whether such shifts in popular perceptions occurred.

An increase in attrition

This section will focus on two prescriptions that are prominently highlighted in the conflict studies literature as being the most efficient means for a government to increase an insurgent actor's loss of personnel. Namely, *the improvement of the government's intelligence collection capabilities*, and *the restriction of civil liberties*.

Improving intelligence collection

Although there are numerous (and fervent) debates in the counter-insurgency and counterterrorism literature about the efficacy of various counterinsurgent measures, there does appear to be a consensus about the 'supreme importance' of enhancing a government's intelligence capabilities as a means of counteracting insurgent threats.[76] To some authors, for instance, a better 'ability to obtain, analyze, and act on information' is crucial, since it allows governments to impede insurgent attacks and, in turn, 'control the psychological dimension of the conflict'.[77] To others, however, the significance of improving a government's intelligence capabilities primarily lies with its likely effect on insurgent attrition. Specifically, the better a government's ability to collect, analyse, and disseminate information about an insurgent actor, the more damage the government will likely be able to inflict on the insurgent actor. Paget alludes to this relationship when he states: 'Good intelligence is undoubtedly one of the greatest battle-winning factors in counterinsurgency warfare'.[78] Thompson, on the other hand, is more explicit:

> Good intelligence leads to more frequent and more rapid contacts. More contacts lead to more kills. These in turn lead to greater confidence in the population, resulting in better intelligence and still more contacts and kills. That, General, is why you should first worry about intelligence.[79]

Underlying this perceived relationship between a government's intelligence capabilities and insurgent attrition is the assumption that the major factor preventing a government from inflicting greater damage on an insurgent actor is its inability to identify and locate members of the insurgent actor. Kitson famously articulated this belief in his seminal work on counterinsurgency, *Low Intensity Operations*: 'If it is accepted that the problem of defeating the enemy consists very largely of finding him, it is easy to recognize the paramount importance of good information.'[80] Byman echoes a similar sentiment when he declares: 'Intelligence is the sine qua non of counterterrorism ... if it [the state] can locate the terrorists, it can usually arrest or kill them.'[81] McCormick, meanwhile, frames the issue in terms of the asymmetry of a government's power. Specifically, '[t]he state ... begins the game with a much greater ability to attack what it sees but a limited ability to see what it wishes to attack'.[82] The primary reason why a government finds it difficult to 'see' an insurgent actor is because the latter, aware of its vulnerabilities in the face of the government's force advantage, deliberately seeks to obscure its presence. It achieves this by: avoiding frontal assaults and static clashes, preferring instead to rely on hit-and-run tactics; foregoing uniforms and other distinguishing features of 'traditional' armies; and operating in environments (such as jungles, mountains, or cities) which provide numerous opportunities for concealment.[83]

Previous testing of this notion that enhancing a government's intelligence capabilities will lead to an increase in an insurgent actor's loss of personnel has been generally supportive. Short, for instance, in his study of the Malayan Emergency, states that the 'most important reason' why the British and Malayan security forces were able to inflict an increasing rate of casualties on the MRLA from 1950 to 1952, and then continue to inflict a significant rate of casualties over the next four years, 'was intelligence. Higher grade information was being received from the public; it was being more efficiently collated; and was therefore used more profitably'.[84] Likewise, such authors as Alexander and Keiger, Horne, and Martin argue that the French Army in Algeria was able to capture and kill an increasing number of *Front de libération nationale* members from 1956 to 1958 because of a series of improvements in its intelligence capabilities.[85] These included: the undertaking of a thorough census of the Algerian population and the issuing of identity cards to all residents; the establishment of a vast network of Muslim-Algerian informants; and the integration of French units amongst Muslim-Algerian communities.

As part of the second level of its examination, this book will seek to subject the relationship between enhancing a government's intelligence capabilities and an increase in insurgent attrition to further empirical scrutiny. However, a 'government's intelligence capabilities' is an expansive – and thus potentially unruly – topic of inquiry. Accordingly, this book will limit its examination to only one component of a 'government's intelligence capabilities'. Specifically, a government's ability to collect information about an insurgent actor. This book has chosen to focus on this component rather than others (such as a government's ability to analyse or disseminate intelligence) because it is the collection of intelligence that most scholars emphasise when they discuss how governments should improve their intelligence capabilities. Thus, this book will examine, *if the FLQ, MLN-T, and PIRA's capacity to regenerate weakened because of an increase in attrition, whether this shift was the result of an improvement in the government's ability to collect intelligence about the insurgent actor.*

The restriction of civil liberties

Following the attacks of 11 September 2001 (and later the bombings of Bali, Madrid, and London) liberal democratic governments around the world have sought to mitigate the terror threat by introducing a range of anti-terrorism laws. Many of these have attracted considerable controversy; primarily due to their curtailment of civil liberties. For instance, since 2002, the Australian Government has: (1) provided the country's Attorney General with the power, largely free of judicial review, to outlaw specific organisations on the basis that s/he believes they pose a threat to national security;[86] (2) authorised the Australian Security Intelligence Organisation to detain people for up to seven days for questioning, even if they are not suspected of, or charged with, any crime;[87] and (3) introduced 'preventative detention' and 'control' orders that allow the Australian Federal Police (AFP) to detain or severely restrict the freedom of individuals who are suspected of possible involvement in a future 'terrorist' offence.[88] Commentators such as Grattan, Harris, and Michaelsen have respectively described these measures as: 'unnecessary' with 'obvious dangers';[89] 'dangerous and disingenuous';[90] and 'ill-conceived' and a 'clear overreaction'.[91]

In the face of such criticism, liberal democratic governments have employed a variety of arguments to justify their 'anti-terrorism' laws. These range from: highlighting the 'exceptional' nature of the jihadist threat (necessitating, of course, 'exceptional measures' to counteract it);[92] to comparing the fight against Salafabist violence to a 'war' (thus requiring 'wartime' sacrifices in individual freedoms).[93] However, perhaps the most common argument liberal democratic governments have used to justify their anti-terrorism laws is 'that they cannot be effective against the threat [of terrorism] unless they sacrifice some of their democratic substance'.[94] Or, to phrase this differently, that a negative relationship exists between the extent of a country's civil liberties and the efficacy of its government's counterterrorism response. John Howard, the former Prime Minister of Australia, implicitly provides an example of this argument where he states that the *Anti-Terrorist Act (No. 2) 2005* (which introduced 'preventative detention' and 'control' orders, and gave the AFP greater powers of stop, search, and arrest) is necessary because it enables the Australian Government 'to better deter, prevent, detect and prosecute acts of terrorism'.[95]

The key assumption underlying this perceived relationship between restricting civil liberties and increasing the efficacy of a government's counterterrorism capability is that 'the very mechanisms that protect the individual from state power … also hamper the state's ability to respond to the [terrorist] threat'.[96] This assumption is evident in the United States' Bush Administration's defence of the National Security Agency's (NSA) domestic surveillance program. This involved the NSA monitoring certain telephone calls of American citizens without obtaining the necessary warrants under the Foreign Intelligence Surveillance Act (FISA). According to the United States President and his top officials, it was necessary for the NSA to circumvent the FISA process because the latter's requirements for legal oversight were too cumbersome ('FISA involves marshalling arguments, FISA involves looping paperwork around') and prevent the United States Government from effectively engaging an agile adversary like al-Qaeda.[97]

Although most scholars tend to exhibit scepticism about the purported benefits to governmental efficiency derived from restricting civil liberties, only a few have sought to subject this relationship to empirical scrutiny. One of these is Hewitt, who analysed the efficacy of emergency powers as a means of reducing terrorism in Cyprus, Italy, Spain, the United Kingdom, and Uruguay. He concluded that, in all cases, there was no 'recognizable pattern whereby violence declines following the introduction of emergency powers. Sometimes violence declines, sometimes it increases, but most times the legislation has no discernible impact'.[98] Adopting an approach similar to that of Hewitt, Freeman investigated the consequences for four democratic states (Canada, Peru, the United Kingdom, and Uruguay) 'of using emergency powers to fight terrorism'.[99] Freeman's conclusions, however, differed from those of Hewitt. Specifically, Freeman argued that emergency powers *can* be effective (in terms of reducing the number and lethality of terrorist attacks), but their effectiveness is dependent on both the 'size of the active terrorist group in relation to its level of support, and the speed with which the security forces capture suspected terrorists'.[100] Specifically, Freeman contends that '[e]mergency powers are most effective when the state moves quickly against a small terrorist group that has weak support'.[101]

As part of the second level of its examination, this book will seek to provide further insight into the relationship between the extent of a country's civil liberties and the efficacy of its government's counterterrorism response. This book will attempt to achieve this by analysing what effect restricting civil liberties has on an insurgent actor's loss of personnel. After all, it stands to reason that, if a relationship does exist between restricting civil liberties and enhancing governmental efficiency, then those governments which do restrict civil liberties should experience an improvement in their ability to arrest and/or kill members of an insurgent actor; increasing, in turn, the insurgent actor's loss of personnel. Thus, this book will investigate, *if the FLQ, MLN-T, and PIRA's capacity to regenerate weakened because of an increase in attrition, whether this shift was the result of restrictions in civil liberties.*

Before this book can undertake this investigation, it must first delineate what constitutes a 'restriction in civil liberties'. According to this book, a *restriction in civil liberties* is the enactment and enforcement of legislation, specifically designed to combat an insurgent actor, which limits existing freedoms (such as freedom of assembly, *habeas corpus*, and freedom from arbitrary search and arrest). In the FLQ case, the primary restrictions in civil liberties were: the *War Measures Act 1914*; the *Public Order Regulations 1970*; and the *Public Order (Temporary Measures) Act 1970*. In the MLN-T case, the primary restrictions in civil liberties were: the Uruguayan Government's repeated invocation of the *Medidas Prontas de Seguridad* ('Prompt Security Measures', or MPS) during the late-1960s and early-1970s; the declaration of an '*estado de guerra internai*' ('state of internal war') in April 1972; and the *Ley de Seguridad del Estado y el Orden Interno* ('Law of the Security of the State and Internal Order') *1972*. In the PIRA case, the primary restrictions in civil liberties were: the reintroduction of internment (under the *Civil Authorities (Special Powers) Act (Northern Ireland) 1922*) in August 1971; the *Northern Ireland (Emergency Provisions) Act 1973*; and the *Prevention of Terrorism (Temporary Provisions) Act 1974*.

Now that this book has expounded the five prescriptions which form the basis of the second level of its examination, it shall turn its focus to conducting its two-tier examination in the context of its three chosen insurgent actors. The first of these to be placed under the spotlight will be the *Front de libération du Québec*, followed by the *Movimiento de Liberación Nacional – Tupamaros*, and, in turn, the Provisional Irish Republican Army.

3   *Front de libération du Québec*

Generally speaking, the *Front de libération du Québec* (FLQ) is not a *sexy* insurgent actor. It lacks the celebrity of the Palestine Liberation Organisation; the demonstrated prowess of the Liberation Tigers of Tamil Eelam; or the sheer brutality of the Algerian *Groupe Islamique Armé*. However, from a regenerative perspective, the FLQ is both an intriguing and noteworthy case. From its inception in 1963 until 1970, the FLQ enjoyed a robust capacity for regeneration. As Gellner states, the movement was able 'to renew itself, to grow new heads, like Hydra, whenever any were chopped off'.[1] Yet, following the 'October Crisis' of 1970, the FLQ gradually lost its ability to replace its arrested, deserted, and killed members with new recruits. The consequences were disastrous for the movement. An insurgent actor that, in mid-1970, seemed to be gaining both in strength and purpose; had instead, by the end of 1972, disappeared from Quebec's political landscape.

The overarching goal of this chapter is to shed greater light on why this deterioration in the FLQ's capacity to regenerate occurred. To facilitate this task, this chapter is divided into six sections. The first three of these are contextual in nature, outlining: (1) the rise of Quebec nationalism during the mid-twentieth century; (2) characteristics of the FLQ itself (such as its operational history and collective action frame); and (3) very briefly, the security forces which were responsible for counteracting the FLQ threat. The fourth and fifth sections, meanwhile, will focus on the FLQ's capacity to regenerate; describing the movement's regenerative experience before and after October 1970, as well as analysing the relative strength of an increase in attrition and a decrease in recruitment as catalysts of regenerative decay, and the dynamics of these factors. Finally, the sixth section will provide a summary of the chapter and its key findings.

The rise of Quebec nationalism

The 1950s and 1960s were a time of remarkable and often dramatic change in Quebec's history. One of the most significant transformations of this era – especially in relation to understanding the dynamics of the FLQ's recruitment – was the rise of Quebec nationalism. In many respects, the emergence of this new strain of French-Canadian nationalism represented a realignment of the historic *Canadien* nationalist impulse with the 'realities' of modern Quebec life.

Arguably the most public and conscious driver of this realignment was a growing band of young nationalists who were dissatisfied with the strictures of the traditional nationalist discourse. Though the first strain of *Canadien* nationalism was relatively liberal in character;[2] for most of the nineteenth and early-twentieth centuries, the Catholic clergy (strict adherents of papal orthodoxy) exerted a significant influence over nationalist thought. This clerical or ultramontane nationalism was based on three central components. These were, *l'agriculturisme* (a linking of rural life with French-Canadian identity and the survival of the nation);[3] *le messianisme* (the belief that the French-Canadian people had a religious mission to fulfil on the North American continent – a mission which required both clerical leadership and a strong Catholic Church);[4] and *l'anti-étatisme* (an inherent distrust of the state and an associated preference for autonomous French-Canadian institutions).[5]

To the dissenting young nationalists, however, these 'myths' (as Brunet so famously described them) were not only increasingly irrelevant in the postwar era, but also potentially damaging to the French-Canadian nation's chances of survival.[6] For instance, authors such as André Laurendeau and Jean-Marc Léger observed that: (1) given the incredible rate of urbanisation and industrialisation that had occurred in Quebec since the end of the Second World War, there was 'no longer a rural and agricultural French Canada, but primarily an urban/ industrial French Canada';[7] and (2) traditional French-Canadian nationalism, with its glorification of rural life, prevented the existing nationalist elite from engaging with the burgeoning ranks of urban, industrial workers and preventing their 'denationalisation'.[8] What was needed, these nationalists argued, was a new nationalist doctrine: one which would be urban and secular in nature, as well as embrace the state as an instrument of advancing the interests of the French-Canadian people. It was these central tenets which would later form the ideological base of Quebec nationalism.

However, the most important 'reality' reflected in Quebec nationalism was not its progressive character; but rather, its demarcation of the nation's borders. Notwithstanding its long history in the French-Canadian political consciousness, for most of the nineteenth and early-twentieth centuries, French-Canadian nationalism lacked an accurate conception of where the spatial boundaries of the nation lay. This confusion was primarily the result of an astonishing (and equally traumatic) wave of French-Canadian emigration that occurred from the 1830s to the 1930s. In all, an estimated 900,000 *Canadiens* emigrated from the Saint Lawrence River area (the historic centre of French settlement) over this period;[9] driven by a ballooning population (doubling nearly every 25 years during the nineteenth-century),[10] a lack of available land along the Saint Lawrence River,[11] and the lure of economic opportunity.[12] These *émigrés* established a remarkably broad presence across North America; primarily settling in Ontario, northern New Brunswick, New England, and the American Midwest. The problem, of course, with such a broad presence was that it obscured the precise borders of the French-Canadian nation. As Bélanger states: 'Clearly, one could not create a nation-state any more, except in imagination.'[13]

However, as the twentieth-century progressed and the surge of French-Canadian *émigrés* abated, a distinct trend emerged amongst North America's Francophones. Specifically, the further a 'community of French origin' was from Quebec, the higher its rate of assimilation with its English-speaking neighbours.[14] Indeed, the proportion of Canadians living outside Quebec with French ethnic origin whose 'mother tongue' was English doubled between 1931 and 1961.[15] In other words, the French-Canadian presence in North America was gradually contracting, becoming increasingly limited to (and identified with) the solidly French-speaking province of Quebec.[16] Quebec nationalism mirrored this demographic trend by redefining the boundaries of the French-Canadian nation to those of Quebec. Thus, *le nation Canadien Français* became *le nation Québécois*.

Though there were many differences between the newly-emerged Quebec nationalism and its French-Canadian predecessors, it did share their preoccupation with the survival of the French-Canadian nation in a hostile, Anglophone environment. Unlike traditional nationalists, however, who sought to ensure the continued existence of the nation by protecting and upholding minority rights across Canada;[17] the Quebec nationalists believed that the best way to secure the nation was by protecting and upholding the rights of the majority in Quebec. To this end, the Quebec nationalists sought (and still seek) the transformation of Quebec's relationship with the Federal Government, so as to ensure that the political structures governing Quebec most suitably met and reflected the will of the Quebecois.

One of the earliest and most prominent group of nationalists who attempted to achieve this goal was the provincial administration of Jean Lesage. Holding office from 1960 to 1966 (a period later known as *la révolution tranquille*, or 'the Quiet Revolution'), Lesage's government enacted a host of nationalist-inspired and often dramatic reforms. These included: the creation in 1961 of a *Département de relations provinciales-fédérales* ('Department of Federal-Provincial Relations') which 'began scrutinising every aspect of relations with Ottawa';[18] the expansion of the provincial bureaucracy (the number of public employees increased from 36,766 in 1960 to 56,258 in 1965);[19] and the 1963 nationalisation of the province's various hydroelectricity municipalities (forming Hydro Quebec). This last measure was the central issue of the 1962 general election; during which Lesage famously campaigned under the slogan '*Maîtres chez nous*' ('Masters in our own house'). Despite such rhetoric and the obvious strains that arose between Quebec and Ottawa during its tenure, the Lesage Administration was, ultimately, autonomist in character. That is, while Lesage and (most of) his ministers agitated for greater provincial control of government services, they nonetheless accepted Quebec's status within Confederation.

The same could not be said of such Quebecois figures as Michel Chaput, Pierre Bourgault, and René Levesque. To these nationalists, the solution to Quebec's problems lay not in merely readjusting the province's role within Confederation; but rather, in removing Quebec from Canada altogether. This separatist perspective was generally based on two lines of reasoning. First, the history of

Canada since 'the Conquest' of 1763 had demonstrated that, while English-Canadians had earnestly tried to accommodate their French-speaking brethren, when the interests of both groups clashed, the 'English' would simply 'rely on their numerical majority to achieve their goal'.[20] Second, the provincial government lacked the authority (and was unlikely to be granted the authority) to implement the measures – such as controlling immigration flows – that were needed in order to secure the future of the nation. Thus, only a sovereign Quebec, free of the institutionalised domination of Confederation and able to utilise the full gamut of policy options available to a nation-state, could both secure and safeguard the needs of Francophone Quebec.

Initially, public support for this separatist perspective of Quebec nationalism was low. Hamilton and Pinard note that, in 1962, only eight per cent of male Francophones living in Quebec were in favour of the province becoming independent.[21] As the 1960s progressed, however, popular support for separatism rose. As Figure 3.1 illustrates, the percentage of male Francophones living in Quebec who were in favour of independence grew by an average of one point each year between 1962 and 1973.[22] The emergence of numerous political organisations advocating Quebec's independence reflected this increase in support. The first of these to surface was *Alliance laurentienne* in 1957; followed by the *Action socialiste pour l'indépendance du Québec* and *Rassemblement pour l'indépendance nationale* in 1960, the *Parti républican du Québec* in 1962; the *Ralliement national* in 1966; and, most famously, the *Parti Québécois* in 1968.[23] It was from this milieu of separatist politics that the FLQ emerged.

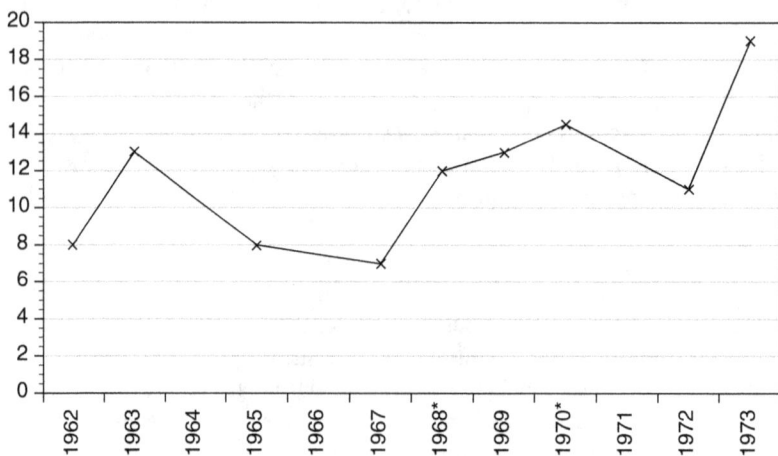

Figure 3.1 Male Francophones favouring Quebec independence, 1962–73 (source: R. Hamilton and M. Pinard, 'The Quebec Independence Movement', in C.H. Williams (ed.) *National Separatism*, Vancouver and London: University of British Columbia Press, 1982, 211).

Note
* Indicates average percentage.

The FLQ

During the night of 7 March 1963, four youths, after spraypainting the letters 'FLQ' on a nearby wall, threw an incendiary device (glass bottles surrounded by a mesh net) at the Royal Montreal Regiment Armoury in Montreal. Given that the perpetrators had used kerosene as their accelerant – a substance which only ignites at very high temperatures – the apparatus smashed harmlessly. Nonetheless, the FLQ's campaign for an independent Quebec had begun. Over the next ten years, the movement would be responsible for an additional 212 violent acts.[24] The majority of these (144) were bombings (both attempted and actual); followed by thefts and robberies (48), arson attacks (17), kidnappings (two), and one assault. Although the FLQ generally ascribed to Jenkins' characterisation (i.e. they wanted 'a lot of people *watching*, not a lot of people *dead*'),[25] FLQ violence did claim the lives of five civilians (as well as two FLQ members).[26] The most common targets of FLQ violence were: institutions associated with the Federal Government (such as Canada Post, Canadian National Railways, and the military); symbols of Anglo-Saxon domination (in particular, the predominately Anglophone suburb of Westmont in Montreal); and businesses involved in protracted labour disputes. This latter target was a reflection of the growing influence of Marxist/Leninist thought amongst some *felquistes* (the colloquial term for a member of the FLQ) from the mid-1960s onwards.

The key to understanding and conceptualising the FLQ is to realise that, in the words of Charters, '*there never was a single organization called the FLQ*'.[27] Rather, the FLQ was a *movement*; a series of autonomous networks that shared a common ideal of begetting *le Québec libre* through the application of violence. Cross-membership between these networks was minimal; though family and friends of captured *felquistes* would frequently appear in later networks.[28] Likewise, central leadership was virtually non-existent. While certain *felquistes* – Pierre Vallières and Charles Gagnon in particular – were able to exert a significant intellectual influence over sections of the movement, to describe them as '*leaders* of the FLQ ... overstates their contribution'.[29] For the most part, the FLQ's networks emerged, fought, and declined independently from each other. As a consequence, there was little continuity of experience and approach, with each network's strategic and operational decision-making largely a function of each network's membership.

Primarily due to the diffuse and secretive nature of the movement, the exact number and composition of the FLQ's networks has yet to be determined.[30] Nevertheless, this book, drawing on the three main historical accounts of the FLQ (i.e. Fournier, Laurendeau, and Morf), as well as a host of more limited surveys (such as Crelinsten and de Vault and Johnson), has identified 16 networks; comprised of an estimated 150–170 members.[31] It is important to note that these approximations likely *undervalue* the actual number of FLQ networks and members; given that the Canadian authorities never identified all the perpetrators of a series of FLQ-claimed bombings (17, plus ten attempted) from May to July 1970.[32]

Of course, the FLQ's estimated 150–170 members were not spread evenly amongst the movement's 16 networks. As Table 3.1 illustrates, some networks (such as the RQ and Lévesque Networks) had between two and four *felquistes*; while the membership of others (like the First, Vallières-Gagnon, and Lanctôt-Rose Networks) extended to over 20 activists. Similarly, the FLQ's networks varied greatly in terms of productivity and the extent of the threat that they posed. At one extreme, the Geoffrey Network – the most prolific of the FLQ's networks – was responsible for 44 violent acts between March 1968 and March 1969 (including the infamous bombing of the Montreal Stock Exchange on 13 February 1969). At the other end of the spectrum, the Canadian authorities were able to disrupt the Macaza Commando Unit before it could launch 'offensive operations'.

Collective action frame

Notwithstanding its organisational complexity, the FLQ had a relatively consistent collective action frame. Its diagnosis, while drawing on a range of societal

Table 3.1 Lifespan, membership and operational summary of FLQ networks 1963–72

Name	Start	End	Members	Violent acts	Fatalities
First Network	02/63	06/63	21–5	28	1
Résistance du Québec (RQ)	07/63	10/63	3	6	–
Armée de libération du Québec (ALQ)	08/63	04/64	8–9	10	–
La Cognée Network	08/63	04/67	6-?	10	–
Saint-Madeleine Network	04/64	05/64	3–5	1	–
Partisans de l'indépendance du Québec (PIQ) Network	05/64	05/64	3	1	–
Armée révolutionnaire du Québec (ARQ)	06/64	09/64	13	1	1
Macaza Commando Unit	?/65	07/65	7	–	–
Vallières-Gagnon Network	12/65	09/66	13–22	9	1
Geoffrey Network	03/68	03/69	10–11	44	–
Dubreuil Network	05/68	05/72	2–6	10	–
Fundraising Network	11/69	03/70	7–8	8	–
Lanctôt-Rose Network	12/69	12/70	30–5	2	1
Saint-Henri Network	12/69	05/72	2–?	?	–
Université du Québec à Montréal (UQAM) Network	05/70	06/72	21–6	17	–
Lévesque Network	12/70	10/72	2–4	16	–
FLQ (Unidentified Network)	–	–	–	50	1

Sources: R.D. Crelinsten, 'The internal dynamics of the FLQ during the October Crisis', *Inside Terrorist Organizations*, in D.C. Rapoport (ed.), *Inside Terrorist Organizations*, London: Frank Cass, 2001, pp. 59–89; C. de Vault and W. Johnson, *The Informer: Confessions of an Ex-Terrorist*, Toronto: Fleet Books, 1982; L. Fournier, *F.L.Q.: The Anatomy of an Underground Movement*, trans. Edward Baxter, Toronto: NC Press Limited, 1984; A. Kellett *et al. Terrorism in Canada 1960–1989*, Ottawa: Ministry of the Solicitor General of Canada, 1991; M. Laurendeau, *Les Québécois Violents: La Violence Politique 1962–1972*, Montreal: Boréal, 1990; G. Morf, *Terror in Quebec: Case Studies of the FLQ*, Toronto and Vancouver: Clarke, Irwin & Company Limited, 1970.

ills, centred on a single metanarrative. Specifically, that Quebec was *une colonie*. Ruling this colony were the 'Anglo-Saxons' (i.e. English-Canadians and North Americans) who, through their routine and seemingly innate discrimination and exploitation, were not only degrading the lives of the majority Quebecois, but also threatening the Francophone nation's very existence. Aiding and abetting the Anglo-Saxons in their nefarious schemes were a 'French-Canadian ruling class', which was 'absolutely incapable of opposing' the system on which its privileges lay.[33]

As the FLQ's First Network announced in April 1963, the Quebecois' status as a colonised people was evident *'politiquement, socialement, économiquement'*.[34] Politically, because the provincial government lacked the 'vital political levers' (such as full control over the economy) that were necessary for the Quebecois' survival.[35] Furthermore, the Anglo-Saxons constantly relied on their numerical, financial, and constitutional dominance 'to maintain and accentuate the inferiority of the Quebecois'.[36] For instance, *La Cognée* (an FLQ-published journal) high-lighted in October 1963 the attempts by Actor's Equity (an American trade union) to claim jurisdiction over the recently opened *Place des Arts* in Montreal. As *La Cognée* fumed: 'The American artists want to dictate to the Quebecois artists what they must do.... Once again, the legitimate aspirations of our people are betrayed, once again the coloniser reveals his contempt and will for exploitation.'[37]

Socially, the colonisation of the Quebecois was apparent by two phenomena. First, the disdain in which the Anglo-Saxons held Canada's French-speakers (the 'white niggers of America');[38] manifested in both employment discrimination, and the general abuse ('Speak White!') to which Francophones were subjected.[39] Second, the colonial language's gradual conquest of Quebec. 'We are 80% of the population and yet the English language dominates in most areas. Little by little French is relegated to the status of folklore whereas English becomes the working language.'[40] Many *felquistes* expressed extreme anxiety over this last issue. For example, in its first edition, *La Cognée* berated Montreal's Catholic school board (*la Commission des Écoles Catholiques de Montréal*, or CECM) for introducing a new programme that required French-speaking students to learn English for 15 minutes per day. According to the journal's editors, the 'direct consequence' of this measure would be the 'accelerated Anglicisation of our population' and that the CECM was guilty of 'betray[ing] their nation and its past' and 'shamefully collaborat[ing] with the colonizer'.[41] The Liberation Cell of the Lanctôt-Rose network expressed similar concern about the assimilatory pressures of Bill 63 (a provincial language bill, introduced in 1969, which upheld the right of parents to school their children in either English or French) in its manifesto of October 1970.[42]

However, the exploitation and slavery of the Quebecois was most evident (and ruinous) in the realm of economics. As the FLQ's First Network stated in 1963: 'Only one sentence is sufficient to prove it: more than 80% of our economy is controlled by foreign interests. We provide the labour, they collect the profits.'[43] Subsequent FLQ networks would gradually begin to frame Quebec's economic colonisation in terms of Marxist/Leninist arguments. Writing in

1968, Vallières argued that, for the past 350 years, Quebec had been 'subject to the interests of the dominant classes of the imperialist countries: first France, then England, and today the United States'.[44] As a consequence, 'its economy has always been directed, controlled, and organized by factors other than the needs of its population'.[45] This was manifested by Quebec's historic dependence on the export of 'raw or semi-finished' materials (e.g. fur, lumber, asbestos, and electricity) and foreign capital.[46]

According to Vallières, the greatest injustice of the colonial economic system under which the Quebecois lived was its inherent inequality. Specifically, the system allowed a minority (i.e. American imperialists and their allied English- and French-Canadian bourgeoisie) to exploit and direct the energies of the majority (i.e. 'the workers, the farmers, the petty white-collar workers, the students, the unemployed, and those on welfare – that is, at least 90 percent of the population') for their own benefit.[47] As Vallières states, the

> masses ... are being unjustly deprived of the ownership of their means of production, as well as of the wealth produced, culture, etc., and that they are being maintained in slavery in the name of democracy, the democracy of free enterprise and the exploitation of man by man.[48]

The Liberation Cell exuded a similar Marxist tint, castigating 'the patronizing "big bosses" and their henchmen who have made Quebec their hunting preserve for "cheap labour" and unscrupulous exploitation'; the 'hypocrite ... Bourassa [Liberal Premier from May 1970 to November 1976] who relies on Brinks armoured trucks,[49] the living symbol of the foreign occupation of Quebec, to keep the poor natives of Quebec in the fear of misery and unemployment in which they are accustomed to living'; and the Federal Government, whose 'policy of heavy importation' ruined Quebec's indigenous producers 'for the benefit of a clutch of damned money-makers in their Cadillacs'.[50]

The FLQ's solution to Quebec's colonisation and associated problems was, not surprisingly, the independence of Quebec. The earlier networks largely portrayed this objective as a simple transfer of power; that is, wresting control of the 'vital political levers' away from the Anglo-Saxons.[51] However, to latter networks, corresponding with their Marxist/Leninist interpretation of Quebec's ills, such 'political' independence was, by itself, inadequate. As Vallières states:

> OK. Let's tell Ottawa to go to hell. And then? What's going to change? ... The iron of the North Shore, the asbestos of Asbestos, the mines of Abitibi, our forests and hydraulic resources, our commerce, finance, and industry – and the political machines: will not all that still be the exclusive property of the Americans?[52]

True independence, from this perspective, required not only political separation, but also the abolition of the system which was directly responsible for the pervasive inequality of Quebec's society – namely, capitalism. In its place, the revolutionary-minded *felquistes* envisaged 'the construction of an egalitarian society, just and free, based on the collective practice of self-management at all levels (economic, administrative, academic, cultural)'.[53]

The FLQ's various networks sought to achieve this goal of independence (however they conceived it) by relying on the transformative powers of the 'armed struggle'. For example, the First Network announced that its 'principal mission' in bringing about the 'POLITICAL AND ECONOMIC INDEPENDENCE OF QUEBEC' was 'to COMPLETELY DESTROY, through SYSTEMATIC SABOTAGE' a host of Anglo-Saxon, colonial targets.[54] Similarly, *La Cognée* promoted both the necessity of creating '*un mouvement insurrectionnel*', as well as using all possible means, 'whether they are violent or not', to achieve the revolution.[55] Finally, Vallières called on his supporters to reject the 'illusory promise of victory without combat ... Even if violence is a phenomenon detestable in itself, it is nonetheless true that for exploited and colonized people like ourselves, freedom grows out of the barrel of a gun'.[56]

However, while the FLQ advocated the primacy of violence as an instrument of change, it did not provide any real conception of how the use of violence would actually engender the independence of Quebec. The closest any of the FLQ's networks came to establishing a connection between coercive force and Quebec's freedom was in the 1966 document, *Revolutionary Strategy and the Role of the Avant-Garde*. This nine-page strategic analysis maintained that Quebec's war for national liberation would be both long in duration and comprise of three stages. That is, the 'radicalisation of social agitation' (primarily a political stage; the objective of which was to use various means – including violence – to raise class consciousness); the 'organisation of the masses'; and unlimited 'popular insurrection' (utilising both political and military means).[57] However, even this document was, in the words of Charters,

> more of an idealistic call to action than a genuine strategy. It made good propaganda, excited revolutionary intellectuals, and worried the authorities – who apparently took it more seriously than it deserved – but in practical terms, it was too vague to serve as a blueprint for revolutionary warfare.[58]

This seeming lack of strategic depth within the FLQ is most likely a reflection of what Charters describes elsewhere as the 'revolutionary amateurishness' of the FLQ's membership; who, by and large, were motivated less by an understanding or even knowledge of revolutionary theory, and more by a rudimentary 'impulse to action'.[59]

Nonetheless, despite not providing much detail about how it expected the use of violence to achieve its goals; the FLQ did go to considerable length to justify its armed struggle. Consistent with Gurr and O'Boyle, the FLQ framed its justificatory arguments both in moral and utilitarian terms. With regard to the former, the FLQ proffered two lines of reasoning. The first and minor of these was based on the twin assumptions that: (1) 'defensive wars and wars of liberation' (in contrast with 'imperialist wars') are 'morally acceptable' (if not 'worthy of praise'); and (2) the war to liberate Quebec was one of these.[60] As *La Cognée* states: 'one can thus conclude that our war is moral.'[61]

The FLQ's principal moral argument, however, was that the movement's armed struggle was justified because violence is the natural and uncontrollable consequence of oppression and exploitation. Responsibility for the movement's actions thus lay not with the FLQ, but with the oppressors and exploiters. This reasoning is evident in the communiqué which the First Network released in the wake of its bombing of an army recruiting centre on 20 April 1963; an otherwise uneventful attack, except that it unintentionally killed the centre's night watchman, Wilfrid O'Neil. After dismissively claiming that 'a revolution does not occur alas, without the spilling of blood';[62] the First Network stated: 'For the death of O'Neil, the culprits are not the Patriots. They are all the collaborators, the wretched exploiters who compel the Quebecois Patriots to take up arms for the freedom of the nation.'[63] Other networks were also quick to embrace this moral rationalisation. For example, *La Cognée* announced in May 1964 that: 'We did not choose clandestinity and violence: they were imposed upon us.'[64] Likewise, Vallières argued that since revolutionary violence 'is the product of the very contradictions of the colonial, capitalist system, it can disappear only with the system itself'.[65]

Seemingly at odds with this moral calculation was the FLQ's central utilitarian justificatory argument. In essence, this line of reasoning implied that the Quebecois *did* have a choice in the means which they could employ to beget Quebec's independence. However, because the alternative means – limited to pacifism and electoralism – were ineffective, the armed struggle was the most effective by default. The FLQ's rejection of pacifism centred on two arguments. First, that it had proved fruitless in the past. As *La Cognée* proclaimed: 'Two centuries of pacifism did not liberate our fatherland from Anglo-Saxon colonialism ... to persevere with pacifism would be treasonous or insane.'[66] Second, that a campaign of non-violence would delay the realisation of Quebec's liberation and, in doing so, impose unneeded suffering on the proletariat.[67]

The arguments on which the FLQ based its dismissal of electoralism were of varying validity. For instance, *La Cognée* rebuffed the suggestion of prominent *indépendantistes* that 'constitutional freedoms and democratic guarantees' made it possible for separatists 'to seize power by the electoral way', by claiming that there was no 'national parliament' (the Federal Parliament being rejected as a foreign government; the Quebec Parliament as not having control over all the nation's territory) in which the FLQ could 'govern in the name of all the nation'.[68] In a latter issue, *La Cognée* asserted that since elections are held only once every four years, the electoral path would likely 'defer independence for a century or two'.[69] However, the FLQ's strongest argument against electoralism was that it was a process inherently corrupted by money. As the Liberation Cell announced in October 1970:

what we call democracy in Quebec is nothing but the democracy of the rich ... the British parliamentary system is finished and the Front de liberation du Quebec will never allow itself to be fooled by the pseudo-elections that the Anglo-Saxon capitalists toss to the people of Quebec every four years.[70]

This contention was based on the observation that to obtain power via the electoral process, a party required a substantial political machine. Unfortunately, maintaining this machine was expensive; potentially costing the party 'millions of dollars'.[71] In order to meet this cost, the party would have to become increasingly reliant on – if not subservient to – those 'who exploit our people', the 'local and foreign capitalists'.[72] Given this subservience, no party would be able to pursue polices – such as independence – that deviated greatly from the interests of its 'owners'. Thus, as Vallières states: 'We were (and still are) convinced that on the ground of electoralism, the battle is always lost for the wage-earners, that is, for the vast majority of the nation.'[73]

Recruitment process

Not surprisingly, given its diffuse nature, the FLQ lacked a permanent and centralised recruitment network. Rather, each of the movement's networks had its own (in most cases ad hoc) recruitment network. The scope of these was generally limited. That is, a direct relationship tie tended to connect new recruits with current members or (with regard to those who founded new networks) other potential members. In some cases, familial bonds would form the basis of this interpersonal connection. For example, François Lanctôt, and Jacques and Louise Cossette-Trudel joined the Lanctôt-Rose Network through their relationship (as brother, brother-in-law, and sister, respectively) with Jacques Lanctôt. However, in a large number of cases, the direct relationship tie that facilitated recruitment into the FLQ was developed in the context of the various radical separatist groups which were prevalent in Quebecois politics. Generally speaking, these groups sought to achieve *le Québec libre* through the use of various paralegal instruments, such as demonstrations, boycotts, and social agitation.[74] They thus attracted those *indépendantistes* who were already disillusioned with the limits of conventional political action (i.e. those most susceptible to accepting the FLQ's collective action frame) and were important meeting grounds for a host of future *felquistes*. For instance, the founders of the First Network – Georges Schoeters, Raymond Villeneuve, and Gabriel Hudon – met each other while they were members of *Réseau de résistance* (RR), a radical group established in November 1962;[75] a large proportion of the Vallières-Gagnon Network knew each other from their membership in the *Mouvement de libération populaire;*[76] and Francis Simard met Paul Rose (both members of the Lanctôt-Rose Network) during their mutual affiliation with the *Rassemblement pour l'indépendance nationale.*[77]

The Canadian Government and its security forces

Since 1867, Canada has maintained a federal system of parliamentary government. While the Federal Government, based in Ottawa, is accountable for such matters as the 'raising of Money by any Mode or System of Taxation', foreign relations, and 'Militia, Military and Naval Service, and Defence'; the Provincial Governments (of which there were 12 in the mid-twentieth century) are amenable for concerns like public health, the 'Administration of Justice' and the 'Imposition of Punishment by Fine, Penalty, or Imprisonment'.[78] Given this distribution of powers, the Government of Quebec had primary responsibility for counteracting the FLQ threat. However, due to concerns within the Federal Government about the rise of separatist sentiment in Quebec, and that a number of *felquiste* targets (e.g. military armouries and diplomatic personnel) fell under the purview of Ottawa's liability, successive Federal Administrations (specifically, those of Lester Pearson and Pierre Trudeau) sought to play a significant role in anti-FLQ efforts.[79]

The Federal and Quebec Governments deployed four major security forces against the FLQ. The first three of these were police forces; specifically, the Royal Canadian Mounted Police (RCMP), the *Sûreté du Québec*, and Montreal's municipal police. The difference between these agencies was largely one of jurisdiction. Whereas the RCMP was Canada's federal police force,[80] Montreal's municipal police were tasked with maintaining law and order within the confines of Greater Montreal. The *Sûreté du Québec*, meanwhile, was responsible for policing: in provincial areas not covered by Quebec's various municipal police forces; and with regard to certain provincial laws, such as those regulating gambling, racketeering and political violence.[81] Though statistics for the 1960s and early-1970s are unavailable, in 1975, the RCMP had a strength of approximately 6,500 officers, the *Sûreté du Québec* 4,049, and Montreal's municipal police 5,735.[82]

The fourth security force was the Canadian Army. Its campaign against the FLQ was a relatively limited one; both temporally (the Federal Government only deployed the army against the FLQ from 15 October 1970 to 4 January 1971) and operationally (it was largely restricted to guarding Federal and other important buildings in Montreal, Quebec City and Ottawa). Nevertheless, the Canadian Army's deployment did have a significant impact on the Quebecois political psyche (an issue that will be discussed in greater detail below). In 1970, the Canadian Army comprised 37,300 regular soldiers;[83] though only 12,500 of these were deployed in the campaign against the FLQ.[84]

The FLQ's regenerative experience

From its inception in February 1963 to October 1970, the FLQ enjoyed a strong regenerative capacity. The movement's rate of attrition over this period was both high and constant. As Table 3.2 illustrates, the primary source of this incessant loss of personnel was security force pressure. In all, the RCMP, the *Sûreté du*

Table 3.2 Attrition of FLQ networks, 1963–70

Year	Arrests	Exiles	Deaths	FLQ networks formed	FLQ networks declined
1963	23	1	–	First, *La Cognée* Networks and the ALQ and RQ	First and RQ Networks
1964	28	–	–	PIQ, Saint-Madeleine Networks and the ARQ	PIQ, Saint-Madeleine Networks and the ALQ and ARQ
1965	10	–	–	Vallières-Gagnon Network and the Macaza Commando Unit	Macaza Commando Unit
1966	13	–	1		Vallières-Gagnon Network
1967	–	–	–		*La Cognée* Network
1968	–	–	–	Geoffrey and Dubreuil Networks	
1969	3	4	–	Fundraising, Lanctôt-Rose, Saint-Henri Networks	Geoffrey Network
1970†	13	–	–	UQAM Network	Fundraising Network

Sources: R.D. Crelinsten, 'The internal dynamics of the FLQ during the October Crisis', *Inside Terrorist Organizations*, in D.C. Rapoport (ed.), *Inside Terrorist Organizations*, London: Frank Cass, 2001, pp. 59–89; C. de Vault and W. Johnson, *The Informer: Confessions of an Ex-Terrorist*, Toronto: Fleet Books, 1982; L. Fournier, *F.L.Q.: The Anatomy of an Underground Movement*, trans. Edward Baxter, Toronto: NC Press Limited, 1984; A. Kellett *et al. Terrorism in Canada 1960–1989*, Ottawa: Ministry of the Solicitor General of Canada, 1991; M. Laurendeau, *Les Québécois Violents: La Violence Politique 1962–1972*, Montreal: Boréal, 1990; G. Morf, *Terror in Quebec: Case Studies of the FLQ*, Toronto and Vancouver: Clarke, Irwin & Company Limited, 1970.

Note
† 1970 is prior to October only.

Québec and Montreal's municipal police arrested 90 *felquistes*; as well as compelling a further five to flee into exile. Though far from perfect, the security force's response to the FLQ benefited from three factors: (1) institutionalised cooperation between the RCMP, *Sûreté du Québec* and Montreal's municipal police in the form of the Combined Anti-Terrorist Squad (CATS), a multi-agency taskforce created in 1964; (2) high-level concern within the Federal Government about the FLQ (a reflection of Ottawa's intrinsic sensitivity towards the rise of separatist sentiment in Quebec); and (3) the general ineptitude of some *felquistes*. This ineptitude, unfortunately, was evident on 14 July 1966, when Jean Corbo, a 16-year-old member of the Vallières-Gagnon Network, was killed by a premature explosion. In addition to deaths and arrests, the FLQ also suffered from an indeterminate number of desertions prior to October 1970. For instance, Fournier contends that, by 1967, 'almost all' of the *La Cognée* Network's members had abandoned the armed struggle and joined 'the "legal" independence movement'.[85]

The FLQ was able to withstand the significant and persistent attritional pressure of the 1960s because new recruits kept coming forward; either to join existing networks or, with the assistance of like-minded acquaintances, form new networks. For instance, on 29 May 1963, the security forces, acting on information provided by an informer, launched a series of raids on suspected FLQ residences around Quebec. This operation was a considerable success, with the police arresting 19 *felquistes* and effectively crippling the First Network's ability to conduct further attacks. However, within three months, between 15 and 20 new *felquistes* had stepped forward; creating the *Armée de libération du Québec* (ALQ), the *Résistance du Québec* (RQ) and the *La Cognée* Network. This pattern of regeneration would be replicated time and time again over the next six years. The only real aberration was the 18-month gap between the demise of the Vallières-Gagnon Network in September 1966 and the rise of the Geoffrey and Dubreuil Networks in early-to-mid 1968; a significant pause in the FLQ's regenerative impulse. Nevertheless, by October 1970, even though the movement had lost approximately 100 members over the previous seven years, there were four FLQ networks in existence, with an estimated combined membership of 40 to 50 *felquistes* – the largest number of *felquistes* to be operational at any one time.

The October Crisis

The beginning of the end for the FLQ was the 'October Crisis' of 1970. This ultimately defining event began on 5 October, when the 'Liberation Cell' (seven members of the Lanctôt-Rose Network, led by Jacques Lanctôt) kidnapped James Cross, the British Trade Commissioner to Montreal. In return for his freedom, the Liberation Cell demanded (amongst other things): the cessation of all police activities designed to find the kidnappers; a 'voluntary tax of $500,000 in gold bullion'; and the release of 23 imprisoned *felquistes* and their guaranteed free passage to either Algeria or Cuba.[86] Three days later, the Federal Government acquiesced to the Liberation Cell's 'minimum demand for continued dialogue' and authorised Radio-Canada to broadcast the group's manifesto.[87] Within 48 hours, on the evening of 10 October, four other members of the Lanctôt-Rose Network (operating independently of Lanctôt's group, and calling themselves the 'Chenier Cell')[88] sought to bolster the Liberation Cell's negotiating position by abducting Pierre Laporte, Deputy Premier and Minister for Employment and Immigration of Quebec.

This second kidnapping had a 'profound psychological impact on the provincial and federal governments';[89] not only because of the victim's high profile and close relationships with many inside the corridors of power (including the Prime Minister, Pierre Trudeau), but also because it suggested (erroneously, in hindsight) that the FLQ was larger and more capable than had been previously assumed. Of greater concern to the authorities was the apparent outpouring of Quebecois sympathy for the Liberation Cell's manifesto and, to a lesser extent, the FLQ itself.[90] Evidence (at least from the Federal and Quebec Governments' viewpoint) of this sympathy included: (1) favourable editorials in such Franco-phone newspapers as *Québec-Presse*, which on 11 October rebuked condemnations of the FLQ's actions and declared 'that the struggle for the liberation of Quebec is a basic requirement';[91] (2) the publication on 14 October of a statement by 16 prominent Quebecois journalists, politicians, and trade unionists, calling on Trudeau to negotiate with the FLQ, while also 'virulently attacking Ottawa's hard-line';[92] (3) a demonstration on 15 October by approximately 3,000 students at the *Université de Montréal* in support of the Liberation Cell's manifesto and the release of the imprisoned *felquistes*;[93] and (4) most disturbingly from Ottawa's perspective, a notable absence of Quebecois outrage over the kidnappings.[94]

By 15 October, the Federal and Quebec Governments had reached the conclusion that an 'apprehended insurrection' existed in the province of Quebec.[95] The essence of this concept (which has attracted considerable controversy)[96] was not that an insurrection was actually ongoing, or necessarily even planned; but rather, given the seeming strength of the FLQ and its growing support, that an insurrection 'was a *possible* outcome' if conditions in Quebec were left unchecked.[97] Thus, the Federal and Quebec Governments decided to abandon their traditional 'criminal justice' approach to combating the FLQ,[98] and instead launch a vigorous campaign aimed at incapacitating the violent separatist movement and 'shock[ing] the Quebec public out of its confusion into support for established authority'.[99]

The first step in this campaign was the deployment of Canadian Army troops (ultimately numbering 12,500) to Quebec City and Montreal on 15 October; tasked with aiding the local police forces and protecting public buildings. Next, in the early hours of 16 October, Trudeau invoked the *War Measures Act 1914* (WMA). This emergency statute (which had only been invoked twice before in Canada's history – both in wartime) provided the Federal Government with extensive powers; covering such areas as censorship, exclusion and deportation, control of Canada's territorial waters, transportation, exportation and importation, and the appropriation of property.[100] Under this 'umbrella of powers', the Federal Government also passed the *Public Order Regulations 1970*.[101] This decree enacted a series of measures specific to the government's anti-FLQ campaign. Specifically, the *Public Order Regulations 1970* declared that the FLQ was 'an unlawful association'; introduced penalties for membership of, and support for, the FLQ; permitted police officers to conduct searches and seize property without warrant; and, most controversially, allowed suspects to be detained for 21 days without charge and 90 days without trial.[102] Using these last powers, the various police agencies operating in Quebec detained without charge 238 suspected FLQ members and sympathisers within hours of the WMA's invocation, and a further 230 people during the remainder of the year.[103]

The October Crisis reached its nadir, however, on the night of 17 October, when Pierre Laporte (under still uncertain circumstances) was killed.[104] After police found his body in the boot of a car the next day, a wave of revulsion swept over Canada. However, despite this public outrage and the security force's extensive new powers, it was not until 6 November that the police scored their first breakthrough in relation to the kidnappings; arresting Bernard Lortie of the Chenier Cell. The security force's next success was the capture of Jacques and Louise Cossette-Trudel of the Liberation Cell on 3 December. However, the Cossette-Trudels' time in detention was brief, as the authorities negotiated safe passage to Cuba for them and three other members of the Liberation Cell in exchange for Cross's release.[105] These five *felquistes* remained in exile (both in Cuba and in France) until the late-1970s, when, after obtaining permission from the ruling *Parti Québécois*, they slowly returned home; receiving (relatively) short prison sentences for their actions during the October Crisis. Meanwhile, on 27 December 1970, the last three members of the Chenier Cell were eventually detained. A week later, the troops in Quebec City and Montreal returned to their barracks and on 30 April 1971 the *Public Order Act*, which had succeeded and mirrored the WMA, was withdrawn, 'returning Canada to a state of normalcy'.[106]

The weakening of the FLQ's regenerative capacity

In the wake of the October Crisis, the FLQ's capacity to regenerate began to irrevocably weaken. This deterioration was the result of less a change in the movement's rate of attrition (which remained both high and constant), and more the gradual decline in the movement's recruitment. In other words, unlike the FLQ's prior-experience, new recruits were not coming forward to replace the movement's often-devastating loss of personnel. This dynamic was increasingly evident from November 1970 to the end of 1971. During this period, the police arrested 28 *felquistes* and forced five others into exile; effectively dismantling the Lanctôt-Rose Network and seriously degrading the operational capability of the UQAM Network. The FLQ also suffered one death (Pierre-Louis Bourret on 24 September 1971), and an indefinite number of desertions; with key *felquistes* such as Robert Comeau, Nigel Hamer, and Gilles Cossette gradually disassociating themselves from the UQAM Network and joining other, non-violent separatist organisations, like the *Front d'action politique*. However, over these same 14 months, only an estimated dozen new recruits emerged. Four of these established the Lévesque Network in December 1970, while the remaining eight joined the UQAM Network.[107]

As 1972 progressed, the divergence between the FLQ's rates of attrition and recruitment expanded even further. For instance, on 25 May, the police detained the seeming last two active members of the Saint-Henri Network. A month later, the UQAM Network was subdued after four of its *felquistes* were arrested. Finally, in August and September, following its robbery of a credit union in Montreal (the last recorded act of FLQ violence), the police arrested the four members of the Lévesque Network. In earlier times, the FLQ would have responded to these losses with an influx (possibly belated) of new recruits; launching the struggle for Quebec's independence anew. However, with the demise of the Saint-Henri, UQAM and Lévesque Networks, no new recruits emerged. As a result, both the FLQ and its campaign of violence came to an end. The FLQ's name would be associated with a number of future violent incidents. In particular, a bomb threat during the 1976 Olympic Games in Montreal, and two firebomb attacks in 1986 and 1989. However, as Kellett states: 'The police assessed these incidents as the work of a few crackpots, and discounted the possibility of a resurgent FLQ.'[108]

Analysis

From the above account of the FLQ's regenerative experience, it appears that a decrease in recruitment played a greater role than an increase in attrition in weakening the movement's capacity to regenerate. Underlying this judgment is the observation that the deterioration of the FLQ's regenerative capacity coincided with a notable reduction in the number of aspiring *felquistes* willing to join an existing, or form a new, network; but *not* with a discernible increase in the number of *felquistes* who were arrested or killed, or who deserted. This is not to deny that the FLQ's losses following the October Crisis were both considerable and relentless. However, while the FLQ's loss of personnel during this period was certainly debilitating, it was no more debilitating than before the kidnappings of Cross and Laporte.

In light of the above findings, the remainder of this chapter will focus on exploring whether the FLQ's decrease in recruitment from October 1970 onwards was the result of the amelioration of grievances, selective government repression, and/or the discrediting of the insurgent actor's ideology.

The amelioration of grievances

There is little support for the notion that the FLQ's intake of recruits declined because of the amelioration of grievances. Rather, by the early-1970s, the grievances which lay at the heart of the movement's collective action frame had only been slightly alleviated (if at all). As aforementioned, the FLQ framed its diagnosis in terms of Quebec's alleged political, economic and social colonisation. Arguably the most improvement had been made with regard to the former. Beginning with the election of Jean Lesage in 1960, Quebec's governing class had become increasingly assertive in demarcating the province's autonomy. Though Ottawa rejected some of the Quebec Government's demands (particularly those that touched on the sensitive issue of Quebec's international status), it acquiesced to many. For instance, by the early-1960s, the Lesage Administration had formalised the doctrine of 'opting-out'. That is, the notion that Quebec should be able to receive full federal funding 'without condition of sponsorship'.[109] Successive administrations were also able to convince Ottawa that, '[i]n order to organize Quebec's social and economic life in conformity with its own spirit', the Quebec Government should control the administration of federal programs in the province.[110]

The Federal Government's response to the October Crisis, however, overshadowed these political achievements. By deploying troops and invoking emergency powers, the Trudeau Administration essentially confirmed one of the FLQ and broader separatist movement's central complaints against the Federal-Provincial relationship. Specifically, while Ottawa may have seemed eager to accommodate Francophone Quebec, when its vital interests were at stake, it would not hesitate to use every aspect of its power to 'subordinate Quebec to its will'.[111] The impact of the October Crisis on separatist and general Quebecois sentiment was thus dramatic. As Charters states, 'the enduring image of the October Crisis is not the body of Pierre Laporte, the victim of an FLQ assassination; it is the troops on the streets of Montreal, the symbol of federal *repression*'.[112] Indeed, Premier Jacques Parizeau made reference to the WMA and the detention of hundreds of suspected *felquistes* as late as the 1995 referendum campaign on Quebec's independence; a clear sign of the lasting resentment that the Federal Government's actions during October 1970 generated.[113]

Likewise, the grievances which underscored the FLQ's indictment of Quebec's economic colonisation had only been marginally ameliorated by the time the movement's recruitment had evaporated. Beginning in the early-1960s, successive Federal and Quebec Governments introduced numerous measures to improve the economic lot of Quebec's Francophones. For instance, Loomis describes how Lester Pearson, Prime Minister from 1963 to 1968, created such initiatives as the Canada Development Corporation and the Economic Council of Canada with the twin objectives of winning the 'hearts and minds' of Canada's French-speaking peoples and combating the FLQ's exploitation of 'the so-called contradiction of "economic colonisation"'.[114] Trudeau continued Pearson's general strategy; establishing the Department of Regional Economic Expansion in 1969. Under this new agency, the Federal Government provided incentives for 'private companies willing to set up new enterprises in designated areas – mainly in eastern Quebec and the Maritimes'; as well as allocating approximately $80 million for economic development in Quebec and New Brunswick over 1970 and 1971.[115] Quebec's various Provincial Governments, meanwhile, had been attempting to address the Anglo-Saxon domination of the local economy. For example, in June 1962, the Lesage administration created the *Société générale de financement*. The goal of this government-controlled financial institution was to encourage and support the development of Francophone enterprises in Quebec. Three years later, the Provincial Government also established the *Caisse de dépôts et de placements du Québec* (CDP). Charged with administering the province's pension funds, the CDP was envisaged as an indigenous 'source of capital that could be used to advance Quebec's economic development'.[116]

While it is true that the above programmes did eventually bring long-term benefits to the Quebecois; during the first half of the 1970s (the period when the FLQ's recruitment declined), their impact was minimal. For instance, the 1961 census revealed that Quebec's Francophones earned 65.5 per cent of the average income of the province's Anglophones.[117] Ten years later, this figure had only increased to 71.9 per cent.[118] Furthermore, Anglo-Saxon firms continued to dominate Quebec's economy. From 1961 to 1974, the percentage of the province's manufacturing labour force employed by Francophone-owned firms increased by less than seven percentage points (from 21.8 to 28.4 per cent).[119] Likewise, the number of Francophone-owned firms in Quebec's largest 100 companies remained at 20 over this same period.[120] As McRoberts states: 'if the Quiet Revolution goal of *maîtres chez nous* is understood to mean Francophone ownership of the Quebec economy, then clearly it had not been realized by the mid-1970s.'[121]

Of all the grievances identified by the FLQ, the least improvement had been made with regard to those which buttressed the movement's accusation of Quebec's social colonisation. Indeed, *la question linguistique* –the perceived vulnerability of the French language in Quebec – arguably increased in intensity from the late-1960s to the mid-1970s. *L'Affaire Saint-Léonards* triggered this escalation.[122] In November 1967, the Catholic school board of Saint-Leonards (a growing municipality 8 km north of Montreal) voted to eliminate the district's bilingual schools. An acrimonious debate ensued. On one side, the district's Italian community (the largest source of the bilingual school's enrolees) ardently demanded the right to freely choose the 'language of instruction' for their children. Facing them were a growing band of Francophones, concerned that Saint-Leonards' bilingual schools were not assimilating Allophones[123] into French-speaking society; but instead, contributing to the growing 'Anglicisation' of the province. Not surprisingly, given the scope and importance of the issues at stake, the debate surrounding the Saint-Leonards affair soon spread to Greater Montreal. The city was a 'linguistic tinderbox', as 'unilingualists' (i.e. Francophones who argued that French should be the sole language of instruction in Quebec's public schools) formed advocacy groups such as the *Mouvement pour li'intégration scolaire*, while the province's Allophones and Anglophones agitated for official bilingualism; with both sides calling on the government of Jean-Jacques Bertrand for action.[124]

Bertrand's (reluctant) solution was Bill 63, 'An Act to Promote the French Language in Quebec'. On the one hand, this bill did seek to placate Quebec's increasingly anxious Francophones; mandating the teaching of French in all of the province's English-speaking schools, and including measures to encourage new immigrants to learn French over English.[125] On the contested issue of 'language of instruction', however, Bill 63 ultimately sided with those in favour of 'free choice'; stating explicitly that schooling 'shall be given in the English language to any child for whom his parents or the persons acting in their stead so request at his enrolment'.[126] The reaction of Quebec's Francophones was 'unprecedentedly intense'.[127] Nationalists decried Bill 63 as 'a "linguistic Munich", an ignominious surrender on the part of the Bertrand government, a powerful encouragement to the anglicization of Quebeckers'.[128] Tens of thousands of demonstrators descended upon Montreal and Quebec City, urging the bill's repeal.

Even with the eventual ratification of Bill 63 on 27 November 1969, the passion generated by it did not abate. Bertrand's government was the first to experience this fervour, resoundingly losing the 1970 general election.[129] In

March 1971, the various unilingualist groups sought to take their struggle to the next level; creating a common front (the *Mouvement Québec français*) to agitate for the 'repeal of Bill 63 and ... legislation declaring French as Quebec's sole official language'.[130] It was not until 1974 (two years after the last FLQ act, and nearly three years after the movement's recruitment had dissipated), when the Liberal administration of Robert Bourassa introduced a new language bill (*Loi 22*), that Francophone anger over *la question linguistique* began to fade.

Selective government repression

The link between selective government repression and the FLQ's decreasing recruitment is convoluted. On the one hand, there is some evidence that the FLQ's recruitment did decline because of the Federal and Quebec Government's use of repression. The primary evidence in this regard is that the FLQ's intake of recruits waned concurrently with the intensification of the authorities' anti-FLQ campaign. As aforementioned, prior to October 1970, the Federal and Quebec Governments largely pursued the FLQ through the criminal justice system. That is, they issued warrants, laid charges within the established legal framework, and primarily focused their operations on those directly linked to *felquiste* violence. In the wake of the Cross and Laporte kidnappings, however, Quebec witnessed not only the weakening of the FLQ's ability to attract new recruits, but also the use of government repression on a scale unknown since the Conscription Riots of the First World War.[131] Specifically, beginning on 15 October 1970, the Federal and Quebec Governments: deployed thousands of troops to Quebec's major metropolitan centres; invoked emergency powers which placed Quebec 'under what amounted to a state of marital law';[132] and detained without charge hundreds of suspected FLQ members and sympathisers. Even after the Trudeau Administration withdrew the Canadian Army and revoked the *Public Order Act* in early-1971, the security forces continued to mount substantial and high-profile raids on suspected FLQ hideouts. The most notable of these occurred on the symbolically important first anniversary of Cross's kidnapping, when 60 police officers 'carried out a large-scale roundup in Montreal and arrested four FLQ members'.[133]

Another source of evidence that a relationship exists between the Federal and Quebec Governments' use of repression and the FLQ's declining recruitment is scholars who suggest that the authorities' vigorous countermeasures during and after the October Crisis were likely to have deterred potential recruits from joining the FLQ. Ross and Gurr, for instance, state that the 'waves of arrests of FLQ members from 1970 to 1972 undoubtedly had a deterrent effect on many would-be supporters'.[134] Likewise, Charters contends that

> a case can be made that deployment of the [Canadian] army, while perhaps unnecessary in respect of the existing threat (although the government may not have known that at the time), served as a deterrent to potential violent activity that might have arisen spontaneously had nothing been done.[135]

While it is possible to draw a tentative link between the authorities' post-October 1970 repression and the FLQ's declining recruitment, it is much more difficult to describe the Federal and Quebec Governments' use of repression during this period as having been *selective*. Indeed, in the wake of the October Crisis, people directly and knowingly connected with the FLQ formed only a minority of those targeted by the authorities as part of their anti-FLQ campaign. For example, between 16 October and 31 December 1970, the security forces operating in Quebec detained 468 people under the *War Measures Act*. Of these, only 33 were ever charged with terrorism-related offences;[136] while the vast majority (over 90 per cent) 'were not associated with the FLQ, nor did they have anything to do with the kidnappings'.[137]

After the Federal Government revoked its emergency powers in early-1971, the security forces did become more discriminating in who they arrested in relation to the FLQ. However, the RCMP's 'disruptive' or 'countering activities' tempered this renewed selectiveness. During the late-1970s, the RCMP grew increasingly frustrated that it was only reacting to, rather than 'forestalling', acts of separatist violence.[138] To redress this perceived deficiency, the RCMP sought to 'get ahead of the curve' by engaging in a four year campaign of disruption.[139] Specifically, the RCMP decided to employ repression (both overtly and covertly) against individuals and groups (such as the *Mouvement pour la défense des prisonniers politiques*, the *Parti communiste du Québec*, and *En Lutte*) that it believed were likely to conduct separatist violence in the future, though who were not necessarily associated with the FLQ. Examples of the RCMP's repression during this period include: the destruction of private property (the RCMP famously burnt down a barn in rural Quebec on 8 May 1971 to prevent a radical group from meeting there);[140] burglary and theft (e.g. in October 1972, the RCMP broke into the headquarters of the *Mouvement pour la défense des prisonniers politiques*, stealing and destroying 'half a tonne' of documentation);[141] and physical and psychological harassment.[142]

Discrediting the insurgent actor's ideology

There is conflicting support for the notion that the FLQ's recruitment declined because its ideology was discredited. On the one hand, it appears that the FLQ's recruitment problems did not coincide with a contraction of public approval for the movement's *goals* (i.e. the independence of Quebec and the adoption of a socialist socio-economic system). This is evident from two sources. The first of these is Hamilton and Pinard's collation of polls tracking Quebecois opinion about the option of independence between 1962 and 1980 (see Figure 3.2). This data suggests that public support for *le Québec libre* trended upwards following October 1970. The second source is the observation that Quebec's major trade unions – namely the *Fédération des travailleurs du Québec* and the *Confédération des syndicats nationaux* – as well as the *Parti Québécois* (one of the province's largest political parties) adopted increasingly socialistic postures from 1971 onwards.[143] For example, in November 1971, the president of the FTQ,

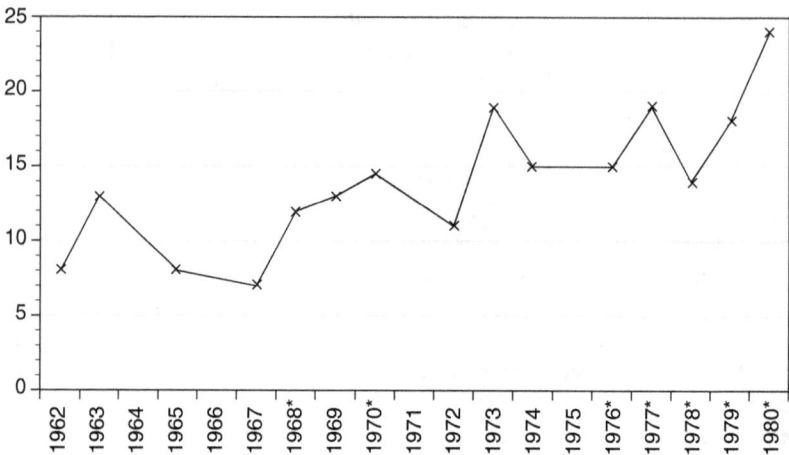

Figure 3.2 Male Francophones favouring Quebec independence, 1962–80 (source: R. Hamilton and M. Pinard, 'The Quebec Independence Movement', in C.H. Williams (ed.) *National Separatism*, Vancouver and London: University of British Columbia Press, 1982, 211).

Note
* Indicates average percentage.

Louis Laberge, 'called for a socialist Quebec and a united front to oppose the capitalist system';[144] while, in the same month, the *Parti Québécois* released a manifesto which advocated the need for 'social revolution' and a 'pro-labour bias'.[145] This seeming 'radicalisation' of the union movement and the ever increasing popularity of the *Parti Québécois* suggests that public support for the adoption of a socialist socio-economic system was likely to have remained at least steady in the wake of the October Crisis.

Conversely, it does appear that the FLQ's recruitment problems following the October Crisis did coincide with a contraction in public approval for the movement's strategy of violence. This is evident from two sources. The first of these are general observations in the secondary literature. Ross, for instance, claims that Laporte's murder represented 'a watershed in the political history of the FLQ. It helped swing public opinion away from the FLQ and toward more conventional forms of political participation'.[146] Charters echoes a similar sentiment, noting the contrasting fortunes of both the FLQ ('when the FLQ murdered Laporte, popular support evaporated almost overnight') and the democratic separatist movement ('a steady trend toward') after October 1970.[147] The second source is the growing number of *felquistes* who came to reject the FLQ's *modus operandi*, while continuing to embrace its goals, from 1971 onwards. The most notable of these 'renouncers' was Pierre Vallières, who announced in December 1971 that he had quit the FLQ and intended to pursue revolutionary separatism through the auspices of the *Parti Québécois*.[148] Similarly, Jacques and Louise

Cossette-Trudel (of Liberation Cell fame) declared in a 1972 letter from Cuba that 'armed agitation must stop. FLQ terrorism is a two-edged sword which has begun to cut the heads off the Quebecois themselves.'[149]

Two beliefs appear to have driven this contraction in public approval for the FLQ's strategy of violence. The first of these was that, in contrast with the FLQ's blithe dismissal of electoralism, the existence of the *Parti Québécois* precluded the need for *indépendantistes* to seek their goals through the use of violence.[150] Founded in October 1968 as the result of a merger between two separatist political parties (the *Mouvement souveraineté-association* and the *Ralliement national*), the *Parti Québécois* strove for both Quebec's independence and various social-democratic reforms.[151] The *Parti Québécois* was also strictly constitutionalist, attempting to achieve its goals solely through the legal, democratic system. According to Vallières in his January 1972 tome, *L'Urgence de choisir* ('Choose!'), the *Parti Québécois* was likely to prove an effective instrument for begetting *le Québec libre* because: (1) Quebec had an accessible electoral system that the masses could use 'effectively';[152] and (2) the *Parti Québécois*, unlike earlier separatist political parties, had not only an accomplished and respected leader (René Lévesque, a minister during the Lesage Administration), but also a potentially successful strategy for achieving the goal of independence.[153] Buttressing Vallières' argument was the *Parti Québécois'* gains in the 1970 provincial election; attracting 23.1 per cent of the vote (the second highest tally, after the victorious *Parti libéral du Québec*). Although it is true that the *Parti Québécois'* meagre return of seven seats, out of a possible 108, from this electoral haul was a source of contention in nationalist circles; the party's 'real accomplishments' (the 1970 election was the *Parti Québécois'* first),[154] the continued perceived legitimacy of Quebec's electoral system,[155] and the seeming upswing of political momentum in the *Parti Québécois'* favour,[156] meant that, to many, the 'democratic road to independence ... seemed a possibility'.[157]

The second belief was that, again in contrast with the FLQ's justificatory arguments, the use of violence was an inefficient means of engendering Quebec's independence. There were two aspects of this perception of violence's inefficiency. First, the 'hostile public reaction' to Laporte's murder showed *indépendantistes* that Quebecois support for political violence was shallow.[158] In Vallières' opinion, this meant that a violent revolutionary movement would unlikely be able to transform itself into an 'authentic people's army' and, in turn, achieve anything more than peripheral and ultimately pointless aggression.[159] The second aspect was that violence was increasingly seen more as a means of 'inviting ... harsh reprisals' on the Quebec independence movement, rather than a means of begetting change.[160] Vallières provided arguably the most paranoid version of this line of reasoning. To the former *felquiste*, the 'major lesson' of the October Crisis was that Ottawa realised its 'main threat' was not the FLQ, 'but the focalising political practice of the Parti Québécois, the union centrals and the citizens' committees'.[161] Consequently, it was in the interests of the Federal Government 'to provoke the opportunity that will allow it to intervene against the independentist and progressive forces of Quebec before the Parti Québécois can acquire the legitimacy of a democratically-elected government'.[162] Vallières maintained that, given the constraints imposed on the authorities by Canada's democratic system, liberal ideals, and free press, only separatist violence would provide the Federal Government with its desired pretext for crushing the Parti Québécois and the province's other legal separatist organs. In other words, Vallières framed violence not as an effective instrument of change, but as a likely instrument of the separatist movement's destruction.

Conclusion

The central focus of this chapter has been to illuminate why the FLQ's previously-robust capacity for regeneration began to weaken irrevocably following the October Crisis of 1970.

It sought to achieve this by first providing a detailed analysis of the FLQ, and the political and strategic environment in which the movement arose and pursued its 'armed struggle'.

Second, this chapter examined the FLQ's regenerative experience from the movement's inception in 1963 to its eventual demise in 1972. It is clear from this investigation that a decrease in recruitment played a greater role than an increase in attrition in weakening the FLQ's regenerative capacity. This finding is in accordance with the prevailing view in the literature that a decrease in recruitment is more important than an increase in attrition in bringing about the deterioration of an insurgent actor's capacity to regenerate.

Finally, this chapter examined whether the post-October 1970 decrease in the FLQ's intake of recruits was the result of the amelioration of grievances, the use of selective government repression, and/or the discrediting of the insurgent actor's ideology.

Regarding the first, this chapter found that the FLQ's recruitment declined even though the grievances which formed the basis of its collective action frame remained more or less unchanged. This suggests that ameliorating grievances is not a necessary condition for reducing an insurgent actor's intake of recruits.

With regard to selective government repression, this chapter observed that, while it is possible that the Federal and Quebec Governments' repression following the Cross and Laporte Kidnappings deterred aspiring *felquistes* from joining the FLQ, the authorities' use of repression during this period was not selective. These results suggest that: (1) as Leites and Wolf contend, a negative and conditional relationship may exist between government repression and insurgent recruitment; yet (2) selectiveness is not necessarily an indicator of whether a government's use of repression will have a deterrent effect.

Last of all, in reference to discrediting the insurgent actor's ideology, this chapter found that, while public approval of the *felquistes'* goal of an independent, socialist Quebec remained steady during the early-1970s, the FLQ's declining recruitment did appear to coincide with a contraction in public support for the movement's strategy of violence. These findings both support and detract from the literature's enthusiasm for discrediting an insurgent actor's ideology as a means of reducing the actor's recruitment. On the one hand, the FLQ case suggests that a link does exist between public approval for an insurgent actor's ideology and the strength of the actor's intake of recruits. However, given that the Canadian authorities were directly and deliberately responsible for only one of the three factors which appear to have discredited the FLQ's ideology, the FLQ case also raises questions about the extent to which governments can influence public perceptions of an insurgent actor's ideology.

4   *Movimiento de Liberación Nacional – Tupamaros*

The *Movimiento de Liberación Nacional – Tupamaros* (MLN-T) has one of the most interesting regenerative histories of any insurgent actor. After an early brush with defeat, the group learnt the importance of being able to replace losses with new recruits. Over the years that followed, the Tupamaros were able not only to develop such a capacity, but also to expand their membership. The group's armed struggle intensified as a result. Indeed, by 1971, *The Economist* suggested that the MLN-T was on the verge of launching an 'armed takeover' of the Uruguayan state.[1] The next 18 months, however, did not witness the formation of a Tupamaro government. Rather, in the face of a concerted and unrestrained assault by the Uruguayan armed forces, the MLN-T's ability to replace its losses with new recruits weakened. Unable to reverse this trend, the MLN-T eventually disappeared from the Uruguayan scene.

This chapter will seek to uncover why the MLN-T's previously-strong capacity for regeneration weakened. To assist this undertaking, this chapter is divided into six sections. The first three of these are contextual in nature, discussing: (1) the flow-on effects of the Cuban Revolution, and Uruguay's socio-economic problems of the mid-twentieth century; (2) characteristics of the MLN-T itself (such as the organisation's structure and recruitment process); and (3) the Uruguayan Government's security forces. The fourth and fifth sections, meanwhile, will focus on the MLN-T's capacity to regenerate; detailing the organisation's three different regenerative phases, as well as analysing the relative strength of an increase in attrition and a decrease in recruitment as catalysts of regenerative decay, and the dynamics of these factors. Finally, the sixth section will provide a summary of the chapter and its key findings.

Cuba and crisis: the foundations of an insurgency

During the 1950s and 1960s, Uruguay witnessed two developments that facilitated the rise of the MLN-T. The first of these was external; specifically, the Cuban Revolution. On 1 January 1959, after suffering a series of military setbacks, Fulgencio Batista, the President of Cuba, fled to the Dominican Republic; handing effective control of the country to the guerrilla forces of the *Movimiento 26 de Julio* (M-26). As Debray observes, these events 'descended like a clap of thunder' on traditional Latin American politics;[2] generating 'shockwaves that resonated across the hemisphere'.[3] These 'shockwaves', however, were not derived from the goals and motivations of the M-26. After all, the concepts of revolution and socialism had long been ensconced in the Latin American political consciousness. Rather, the significance of the Cuban Revolution lay in how it 'redefined revolutionary possibilities'.[4] As Wickham-Crowley states, prior to 1959, a Leninist conception dominated the 'cultural repertoire' of revolutionary action in Latin America.[5] This rejected the option of internal reform; maintaining that capitalist systems could only be overthrown through the use of force. However, it also stipulated that violence could impede the revolutionary process if it was employed before the necessary 'objective conditions' were in place. Thus, from the Leninist perspective, the task of the revolutionary was largely preparatory; that is, establishing an organisation and class-consciousness to take advantage of the 'objective conditions' once they transpired.

The Cuban Revolution, however, introduced a new 'mode of action' – or, in the words of a former Tupamaro, a 'new path to national liberation'.[6] This was initially fragmentary (derived from the speeches of Fidel Castro and Ernesto 'Che' Guevara), but was eventually codified by Che as a theory of revolutionary warfare. Known as *foco* theory, its dual essence was that: (1) 'the countryside is the basic area of armed fighting'; and (2) committed revolutionaries did not have to wait for the 'objective conditions' to exist before launching a revolution; but rather, that insurrectionary violence would create them.[7] As a number of authors have noted, *foco* theory was a deliberate simplification (if not outright distortion) of the Cuban experience; the result of internal politicking and a desire to generalise the M-26's strategy for wider adoption.[8] Nevertheless, *foco* theory did have tremendous appeal to aspiring revolutionaries across Latin America. It offered them a model that not only was drawn from their hemisphere (and was thus seemingly more applicable to the vagaries of their political life); but also forsook the arduous and time-consuming tasks of preparation, emphasising instead the transformative power (and more-glamorous undertaking) of revolutionary action. More importantly, *foco* theory had seemingly succeeded in the shadow of America's economic and military power. As Wickham-Crowley states:

> The thought processes of future guerrillas were probably remarkably neat: if Cuba can carry out a socialist revolution under the very nose, and against the resistance, of yanqui imperialism, then why not here as well, where the U.S. presence is so much less pervasive?[9]

It was the result of this instinctive appeal that the *foquista* approach came to dominate the cultural repertoire of revolutionary action in Latin America. This was evident from the early-1960s onwards, when Latin America witnessed an explosion of insurgent actors who were convinced that the use of force would 'jump-start' the revolutionary process in their countries. Prominent amongst these were: the *Frente Sandinista de Liberación Nacional* of Nicaragua (est. 1961), which, as Nolan notes, maintained a strict adherence to *foco* theory during the 1960s;[10] the

Fuerzas Armadas de Liberación Nacional of Venezuela (est. 1962); the *Fuerzas Armadas Revolucionarias* of Guatemala (est. 1962); and the *Ejército de Liberación Nacional* of Colombia (est. 1964). It was during this 'rush to revolution' that the founders of the MLN-T, similarly inspired by the exploits of the Cuban Revolution, began moving towards their own embrace of revolutionary action.

The second development that came to pass during the 1950s and 1960s was a prolonged crisis in Uruguay's politico-economic system. Since the country's independence in August 1828, two parties have dominated Uruguayan politics: the *Partido Colorado*, with its power base in the capital, Montevideo; and the *Partido Nacional-Blanco*, the traditional representative of the landholding elite.[11] For most of the nineteenth century, the Blancos and Colorados were, in the words of Taylor, 'pseudo-parties'.[12] That is, they were more 'the personal gangs of momentarily dominant *caudillos* rather than conscious articulators of genuine interests';[13] willing to use every means possible (including a frequent and disturbing recourse to violence) to achieve political supremacy. From the 1870s onwards, however, both parties gradually sought to moderate and institutionalise their rivalry. The guiding principle behind this process was that minority party participation should be guaranteed in the administration of government (known in Uruguay as *coparticipación*).[14] By the early-twentieth century, aided by President José Batlle y Ordóñez's crushing of an attempted Blanco uprising in 1904, inter-party violence was largely eliminated.[15]

It was due in part to this factor, as well as a series of labour, education, and social security reforms implemented by Batlle in the 1910s,[16] that Uruguay was able to embark upon an extended period of national growth and prosperity. Indeed, as the twentieth century progressed, scholars came to laud Uruguay as the 'Switzerland of South America'. In many respects, this academic esteem was warranted. After all, by the 1950s, Uruguay's citizenry enjoyed near-universal literacy;[17] the trappings of a modern welfare state;[18] and one of the highest per capita incomes and standards of living of any Latin American country.[19] Furthermore, Uruguay's democratic record for the previous 50 years had been arguably the continent's best. As Kohl and Litt state: '[t]here were honest and regular elections, a free press, civil liberties, few coups, and minimal military interference and civil violence.'[20]

A slump in world meat and wool prices during the mid-1950s dealt a blow to Uruguay's helvetic reputation. Despite the country's seemingly 'modern' character, the Uruguayan economy was essentially dependent on 'two tyrants … Their names are Cattle and Sheep'.[21] This dependency was related not so much to the size of the livestock sector (which was responsible for less than 20 per cent of the nation's GDP and employment), but to the fact that meat, wool, and hides accounted for over 80 per cent of the total value of Uruguay's exports.[22] As Daly thus states: '[t]he Uruguayan economy [was] like an inverted pyramid – it rest[ed] on its smallest sector and [was] held in balance by the flow of international trade.'[23]

During the decade following the end of the Second World War, strong international demand for livestock products helped Uruguay maintain its poise.

Indeed, the country's GDP expanded by an annual average of 4.8 per cent over this period.[24] However, when the end of the Korean War triggered a collapse in world commodity prices, the Uruguayan economy was unable to perform its balancing act any longer. Over the next five years, the country saw its export earnings virtually halve; dropping from an annual average of US$243.5 million between 1950 and 1954, to US$159.9 million between 1955 and 1959.[25] As the value of the country's exports shrank, Uruguay's industrial sector, which was heavily reliant on the international exchange earned by agricultural exports for the importation of necessary machinery and equipment, also began to struggle. Moreover, as the cash inflows of primacy producers contracted, so did their supply of raw materials to, and demand for the products produced by, Uruguayan industry. The government, meanwhile, already carrying a 'heavy burden of social welfare programs, public enterprises, and partially parasitical public employees',[26] had neither the capital nor the room for manoeuvre to stimulate the local economy.

As a consequence of all these factors, Uruguay's economic expansion first decelerated and then stagnated; with the country's GDP growing by an annual average of only 0.4 per cent between 1955 and 1965.[27] Though Uruguay's low rate of population growth (approximately 1.3 per cent) tempered the impact of this stagnation on per capita income, the effect was, nevertheless, still severe.[28] For instance, while Uruguay's per capita income grew by an annual average of 3.4 per cent between 1945 and 1955, it declined by 1.1 per cent between 1955 and 1965.[29] Further manifestations of Uruguay's stagnant economy included a doubling of the ranks of the nation's unemployed;[30] and a dramatic increase in inflation. Indeed, Uruguay's Consumer Price Index grew by an annual average of 23.4 per cent between 1956 and 1960; 30.7 per cent between 1961 and 1965; and an astonishing 66.1 per cent between 1966 and 1970.[31]

As Uruguay's economic conditions worsened, popular dissatisfaction rose. One of the earliest manifestations of this growing discontent was the electorate's rejection of the incumbent Colorado executive in 1958; handing control of the government to the Blancos for the first time in 93 years. As the country's economic crisis continued, the public's anger soon began to express itself in the form of public militancy.[32] In particular, strikes and work stoppages by Uruguay's various labour unions became 'an everyday fact of life in Montevideo'.[33] According to Weinstein, throughout the 1950s, an estimated 1,200,000 total man-days of labour were lost each year as a result of strikes. In 1963, this figure had skyrocketed to 2,500,000.[34] Political protests were also common, with Lyndon Johnson's visit on 11 April 1967 especially provoking 'violent demonstrations'.[35]

The government's response to Uruguay's worsening economic and political conditions was generally ineffectual. Though the Blanco-led administration introduced numerous measures aimed at addressing the country's waning economic fortunes (e.g. the *Ley de Reforma Monetaria y Cambiaria* of 1959); it was unable (and seemingly unwilling) to tackle Uruguay's debilitating structural deficiencies (such as the crippling cost of the government's various social programs and the ingrained politicisation of the bureaucracy).[36] Likewise, the government's response to societal and labour unrest was typically heavy-handed. For example, in February 1963, and in April, September and October 1965, the Blanco-led administration reacted to prolonged strikes by invoking emergency powers.[37] These were used to disperse bothersome strikers and, in some cases, arrest union leaders. Police also frequently clashed with and 'repressed' protestors angry with the government's hostile posture towards revolutionary Cuba between 1961 and 1964.[38]

The MLN-T

It was during this political turmoil of the early-1960s that a number of groups on the Uruguayan left began to embrace unconventional and illegal means of political participation. Though the circumstances of each group were unique, the primary reason for this shift was a general and growing disillusionment with the traditional avenues of political change. The experience of Raúl Sendic, arguably the most famous Tupamaros, provides a good example of this evolution. Beginning in the late-1950s, Sendic and some colleagues from Montevideo embarked upon an attempt to unionise the sugar workers of northwest Uruguay. These activists were motivated not only by a desire to improve the lot of the *cañeros* (traditionally one of the most impoverished sectors of Uruguayan society), but also a belief that unionising the sugar workers would help them shape the national political agenda. As Lopez-Alves describes, Sendic and his associates had faith both in the 'power of public opinion' and the instrumentality of parliamentary politics.[39] They thus believed that, by using conventional labour tactics, they could raise public awareness of the plight of rural workers; and this, in turn, would undermine the legitimacy of Uruguay's political and socio-economic system.

In 1961, Sendic and his compatriots were successful in unionising sugar beet workers in the Department of Paysandú, and cane-cutters in the Department of Artigas; forming the *Union Remolacheros del Este* and *Union de Trabajadores Azucareros de Artigas* (UTAA), respectively. These unions found it difficult, however, to secure major reforms, or even to force the sugar companies to abide by previously negotiated agreements.[40] Consequently, the leadership of the UTAA decided to press their demands at the heart of Uruguayan political life. In June 1962, hundreds of caneworkers and their families marched 600 kilometres from Artigas to Montevideo. Although these demonstrators were well-received by certain sectors of the political community, they were, in the main, ignored by the legislative and executive branches. According to Porzecanski, this seeming disregard was the tipping point for Sendic and his colleagues; as they concluded 'if the political system was not capable of even listening to its constituents, then it was surely time to abandon it'.[41] Over the next 12 months, they thus decided to pursue their revolutionary goals through increasingly violent means.

Sendic's Group was not the only one which chose the path of the armed struggle at this time. Others included: the *Movimiento de Ayuda al Campesino*

(MAC), comprised of disaffected members of the *Movimiento Revolucionario Oriental* (a radical left-wing party); several members of the *Partido Socialista*, who had become 'disappointed with their party's electoral performance in 1962'; the *Movimiento de Izquierda Revolucionaria* (MIR); and the *Federación Anarquista del Uruguay* (FAU).[42] These various groups were in frequent contact with each other. In mid-1963, they decided to form a loose federation called the *Coordinator*. This arrangement allowed them to combine their operational and intelligence capabilities, while also maintaining complete independence over their actions.[43] During the subsequent 12 months, member groups of the *Coordinator* conducted a number of 'revolutionary' actions, such as stealing explosives from a quarry in the Department of Maldonado on 19 April 1964, and firebombing several American businesses and two US embassy cars in Montevideo on 9 September 1964. In late-1964, some member groups (primarily the FAU) split from the *Coordinator* over ideological differences.[44] The remaining four groups – the MAC, the Socialists, Sendic's Group, and the MIR – decided to continue their association by forming a single, unified organisation. They called this new grouping the *Movimiento de Liberación Nacional – Tupamaros*.[45]

From 1965 to 1973, the Tupamaros were responsible for a total of 586 violent acts.[46] This figure includes: 258 robberies and thefts; 135 armed attacks; 81 bombings; 55 firebombings; 16 kidnappings (plus a further eight attempted kidnappings); and nine assassinations (plus an additional three attempted assassinations). The MLN-T also conducted 21 'coercive broadcasts'. That is, the temporary occupation of either a public place (such as a theatre) or a radio station in order to transmit Tupamaro propaganda. Targets of MLN-T violence generally included: perceived corrupt and exploitative businesses; members of the Uruguayan police force; and foreign embassies and their staff.

Despite Uruguay's size, the MLN-T was able to capture significant international attention during its eight-year campaign; influencing revolutionaries not only in neighbouring Brazil and Argentina, but also as far away as Quebec and West Germany.[47] The primary reason for this was the group's reputation as 'romantic revolutionaries'.[48] As Kohl and Litt state: 'Their actions were characterised by flawless planning and execution, and, perhaps most important, by style'[49] – what Connolly and Druehl refer to as the organisation's 'human touch'.[50] For example, during a bank robbery in May 1968, a Tupamaro administered first aid to an elderly bystander who had 'suffered a nervous shock'.[51] On another occasion in February 1969, after learning that the $300,000 they had recently stolen from the San Rafael Casino included tips for the casino operators, the Tupamaros 'returned a portion of the confiscated money earmarked for the workers'.[52]

The MLN-T's 'romantic' approach to revolutionary warfare was also evident (to some extent) in the deaths attributable to the organisation. Of the 37 people that died as a result of Tupamaro violence, only four were non-combatants (Carlos Burgueno, Juan A. Betancour, Professor Armando Acosta y Lara, and Julio Morató).[53] Furthermore, Burgueno's death was unintentional (he was killed in crossfire between the police and the Tupamaros in October 1969), and Acosta y Lara was a recently retired Undersecretary for the Interior (and thus had played a leading role in the Government's anti-Tupamaro efforts). Nevertheless, notwithstanding this apparent discrimination, the MLN-T clearly did not shy away from the use of lethal force. Over the course of their campaign, the Tupamaros killed 21 police officers, 11 members of the *Fuerzas Armadas* (the Uruguayan Armed Forces, or FFAA), and one American embassy official (Dan Mitrione) who had been advising the Uruguayan police on counterinsurgency tactics and interrogation methods.[54] Arguably the most bloodthirsty of the MLN-T's attacks occurred on 18 May 1972, when a Tupamaro cell, in an attempt to assassinate the Commander-in-Chief of the FFAA, Oscar Gravina, brutally killed four of his guards.

Organisationally, the MLN-T was structured to ensure a hierarchical flow of information, while also maintaining the security principle of compartmentalisation (i.e. restricting access to information in order to reduce the likelihood of its discovery by adversaries). The basic building block of this structure was the cell. Comprised of between two and six members, each cell specialised in either 'commando-type operations or service-type work', and upheld strict confidentiality amongst its membership.[55] Cells were coordinated and supervised by an Executive Committee; the organisation's 'primary decision-making organ'.[56] To assist this coordination process, the Executive Committee grouped the MLN-T's various cells into columns, based on either geographic or, in the case of Montevideo's numerous cells, functional requirements. These columns were not decision-making units, but purely administrative entities that sought to take advantage of such tactical benefits as economies of scale.[57] Nevertheless, each column was intended to have a regenerative function. That is, they 'had to be able to continue operating even when the rest of the organization had been dismantled';[58] thus ensuring even if 'only one column survives, the possibility exists of regenerating the whole movement'.[59] In theory, the MLN-T had one further organisational level, the National Convention. Consisting of representatives from each of the organisation's cells, the National Convention was originally intended to appoint the Executive Committee, and to 'deal with broad ideological issues, such as strategies to be pursued or attitudes to be taken'.[60] However, given the security risk involved to the MLN-T in having a large number of its members concentrated in one place at one time, the National Convention met on only two occasions: in January 1966 and March 1968.[61]

Unfortunately, as is the case with most (if not all) insurgent actors, there is a dearth of direct information about the MLN-T's membership. Nevertheless, the industriousness of two scholars has, to some extent, counteracted this deficiency. The first of these academics is Arturo Porzecanski. In the immediate aftermath of the MLN-T's demise, Porzecanski compiled 'all information released to the press by Uruguay's police and armed forces concerning both guerrillas captured and later convicted and guerrillas killed in action' between 12 December 1966 and 22 June 1972.[62] After discarding 'what appeared to be contested or very incomplete entries', Porzecanski obtained a list of 648 Tupamaros.[63]

The second scholar who has shed light on the MLN-T's membership is Astrid Arraras. In her examination of the Tupamaros' journey from violent revolution-aries to respectable members of Uruguay's democratic process, and with the benefit of greater access to primary source material, Arraras sought to expand upon and improve Porzecanski's compilation. Adopting a similar methodology to Porzecanski, Arraras collated 'names and personal information of members and sympathizers of the MLN-T from the police and Armed Forces communi-qués published in the newspaper, *El Día*, from December 12, 1966 to December 31, 1972'.[64] After revising her list with the assistance of former Tupamaros,[65] Arraras estimated that 'a total of 1,549 members (including the founders) or sympathizers of the MLN-T were arrested and prosecuted during 1966–1972'.[66]

Of course, this figure is not an exact measure of the MLN-T's total member-ship. As Arraras concedes, her approximation excludes those Tupamaros whose arrest and prosecution were not publicised, or who managed to avoid arrest and prosecution altogether (primarily by fleeing overseas).[67] Furthermore, the figure of 1,549 does not include those Tupamaros who were arrested and prosecuted during 1973, or the 47 members of the MLN-T who were killed between 1965 and 1973.[68] Once these factors are taken into consideration, it is likely that the MLN-T's total strength lay approximately between 1,700 and 1,800 members and sympathisers. This estimation will be used in the following investigation.

Collective action frame

Not surprisingly, the focus of a significant portion of the MLN-T's diagnosis was Uruguay's deteriorating economic situation. For example, the Tupamaros drew attention to: the country's ballooning inflation;[69] the 'plight of rural wage workers';[70] the reduction of 'pensioners and old people to beggary';[71] and the 'daily deaths' of children in hospital (due not to the incurability of their afflic-tions, but to simple 'malnourishment').[72] The MLN-T also highlighted inequali-ties in Uruguayan society. For instance, the organisation's *Proclama de Paysandú* of 1971 contrasted the wretched conditions of the *cantegriles* (where the 'cold comes through the walls and the *guriserio* [the children] have to sleep embracing the dogs to keep warm'), with the fortunes of the rich (who had 'com-fortable homes, top physicians, vacations houses in the resorts; for them there is never any meat shortage').[73]

From the Tupamaro perspective, the primary culprit of Uruguay's socio-economic problems was capitalism. As Porzecanski states, the MLN-T attributed 'the failure of the agricultural and industrial sectors to grow and expand … to inherent contradictions and malfunctions of Uruguay's primitive capitalist system'.[74] Likewise, the organisation portrayed inflation as a 'redistributive mechanism of the social product in favour of the capitalist'.[75] The MLN-T also attributed blame for Uruguay's economic decline to the country's bourgeoisie. According to the Tupamaros, through the 'rampant' corruption of officials and the infiltration of vital government positions,[76] the 'rich' (i.e. 'the owners of the ranches, the cattle, the factories, the banks') had 'taken over' Uruguay.[77] They thus acted as a brake on the government's ability to reverse the system's exploitation of the poor majority. As the Tupamaros stated in 1971: 'they [the rich] are in the government, occupying ministries, administering what is theirs so that everything continues as it is, the rich rich and the poor poor.'[78]

The Tupamaros provided many examples of what they saw as the government's defence of the 'established order'. These included: the firing of 'hundreds of workers';[79] continued interference in educational matters and the suppression of the student movement;[80] the introduction of a wage freeze (which resulted in a 'drop of income of the poorest, while the interests of those who are responsible for the crisis remain untouched');[81] the banning of strikes and the repression of protesters;[82] the closing down of newspapers; and the imprisonment of people 'without proof of guilt' and the infliction of '[t]orture and beatings ... with complicity of the Judiciary'.[83] The Tupamaros also highlighted the government's inability (and seeming unwillingness) to punish the crimes of the powerful. After a series of financial scandals involving prominent members of Uruguay's elite (the perpetrators of which remained largely untouched), the MLN-T parodied the government's approach to justice:

> A plantation owner can engage in troop contraband at will on behalf of the Brazilian meat packers. Leave the population without meat, leave the country without foreign exchange. This ranch owner can become minister at any moment. Or president. But for a man of the people who steals a sheep in Vichadero [a small, rural town] to feed his children who are dying of starvation, the price is three years in jail.[84]

The MLN-T's diagnosis also consisted of a condemnation of what it saw as Uruguay's subservience to foreign powers. Although this complaint encompassed Uruguay's historically interventionist neighbours, Brazil and Argentina, it was primarily aimed at what the Tupamaros regarded as the region's leading imperialist power, the United States. For instance, the MLN-T declared in 1969 that: '[t]here has never been such shameless direct intervention by the United States embassy. Through the International Monetary Fund and through national organizations, the government of the United States dictates its policies to our worthless government and it obeys.'[85] Similarly, in 1968, the Tupamaros lambasted 'the stranglehold of North American capital on our country, and the increasing interference of neighbouring dictators'.[86]

The MLN-T's solution to Uruguay's many problems was twofold: (1) the seizure of power by the revolutionary movement; and (2) the implementation of major structural reforms.[87] The goal of these reforms was to create a socialist socio-economic system; one which was in line with Uruguay's specific historical and developmental conditions. The MLN-T's proposed reforms included: transferring ownership of all large farms and industries from employers to employees; state control over the economy, especially in such areas as foreign trade, savings and loans, and the development of vital industries; the nationalisation of all foreign investments; the redistribution of 'excess' land and the provision of housing for Uruguay's homeless; the redistribution of wealth on the basis of 'to each according to his needs'; the provision of free education and modern medical services; and the replacement of the nation's capitalist criminal justice system with one 'that takes essential human values into consideration'.[88]

The overarching strategy which the MLN-T advocated to achieve its goals was armed struggle. In this sense, the Tupamaros likened themselves to José G. Artigas and other heroes of Uruguay's struggle for independence during the early-nineteenth century.[89] The MLN-T's articulated strategy had two central tenets. The first of these was its urban focus. This put the MLN-T at odds with *foco* theory, which stressed that 'the countryside is the basic area of armed fighting'.[90] However, to the founders of the Tupamaros, such an emphasis on the countryside did not appear to suit their strategic environment. Uruguay, after all, was one of the most urbanised countries in Latin America, with only 15.1 per cent of its population living in rural areas in the early-1960s.[91] Furthermore, Uruguay's terrain was not appropriate for the type of rural warfare envisioned by Guevara; consisting of 'neither vast jungles nor mountains'.[92] Rather, Uruguay's advantages seemed to lie in its urban centres, specifically Montevideo. With approximately 50 per cent of the country's population, and '300 square kilometres of buildings', the Tupamaros believed that the nation's capital could provide them with not only an ideal clandestine environment, but also ready access to potential recruits and other necessary resources.[93] Thus, the Tupamaros became one of the earliest proponents of urban guerrilla warfare.

The second tenet of the MLN-T's strategy was that the armed struggle would progress in three phases.[94] First, the MLN-T would establish and consolidate a 'revolutionary movement'.[95] Violence during this phase would be used for three purposes: (1) to acquire the necessary materials (such as munitions, money, and medicine) for waging a guerrilla war; (2) to harass and wear down the forces of repression; and (3) to raise popular consciousness about the need for revolution. The MLN-T sought to accomplish this last goal through 'occupation broadcasts' and 'armed propaganda'. That is, acts of violence which would either draw attention to or illustrate the repressive nature of the governing regime.[96] After it had established a revolutionary movement, the MLN-T would then attempt to transform public support for revolution into a 'people's army'. Once this had been achieved, the MLN-T would then embark on the final phase: the destruction of the repressive forces.

The MLN-T justified its armed struggle primarily in terms of efficacy. In all, the organisation deployed three utilitarian justificatory arguments. The first of these was that the underlying conditions were supportive for the waging of an armed struggle. The 'most important' examples of these favourable circumstances included: (1) 'The conviction that the [economic] crisis, far from having been overcome, is becoming worse by the day', thus ensuring the existence of 'popular discontent in the coming years'; (2) Uruguay's 'high degree of unionization', which presented opportunities for synchronising the union movement's ability to paralyse 'the basic services of the state' with the MLN-T's general insurrection; and (3) the poor state of Uruguay's armed forces, which at 'some 12,000 men sketchily equipped and trained, constitute[d] one of the weakest organizations of repression in America'.[97]

The MLN-T's second utilitarian justificatory argument was that armed struggle was the only option available to beget the organisation's goals. Of course, the Tupamaros recognised that there were many instruments for affecting change in Uruguay's political system, such as parliamentary action, demonstrations, and proclamations.[98] They portrayed these as largely ineffective, however; capable of only 'improbable and remote change'.[99] The source of this inefficacy was the bourgeoisie domination of the country's legal and conventional avenues of political reform. As the MLN-T decried, a 'rich minority' controlled the bureaucracy,[100] Uruguay's two main political parties (the Blancos and Colorados),[101] and the security forces;[102] as well as benefiting from a legal system which was 'conceived with the idea of maintaining the private ownership principle of the capitalist system'.[103] The bourgeoisie could thus marshal this explicit and implicit power to frustrate any legislative or popular threat to their interests.[104] As a Tupamaro stated in 1970:

> The masses are learning that whatever action on their part affects the regime always clashes with it in one way or another; that their struggle for wage increases invariably comes up against the regime's wage-freeze laws; that any attempt at demonstrating or holding assemblies aimed against the interests of the regime or the order the regime defends are repressed; and that any means for the expression of ideas that say something critical of the order defended by bayonets is muzzled, as has happened to so many newspapers.[105]

In this context, 'the only means of effective expression and action', the only instrument that 'will allow the complete destruction of the old so that we can begin to build a new, truly free country' was the armed struggle.[106]

The MLN-T's third utilitarian justificatory argument was that armed struggle was an effective means of accomplishing the organisation's goals. Despite rejecting his focus on the countryside, the Tupamaros were heavily influenced in this regard by Guevara's notion of the transformative power of violence. This inspiration is evident in the MLN-T's famous *Thirty Questions to a Tupamaro* of 1967, which stated that 'revolutionary action in itself, the very act of arming oneself, preparing, equipping and pursuing activities that violate bourgeois legality, generates revolutionary consciousness, organization, and conditions'.[107] In other words, the Tupamaros believed that the use of violence against the capitalist system would build support – a 'mass movement' – for its overthrow.[108] The use of force would create this revolutionary consciousness by polarising Uruguayan society. Specifically, the growing intensity of the battle between the government and the Tupamaros would force the broader public to make a choice between 'support or disappearance' of the revolutionary dream; a choice between the inherent ineffectiveness of traditional modes of political expression and 'the direct road embodied by the armed group and its revolutionary action'.[109] To support this line of contention, the MLN-T highlighted China, Cuba and Algeria as examples where 'armed struggle' created 'revolutionary consciousness and conditions ... even before the "classic" conditions for an insurrection existed'.[110]

Although the organisation primarily relied on notions of utility, the MLN-T also justified its armed struggle in terms of morality. Specifically, the Tupamaros framed their use of violence as an 'indispensable' response to the 'veiled and evident violence' which the capitalist regime used to 'defend an unjust order'.[111] However, the MLN-T did not fully develop this line of reasoning; nor did they utilise it frequently.

Recruitment process

Keenly aware of the need for new recruits, the MLN-T had a relatively formal and organised recruitment network. The key feature of this was the *Comandos de Apoyo Tupamaro* ('Tupamaro Support Commands', or CATs). Formed in 1968, the CATs were compartmentalised cells attached to each of the organisation's columns. As well as engaging in a host of propaganda and administrative duties (such as training cadres and collecting intelligence), the CATs were also responsible for recruiting new members. To help facilitate this goal, many CATs integrated themselves in the student movement and Uruguay's various trade unions.[112] The CATs would seek to establish interpersonal linkages with potential members by either: (1) identifying and approaching promising candidates; or (2) simply providing potential members a point of contact with which to volunteer.[113] In addition to the CATs, the MLN-T also encouraged its broader membership base to identify prospective recruits where possible.

Once identified, the Tupamaros subjected their prospective recruits to a lengthy and rigorous investigatory process.[114] As the MLN-T stated in April 1968, its goal was 'not to incorporate into the Organisation every person who wants the Revolution', but only those needed to create and maintain 'a highly efficient, clandestine apparatus'.[115] Thus, the Tupamaros repeatedly interviewed prospective recruits, and compiled extensive reports on their 'life, habits, political and occupational background, personality, friends, health record, and all other aspects that might [have been] significant'.[116] On the basis of these reports, and generally a period of probation, the Executive Committee accepted or rejected prospective recruits' candidatures for membership. It is important to note, however, that, despite this lengthy and seemingly thorough recruitment process, in retrospect, 'many Tupamaro leaders have admitted that in reality they were [neither] cautious nor selective' in recruiting new members.[117]

The Uruguayan Government and its security forces

At the beginning of the 1960s, Uruguay was a constitutional democracy, with a bicameral legislature and a collegial executive.[118] During the mid-1960s, however, the country's political elite was concerned that the nine-member *colegiado* (with its seemingly constant bickering and divided responsibilities) was hindering the government's ability to reverse Uruguay's economic decline.[119] Thus, in December 1966, the government convened a plebiscite on constitutional reform; the central plank of which was the creation of a unitary executive. Passing with 59 per cent of the vote, Uruguay's new constitution was ratified in February 1967. As well as dismantling the *colegiado*, the 1967 Constitution also gave the Uruguayan President the sole ability to invoke *Medidas Prontas de Seguridad* ('Prompt Security Measures', or MPS) 'in the event of serious and unexpected external attack or internal upheaval'.[120] This power would later prove to have an important impact on both the development and decline of the MLN-T's campaign.

The Uruguayan Government maintained two security forces: the *Policía Nacional* (PN) and the *Fuerzas Armadas* (FFAA). The former (along with the Maritime Police; an agency under the supervisory of the Uruguayan Navy) was responsible for maintaining internal security and was the lead actor in the government's counterinsurgency campaign until September 1971. In 1970, the PN was comprised of approximately 17,000 officers; 40 per cent of which were assigned to urban areas.[121] According to Porzecanski, two branches of the PN 'were given the task of containing and eliminating the Tupamaros'.[122] First, the Information and Intelligence Directorate, which utilised various forensic, data management and human intelligence resources to analyse and provide information about the MLN-T. Second, the Metropolitan Guard, a paramilitary organisation under the jurisdiction of the chief of police of Montevideo. Consisting of 600 officers in 1966, the Metropolitan guard 'was originally intended to be an elite police corps', with its members having met strict physical requirements and received training in military-style weapons and crowd-control devices.[123]

As of 1970, the FFAA consisted of 16,000 soldiers. The majority of these (12,000) were members of the Uruguayan Army; split between nine cavalry regiments, two armoured regiments, five infantry regiments, five artillery groups and five engineer battalions.[124] The Army's mechanised units were 'equipped with both light and medium tanks', such as the M-24 and the M-113AI Armoured Personnel Carrier (APC).[125] The Navy and Air Force each consisted of approximately 2,000 personnel; with the former primarily operating escort and patrol vessels and the latter a small number of combat and transport aircraft.[126] In comparison with Uruguay's overall population, the FFAA was one of the largest armed forces in Latin America (ranked third in 1970).[127] However, as Kaufman states, the FFAA's strength was

> still insufficient to prevent aggression from either the Argentinean or Brazilian armed forces. Because of this, the military in Uruguay was for a long time seen as little more than a decorative force, the minimum required for a 'normal' country.[128]

Nevertheless, Uruguay's armed forces were highly professional and 'enjoyed the reputation of being one of the most apolitical in Latin America'.[129] As a result of this political aloofness, the FFAA's share of Uruguay's Gross National Product (GNP) was relatively modest; averaging at 1.4 per cent during the 1960s.[130] The FFAA's political nature began to erode in September 1971, when the government transferred responsibility for combating the Tupamaros from the PN to the Uruguayan armed forces. This decision, and its effects, will be discussed in greater detail below.

The MLN-T's regenerative experience

The preparatory phase, 1965–July 1968

At its inception in early-1965, the MLN-T was comprised of approximately 50 active members.[131] These 'founders' spent the first three-and-a-half years of the organisation's existence engaged in the relatively mundane tasks of effecting a revolution, such as establishing training and administrative facilities, as well as workshops for the manufacture of explosives, propaganda, and forged documentation.[132] The MLN-T was rather inconspicuous during these formative years; conducting only 34 violent acts between January 1965 and July 1968.[133] These were primarily aimed at securing arms and money; building public support for the organisation (i.e. armed propaganda), as well as providing the Tupamaros with much needed 'target practice'.[134]

Initially, the MLN-T did not place a great emphasis on recruiting new cadres. While this process was certainly not discouraged, the 'founders' were more interested in consolidating their revolutionary organisation and maintaining clandestinity. As Fernández Huidobro (a former Tupamaro and founder) admitted, growth was not a task of the 'first order' for the MLN-T.[135] A series of clashes with the police in late-1966 challenged this attitude. On 22 December, several Tupamaros in a stolen car stumbled upon a police patrol. In the ensuing shoot-out, one Tupamaro, Carlos Flores, was killed. During the subsequent police investigation, a number of hide outs were discovered, approximately 25 Tupamaros were forced underground, several Tupamaros were arrested, and a police-officer (Silveira Regalado) and a Tupamaro (Mario Robaina) were killed.[136]

Although these events did not lead to the destruction of the MLN-T, they did constitute a defeat; compelling the organisation to engage in a period of reconstruction and reflection. One of the most important insights that emerged from this process was that '[l]osses are relatively high in the city'.[137] Indeed, the MLN-T came to perceive attrition as 'unavoidable'; 'a natural and therefore calculable and foreseeable law' of urban guerrilla warfare.[138] The Tupamaros also realised that, before December 1966, they had neglected the issue of recruitment; especially the political action which was required to attract new personnel. This neglect had placed the MLN-T in a precarious position, as the group was not able to adequately replace 'those who [were] captured'.[139] As a consequence of these insights, the Tupamaros decided to shift greater emphasis to the issue of recruitment; claiming that 'only growth can save us'.[140] To facilitate this membership drive, the MLN-T created two new columns, and stepped-up its propaganda campaign.[141] For instance, in 1967, the organisation released *Treinta Preguntas a un Tupamaro* ('Thirty Questions to a Tupamaro'); a 'document destined to attract new members'.[142] Over the next 18 months, the organisation gradually expanded, while conducting few operations in a deliberate attempt to avoid possible confrontations with the security forces.

The rise of the Tupamaros, August 1968–August 1971

On 13 June 1968, in an attempt to address the nation's spiralling inflation and recent social disturbances, Uruguayan President Jorge Pacheco Areco invoked MPS and introduced a series of draconian 'reforms', such as price and wage freezes, and the 'militarization of striking bank workers'.[143] Two weeks later, Pacheco Areco followed up these initial measures by declaring martial law, which subjected newspapers to 'official rather than self-censorship', and decreed courts martial for anyone 'demanding wage increases'.[144] It was during this turmoil that the MLN-T judged its strategic environment to be favourable for the intensification of its revolutionary campaign. Thus, on the morning of 7 August 1968, the Mario Mendez commando unit of the MLN-T kidnapped Ulysses Pereira Reverbel; a close friend of the Uruguayan President, and director of the *Administración Nacional de Usinas y Transmisiones Electricas*.[145] After holding Pereira Reverbel for four days in their 'people's prison', the Tupamaros released him unharmed. This episode, which shocked both the authorities and the general public, marked the beginning of a new chapter in the MLN-T's armed struggle.

Over the next three years, the Tupamaros' campaign would be characterised by two trends. The first of these was the MLN-T's increasing rate of violence. Prior to August 1968, the Tupamaros had conducted an average of less than one violent act per month. However, after Pereira's kidnapping, the MLN-T's monthly average skyrocketed; from four during the latter months of 1968, to six in 1969, 13 in 1970, and 16 in 1971 (see Figure 4.1).[146] Indeed, by mid-1971, the MLN-T had earned the reputation of being 'the most effective guerrilla group in Latin America';[147] with *The Economist* declaring that:

> Uruguay's urban guerrillas, the Tupamaros, can no longer be shrugged off as a gang of romantic conspirators, out of touch with the people. In Monte-video ... they are running what is virtually a parallel government, and the country is facing the threat of an armed takeover.[148]

The second trend of the MLN-T's campaign from August 1968 to August 1971 was the organisation's increasing rate of attrition. During the first three years of their existence, notwithstanding their 'defeat' of December 1966, the Tupamaros had few confrontations with Uruguay's security forces. In all, the organisation suffered only four arrests and two deaths from January 1965 to July 1968.[149] However, from August 1968 onwards, the MLN-T's losses began to mount. For example, during the last five months of 1968, the Tupamaros suf-

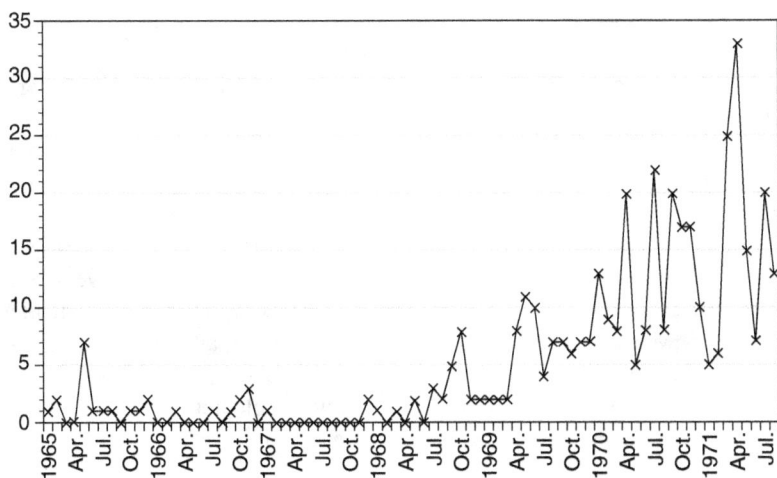

Figure 4.1 MLN-T violent acts, 1965–August 1971 (source: Documentación y Archivo de Lucha Armada DC. 'Cronología Básica 1954–1973'. Montevideo: Facultad de Humanidades, la Universidad de la República, 2006).

fered an average of three arrests per month. In 1969, this figure rose to nine; climbing again to 13 in 1970 and 14 during the first eight months of 1971 (see Figure 4.2).[150] Altogether, 389 Tupamaros were arrested (and an additional 13 were killed) between August 1968 and August 1971. Notable clashes with the police during this period included: the loss of 20 Tupamaros (17 arrested,

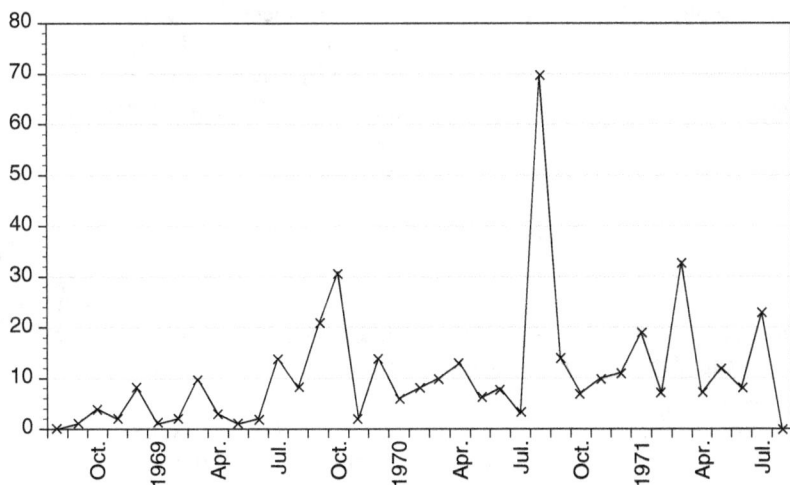

Figure 4.2 MLN-T arrests, August 1968–August 1971 (source: Documentación y Archivo de Lucha Armada DC. 'Cronología Básica 1954–1973'. Montevideo: Facultad de Humanidades, la Universidad de la República, 2006).

three killed) during the MLN-T's Pando Operation of 8 October 1969; and the capture of nine members of the MLN-T's central leadership (including Sendic, Edith Morales and Raul Bidegain) on 7 August 1970.

The MLN-T's losses during 1968–71 did cause the organisation some consternation. For example, while reviewing their performance in 1969, the Tupamaros acknowledged that 'there are too many prisoners', and proposed to 'reinforce internal security' by creating a centralised 'security service' which would operate in each column.[151] The MLN-T also stressed the importance of training and 'military preparation', especially in such areas as discipline, '[o]peration of the cells', and 'conduct in front of the police' (i.e. what to say and how to behave when stopped by the security forces).[152] However, this concern notwithstanding, the MLN-T's losses were not debilitating. As highlighted above, although the organisation's rate of attrition increased from August 1968 to August 1971, so did its rate of operations. In other words, the Tupamaros were able not only to withstand the police's counterinsurgency, but to thrive in the face of it.

The decline of the Tupamaros, September 1971–73

The primary reason why the Tupamaros were able to accomplish this feat was because of their strong regenerative capacity. Through a 'massive influx' of new recruits, the MLN-T was able to both offset its losses and expand.[153] As aforementioned, this growth began in 1967 and continued until 1971.[154] Unfortunately, a lack of accurate data prevents this book from identifying exactly when and how many new recruits joined. However, some indicative factors include: the expansion of the MLN-T's structure in September 1968 from two to seven columns;[155] Colonel d'Oliveira's statement that, in the wake of Pereira Reverbel's kidnapping, '[n]ew recruits flocked to the movement';[156] a Tupamaro interviewed by Lopez-Alves noting that recruitment increased during 1969 – a phenomenon reflected in that year's *Balance*, which hoped that the organisation 'continued its growth' over the next 12 months;[157] and Kohl and Litt's observation that neither the MLN-T's 'recruitment nor technical capacity nor leadership capability was, in fact, seriously impaired' by the August 1970 seizure of Sendic and other prominent Tupamaro leaders.[158]

Somewhat surprisingly, the catalyst for the demise of the MLN-T and its regenerative capacity was an event that, at the time, both the Uruguayan Government and the Tupamaros perceived as a tactical success for the insurgent actor. On 6 September 1971, 100 Tupamaros, including Sendic and other high-profile leaders, escaped from *Punta Carretas* (the country's main penitentiary for holding convicted subversives). This dramatic breach came in the wake of a similar mass breakout by 38 female members of the MLN-T (known as *Tupamaras*) from the *Penal de Mujeres* two months earlier. These escapes represented a breaking point for Pacheco Areco and his confidence in the PN's ability to contain and counteract the Tupamaro threat. Thus, on 9 September 1971, the Uruguayan President transferred primacy of the government's counterinsurgency efforts from the police to the armed forces by decree 566/971.

The impact of this shift, however, was not immediately apparent. On the one hand, the leadership of the FFAA decided not to launch an instant counteroffensive; but rather, to engage in an extended period of training and organisation. For example, Porzecanski describes how the FFAA's Intelligence Service began in September 1971 (with the assistance of the PN's Information and Intelligence Directorate) to prepare 'the background information and plans' required for future counterinsurgency operations.[159] The Tupamaros, meanwhile, had declared a unilateral ceasefire. The reasoning behind this decision was linked to the creation of the *Frente Amplio* ('Broad Front', or FA), a coalition of more than a dozen leftist parties, in late-1970. Initially, the MLN-T was concerned about the FA's potential to 'marginalise' the organisation.[160] Thus, in an attempt to maintain both their role as the 'vanguard' of the revolution and the legitimacy of the armed struggle, the Tupamaros announced their limited support for the FA in December 1970.[161] In the wake of the September breakout, the MLN-T decided to strengthen its support by declaring a unilateral ceasefire to coincide with the FA's campaign for the November presidential election. This move was unexpected, given both the MLN-T's intrinsic rejection of the electoral process as a means of engendering desired reforms, and the seeming success the organisation had attained through the use of revolutionary violence. However, it appears that the Tupamaros took the 'calculated risk' of declaring a ceasefire in order to further prevent their isolation from the broader Uruguayan left.[162] Specifically, the MLN-T was seeking to allay FA concerns that continued Tupamaro violence might give the government a pretext to postpone the election, as well as encourage the burgeoning number of right-wing, anti-Tupamaro vigilante groups (which had first appeared in early-1971) to harass and intimidate FA supporters.

Notwithstanding the MLN-T's ceasefire, the next two months witnessed a campaign 'accompanied by a level of violence unparalleled since the civil war period at the beginning of the century', and the eventual loss of the *Frente Amplio* (polling just over 18 per cent of the vote).[163] In response to this defeat, and widespread suspicion about voting irregularities, the Tupamaros revoked their ceasefire in December 1971.[164] One of the organisation's first major actions was the kidnapping of Nelson Bardesio on 25 February 1972. A police officer, Bardesio was suspected of, and later confessed to, being a member of a right-wing vigilante group. On the basis of information provided by Bardesio, the Tupamaros issued a communiqué on 14 April 1972 sentencing to death a host of government officials and members of the security forces for their alleged role in controlling the anti-Tupamaro groups. Within hours of the communiqué's release, the MLN-T had killed three of those listed: Oscar Delega Luzardo (a senior police officer), Ernesto Motta (a naval counter-intelligence officer), and Professor Armando Acosta y Lara.[165]

These assassinations shocked the administration of newly-elected President Juan Maria Bordaberry (Pacheco's hand-picked successor); as well as the FFAA, which had just lost its first officer to Tupamaro violence. Bordaberry, under strong pressure from the military, acted swiftly; immediately asking the General Assembly for fresh emergency powers and a declaration affirming the existence of an 'estado de guerra interno' ('state of internal war'). The next day, the legislature acceded to the President's demands. Martial law descended on Uruguay, as the FFAA were given free reign to fulfil their counterinsurgency mandate 'without regard for judicial accountability of individual rights'.[166] After an eight-month 'phoney war', the battle between the military and the Tupamaros was finally joined.

It was at this point that the MLN-T's capacity to regenerate began to irrevocably weaken. This deterioration was the function of two factors. The first of these was a dramatic increase in the MLN-T's rate of attrition. Previously, the Tupamaros' losses had been sustainable. However, the advent of the military's counteroffensive significantly altered the MLN-T's strategic environment. Striking with both speed and ferocity, the FFAA instantly 'dominated the street scene'; manning roadblocks and systematically raiding houses across the country.[167] Hundreds (and eventually thousands) of Uruguayans suspected of 'subversive' behaviour – including members of the FA, as well as the student and union movements – were swept-up in mass arrests.[168] The military subjected these detainees to abusive yet methodical interrogation sessions; the information from which was used to launch new waves of arrests.

The Tupamaros were simply unable to withstand this onslaught. By the end of April, 84 Tupamaros had been arrested and a further 11 killed. As 1972 progressed, the MLN-T's attrition continued to mount, with the organisation recording 116 arrests in May; 329 arrests and seven deaths in June; 251 arrests and six deaths in July; and 171 arrests and four deaths in August. Over the remaining months of 1972 and the first half of 1973, the organisation lost a further 183 members. In addition to these arrests and deaths, approximately 100–200 Tupamaros fled into exile after April 1972; primarily settling in Argentina, Brazil, and Chile.[169]

The second factor responsible for the weakening of the MLN-T's regenerative capacity was the organisation's declining ability to attract new recruits. Interestingly, the Tupamaros had highlighted problems with their recruitment as early as March 1972; arguing that Uruguayan society (both the oligarchs and the people) had grown 'accustomed' to their presence.[170] As the FFAA intensified its counterinsurgency efforts after April 1972, the MLN-T's recruitment problems worsened.[171] While publicly claiming that the organisation continued to receive 'popular support', which meant, 'on a day-to-day basis, new fighters, new hideouts';[172] in private analyses, the MLN-T acknowledged that, after the 'blow of 72', its 'possibilities of recruitment' had 'diminished'.[173]

As a consequence of these two factors, the MLN-T began to shrink. The organisation's rate of operations reflected this contraction. Initially, the Tupamaros met the FFAA's counteroffensive with a dramatic increase in activity. Indeed, April, May, and June of 1972 recorded some of the MLN-T's highest monthly tallies of violent acts. However, as Figure 4.3 illustrates, the Tupamaros' rate of operations started to decline from July to September; with the organisation unable to conduct more than a handful of violent acts from October 1972 to July 1973.[174] By this time, virtually every member of the

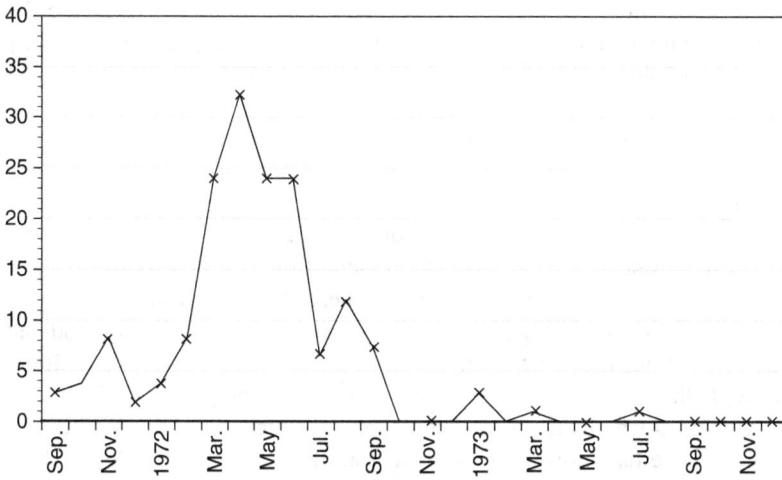

Figure 4.3 MLN-T violent acts, September 1971–December 1973 (source: Document-ación y Archivo de Lucha Armada DC. 'Cronología Básica 1954–1973'. Mon-tevideo: Facultad de Humanidades, la Universidad de la República, 2006).

MLN-T was either dead, in prison, or in exile.[175] Over the next few years, those Tupamaros living in Argentina, Chile, and Brazil would attempt to revive the organisation in Uruguay. To assist the achievement of this goal, they published numerous items of propaganda, and even sought guerrilla training in Cuba.[176] However, divisions soon emerged amongst the expatriates over the future direction of the MLN-T. This schism, as well as the continued dominance of the FFAA, hindered efforts to relaunch the armed struggle. For all extents and purposes, by the end of 1973, the MLN-T, as an organisation actively seeking the violent overthrow of Uruguay's socio-economic system, ceased to exist.[177]

An important postscript to the MLN-T's decline was the FFAA's gradual subjugation of the Uruguayan political system. As its campaign against the Tupamaro wound down, the military, concerned about the quality of Uruguay's civilian leadership, became increasingly interventionist. This culminated in February 1973, when the FFAA refused to accept the President's choice for Minister of Defence, General Antonio Francese. At first, Bordaberry sought the assistance of other civilian political leaders to resist the military's encroachment. However, after realising that he commanded little support both within and without his party, Bordaberry formed an alliance with the FFAA. Under the terms of this agreement, the President accepted that 'government policy would be supervised by a newly created National Security Council [COSENA] clearly dominated by the military'.[178] However, this was not the final blow against Uruguay's democratic system. On 27 June 1973, after several months of tension with the Senate over the immunity of Senator Enrique Erro (whom the FFAA suspected of complicity with the Tupamaros), Bordaberry launched a military-backed coup. As a result, the Uruguayan Parliament was closed down (replaced by a presidential-nominated, 25-member council), and the FFAA was empowered to ensure the functioning of public services. For the next 12 years, Uruguay was governed by a military dictatorship, until democracy was restored on 1 March 1985.

Analysis

From the above account of the MLN-T's regenerative experience, it appears that an increase in attrition played at least an equal, and arguably greater, role than a decrease in recruitment in weakening the organisation's capacity to regenerate. Three observations form the basis of this judgment. The first of these is that the deterioration of the MLN-T's regenerative capacity coincided with both an increase in attrition and a decrease in recruitment. The second observation, meanwhile, is that the MLN-T's loss of personnel seemingly increased at a rate greater than that at which the organisation's intake of recruits declined. Although a lack of adequate data prevents this book from quantifying the scale at which the MLN-T's recruitment decreased following Bordaberry's declaration of a 'state of internal war'; the language used by the Tupamaros to describe their recruitment problems during 1972 (such as noting that their 'possibilities of recruitment' had 'diminished', and complaining that Uruguayans had become 'accustomed' to their presence) does not convey an impression of either urgency or fervency. The MLN-T's loss of personnel, on the other hand, clearly increased at a phenomenal, frenzied, and ultimately catastrophic rate. Where 502 Tupamaros were arrested over the 44 month period from August 1968 to March 1972 (at an average of approximately 11 per month); more than double this amount (1,008) were arrested over the six months between April and September 1972 (at an average of 11 Tupamaros every two days).[179]

The final observation is that the MLN-T's burgeoning loss of personnel appears to have had a greater impact on the organisation's decision-making process than its declining intake of recruits. Beginning with its loss of 61 Tupamaros (including several members of the Executive Committee and a column leader) within seven days of the 'state of internal war', the MLN-T's burgeoning rate of attrition seemingly threw the organisation into a state of disorientation. As David Cámpora, a former Tupamaro, later acknowledged; reeling under the FFAA's onslaught, the Tupamaro leadership 'lost control, the Organisation galloped, without knowing where it was going'.[180] Or, in the words of Arraras, the 'Tupamaros experienced internal chaos as the Armed Forces dismantled their organization'.[181] The MLN-T's declining intake of recruits, in contrast, was ostensibly a secondary concern – with the Tupamaros and their supporters seemingly more interested in 'avoid[ing] arrest', rather than problems of recruitment.[182]

In light of the above findings, the remainder of this chapter will seek to provide greater insight into why the above shifts in Tupamaro recruitment and attrition occurred. Specifically, this section will examine: (1) whether the MLN-T's increase in attrition was the result of the improvement in the government's intelligence collection capabilities and/or restricting civil liberties; and (2) whether the MLN-T's decrease in recruitment was the result of the amelioration of grievances, selective government repression, and/or the discrediting of the insurgent actor's ideology.

The improvement of the government's intelligence collection capabilities

The MLN-T case provides strong support for the notion that an insurgent actor's loss of personnel will increase if the opposing government's ability to collect information about the insurgent actor improves. Prior to September 1971, 'poor intelligence' hampered the Uruguayan Government in its attempts to counteract the Tupamaro threat.[183] As the United States Agency for International Development (USAID) (which was tasked with advising and training Uruguay's police during the 1960s) stated in 1968, the PN's 'intelligence apparatus [was] deficient'[184] – lacking the ability to collect not only high-end intelligence derived from 'penetrating' the insurgent actor, but also 'low-level, "listening post" information'.[185] However, from April 1972 onwards, the Uruguayan Government was able to inflict an increasing level of casualties on the MLN-T because, in part, its ability to collect information about the Tupamaros improved.

This improvement had three primary sources. The first of these was the military's expanded and systematic use of torture as a means of acquiring information. Of course, the FFAA was not the first government institution to use torture against the MLN-T. According to the former chief of police intelligence, Alejandro Otero, the PN first began to employ torture against suspected Tupamaros in 1968; largely on the counsel of US security 'advisor' Dan Mitrione.[186] Indeed, a bipartisan congressional committee tasked with investigating the subject 'concluded unanimously' in June 1970 'that "inhumane" torture, including electric shocks, cigarette burns and psychological pressure, was used by police as a "normal, frequent and habitual" manner on Tupamaros, common criminals and innocents alike'.[187] However, according to Servicio Paz y Justicia's (SERPAJ) investigation of human rights violations in Uruguay, it was not until April 1972, when 'political prisoners were moved to the jurisdiction of the military courts, that the practice of torture reached truly alarming levels'.[188] To support this claim, SERPAJ cites its survey of 313 former Uruguayan prisoners (arrested between 1972 and 1985), in which 'only 1 per cent of the men and 2 per cent of the women said they had not been tortured'.[189]

Similarly, under the military, the use of torture 'became much more prolonged, systematic, and "sophisticated"'.[190] During the police' anti-Tupamaros campaign, torture was used in a 'brutal' yet 'haphazard' manner.[191] The FFAA, however, deliberately sought to maximise the provision of information from its interrogations. Interrogatees were thus subjected to a range of physical and psychological abuse, including: prolonged standing in a rigid position without food or rest (known as *plantón*); repeated electrocution below 220 volts ('the death threshold'); repeated submersion under water 'to the limit of asphyxia' (known as *tacho* or *submarinos*); extended use (up to months) of hoods and blindfolds; and simulated firing squads.[192] Of course, the information obtained from the use of these cruel measures was not always reliable.[193] Nevertheless, it does appear that the sheer quantity of information obtained from the FFAA's '[e]nergetic and professional' interrogations did lead to the arrest of numerous Tupamaros.[194] This seeming variance in the efficacy of the Uruguayan military's use of torture as a means of acquiring information is in accordance with the literature's general understanding of the complex relationship between torture and intelligence collection.[195]

The second source of the authorities' improved ability to collect actionable intelligence was Tupamaro defectors. Beginning in March 1972, a number of detained members of the MLN-T decided to collaborate with the FFAA's intelligence apparatus. The most important of these was Héctor Amodio Pérez; a former leader of the General Command of Montevideo 'with seven years combat experience'.[196] After his arrest on 25 February 1972, Amodio Pérez is believed to have revealed the 'whereabouts of at least 30 Tupamaro hideouts, including the *carcel de pueblo*, a principal field hospital, and a number of arsenals and documentation centres'.[197] However, as Porzecanski contends, the true value of Amodio Pérez's betrayal came not from the capture of such Tupamaro facilities, but from the information he supplied about the 'workings of and individuals involved in the Tupamaro organization'.[198] Other prominent Tupamaro collaborators included Marcos Píriz Budes (leader of the Interior, arrested 9 May 1972) and Alicia Rey (also a former leader of the General Command of Montevideo, detained 19 May 1972).[199] The reasons why these Tupamaros decided to defect is unknown. Some authors have speculated about the impact of leadership tensions on Amodio Pérez's decision; caused by either his own personal ambition, or the reintegration of senior Tupamaros who escaped from *Punta Carretas* back into the organisation.[200]

The third source of the improvement in the authorities' ability to collect actionable intelligence was a breakdown in the MLN-T's internal security. As aforementioned, the Tupamaros' primary mechanism to frustrate government intelligence was the principle of compartmentalisation. That is, the organisation maintained strict confidentiality amongst its membership, limited contact between cells and columns, and dispensed operational information on a rigid 'need-to-know' basis. Thus, any information a Tupamaro could pass on to the security forces (either voluntarily or involuntarily) would necessarily be limited. The MLN-T also provided its members with a plethora of security rules and tips. These included: methods of detecting and avoiding intelligence monitoring (such as using the reflection of glass mirrors to observe suspicious bystanders);[201] how to evade pursuers; and how to neutralise technical devices, such as microphones and telephonic lenses.[202]

According to Lopez-Alves and d'Oliveira, stresses had already begun to emerge in the MLN-T's security regime during 1970 and 1971; primarily due to the dramatic expansion of the organisation over the previous few years.[203] However, it was not until the gaolbreaks of July and September 1971 that the

MLN-T's internal security truly began to unravel. The main problem was that the 'captured guerrillas obviously got to know one another well during their imprisonment'.[204] While this familiarity was undoubtedly beneficial for the prisoners' mental stability, it did undermine the MLN-T's compartmentalisation once the incarcerated Tupamaros reintegrated back into the organisation. Not only were the escapees acquainted with a great number of guerrillas across a variety of cells and columns (facilitating later military interrogations); but their obvious familiarity also encouraged the broader erosion of the principle of compartmentalisation throughout the remainder of the organisation. A further problem triggered by the 1971 gaolbreaks was the escapees' general lack of recent operational experience. Many forgot security codes, the location of hideouts, and correct operating procedures. Thus, as Arraras states, 'it was not surprising that numerous Tupamaros broke security rules'.[205]

Miller proposes a fourth source for the authorities' improved intelligence: the Uruguayan public. According to Miller, during the 1960s and early-1970s, the majority of Uruguayans maintained a passive demeanour towards the government's anti-Tupamaro campaign. This passivity was borne out of a distrust of the police and 'Tupamaro intimidation'.[206] However, Miller contends that, when the FFAA assumed control of Uruguay's counterinsurgency campaign, the public's inertia evaporated; as individuals 'rushed to military headquarters with information on suspected guerrilla personnel and activities'.[207] Miller credits this popular embrace to the public's general respect for the Uruguayan military; a respect associated with the FFAA's apolitical and effective reputation.

Notwithstanding the confidence in which Miller frames his assertions, it is difficult to judge the veracity of this alleged shift in public attitude and action. On the one hand, central aspects of Miller's argument – i.e. the police' unpopularity, the public's passivity towards counterinsurgency operations, the respect accorded to the military (at least up until early-1972) – have been documented elsewhere.[208] On the other hand, few other authors have noted a similar rise in public informants after September 1971. Furthermore, Gallup polls taken in 1971 and 1972 indicate that public sympathy for the MLN-T was at least stable during the FFAA's campaign. For instance, the proportion of respondents who believed that the Tupamaros were 'well-intentioned revolutionaries' averaged at 41 per cent across eight polls over this period, with a high of 52 per cent and a low of 35 per cent. Similarly, the proportion of respondents who believed that there was some justification for the MLN-T's campaign rose from 38 per cent in early-1971 to 51 per cent in mid-1972.[209] This opinion polling data suggests that greater research is required on the Uruguayan public's receptiveness towards the government's counterinsurgency efforts before a definitive conclusion can be reached.

Restricting civil liberties

At first glance, the notion that the MLN-T's loss of personnel increased because the Uruguayan Government restricted civil liberties does appear to have some validity. After all, the MLN-T's skyrocketing attrition did coincide with the Bord-aberry Administration's introduction of a series of laws that severely circum-scribed the freedoms and protections of Uruguay's citizenry. The first of these legislative measures was the declaration of a 'state of internal war'. Approved by the Uruguayan Parliament on 15 April 1972, this decree: authorised preventative detention; suspended the right of habeas corpus; 'derogated the inviolability of the domicile, the right of assembly, association, and speech'; 'extended the time that an individual could be held before being presented to a magistrate'; transferred the prosecution of civilians accused of 'subversion' from civilian to military courts; and stripped the judiciary and parliament of 'control over arrests'.[210] On 10 July 1972, the Uruguayan Parliament, at the urging of President Bordaberry, lifted the 'state of internal war' and, in its place, enacted the *Ley de Seguridad del Estado y el Orden Interno* ('Law of the Security of the State and Internal Order', or LES).[211] This measure essentially institutionalised the 'state of internal war', while also expanding the jurisdiction of military courts to the civilian realm.[212] The LES remained as part of Uruguay's legal framework until its repeal in 1985.[213]

A number of authors have also attested to the seeming importance of the Uru-guayan Government's restriction of civil liberties to the MLN-T's post-April 1972 burgeoning loss of personnel. For instance, d'Oliveira, a then-Colonel in the Uruguayan Army, declares '[i]t was with' the 'legal weapons' of suspending habeas corpus, allowing 'searches of private property without a warrant', permit-ting preventative detention, and subjecting Tupamaros 'to the more summary and severe process of military justice', that 'the armed forces obtained the results which are a matter of record'.[214] Likewise, Weinstein contends that, due to it being 'given carte blanche and unhampered by judicial or constitutional con-straints', the FFAA was able to enjoy 'almost total success against the guerrillas, all but destroying their infrastructure, capturing hundreds of active supporters, and detaining thousands of other suspects'.[215]

Two observations, however, suggest that the relationship between the Borda-berry Administration's restriction of civil liberties and the MLN-T's post-April 1972 increase in attrition was more coincidental, and less causative, than the above accounts assume. The first of these is that the declaration of a 'state of internal war' and the LES were not the first time that the Uruguayan Govern-ment had restricted civil liberties as part of its anti-Tupamaro campaign. Rather, the Administration of Pacheco Areco curtailed individual freedoms on three occasions during its approximately four year tenure (December 1967 to March 1972). First, by invoking *Medidas Prontas Seguridad* (MPS) between 13 June 1968 and 15 March 1969; second, by once again invoking MPS between 24 June 1969 and 29 August 1969; and third, by declaring a twenty-day 'state of siege' on 10 August 1970. Both of Pacheco Areco's invocations of MPS 'limited the right to strike, to hold meetings, and freedom of speech, restricted the right to judicial due process, habeas corpus, and increased police powers and weakened those of the legislature'.[216] The 'state of siege', meanwhile, essentially mirrored that 'state of internal war', except that it did not transfer jurisdiction over civil-ians accused of subversion to the military courts.[217]

The second observation is that the Uruguayan Government's pre-April 1972 restriction of civil liberties did not trigger an increase in Tupamaro attrition. Indeed, it appears that, if a relationship did exist between Pacheco Areco's emergency powers and the MLN-T's loss of personnel, it was most likely negative. For example, over the 24 non-consecutive months between August 1968 and September 1971[218] during which the Uruguayan Government *did not* curtail civil liberties, the MLN-T lost a monthly average of 10.4 members. However, over the other 12 months during which the Uruguayan Government *did* restrict individual freedoms, the MLN-T lost a monthly average of 10.0 members.[219] It is important to note that this latter figure is inflated, given that 34 of the 69 Tupamaros arrested in August 1970 were detained prior to the government's declaration of a 'state of siege'.

A possible explanation for why the MLN-T's attritional experience varied under Pacheco Areco and Bordaberry's restrictions of civil liberties is that Bordaberry's emergency powers were more restrictive than Pacheco Areco's, and thus more likely to have had an impact on Tupamaro attrition. Although this line of reasoning does have some intuitive appeal, it is undercut by the twin observations that: (1) as aforementioned, Pacheco Areco's 'state of siege' was, in essence, equally restrictive as Bordaberry's 'state of internal war'; and (2) despite this, Pacheco Areco's 'state of siege' had no discernible impact on the MLN-T's loss of personnel. For instance, from 10 to 30 August 1970 (the period during which the 'state of siege' was in effect), the Uruguayan police arrested 35 Tupamaros.[220] While this figure may seem impressive, especially given that the MLN-T lost a monthly average of 13.3 members during 1970, it is slightly less than the 43 Tupamaros that the PN arrested during the ten days before and after the 'state of siege'.[221]

The amelioration of grievances

The notion that an insurgent actor's recruitment will decline if its grievances are ameliorated has little explanatory power with regard to the MLN-T. Rather, the MLN-T's intake of recruits waned even though the grievances which comprised the organisation's collective action frame remained more or less unimproved. This is arguably most evident concerning the MLN-T's central grievance, the poor state of the Uruguayan economy. Indeed, over the last six years of the MLN-T's campaign, the organisation's recruitment exhibited a positive relationship with Uruguay's economic welfare. For instance, during the late-1960s – a period when the Tupamaros experienced a massive influx of new recruits – Uruguay began to emerge from its economic doldrums. Through such measures as the devaluation of the peso and the introduction of wage and price freezes, the Pacheco Areco Administration managed to stimulate economic growth (e.g. in contrast with an annual average of 0.1 per cent between 1958 and 1967, Uruguay's GDP expanded by 1.6 per cent, 6.1 per cent. and 4.7 per cent in 1968, 1969, and 1970, respectively) and bring the country's rampant inflation under some semblance of control (e.g. the rate of change in the consumer price index shrank from 125 per cent in 1968, to 21 per cent in 1969 and 16 per cent in 1970).[222]

Pacheco Areco's reforms, however, while seemingly successful, merely suppressed, rather than eliminated, the structural problems afflicting Uruguay's economy. Thus, the early-1970s – a period when the MLN-T's recruitment began to decline – witnessed the return of stagnation, with the country's GDP contracting by 1.0 per cent and 3.6 per cent in 1971 and 1972, respectively, and growing by a meagre 0.8 per cent in 1973.[223] Though the Uruguayan economy would expand by 3.1 per cent and 4.4 per cent over the next two years, three factors would overshadow this growth.[224] First, the country's rate of inflation, which had tempered somewhat during the late-1960s, once again began to mushroom; rising from 23.9 per cent in 1971 to an average of 83 per cent over the 1972–74 period.[225] Second, and related to the first factor, Uruguay's real wages started to steadily decline; contracting by an annual average of 7.1 per cent between 1971 and 1975.[226] Lastly, Uruguay's unemployment rate continued to increase; rising from 7.1 per cent in 1971 to 12.9 per cent in 1976.[227] From these figures, it is difficult to conclude that the Uruguayan economy was in any better shape when the MLN-T's campaign faded compared to when it began.

A similar dynamic to that outlined above is apparent with regard to the MLN-T's second major grievance, the authorities' defence of the 'established order'. Of course, determining the extent to which this grievance was ameliorated is difficult, given its highly subjective nature. However, it stands to reason that perceptions of the Uruguayan Government's favouritism towards the 'rich and powerful' would likely have worsened in the wake of the declaration of a 'state of internal war'. After all, beginning on 15 April 1972, the FFAA launched an unrestrained and unprecedented assault on Uruguayan society; targeting not only Tupamaros, but also those generally associated with the pursuit of societal change (such as students, left-leaning activists and politicians, and union members). Furthermore, as Arraras describes, from 1971 to 1975, the military and President Bordaberry 'disarticulated institutions of the opposition and exercised control over society in general'; pursuing 'neoliberal economic policies which resulted in the demobilization of the nation's popular sectors'.[228] In this environment, it is unlikely those who sympathised with the MLN-T's collective action frame would have reached the judgement that the authorities had abandoned, rather than escalated, their defence of the established order.

Selective government repression

There is mixed support for the notion that the MLN-T's recruitment declined because of selective government repression. On the one hand, it is feasible that the Uruguayan Government's use of repression from mid-April 1972 onwards deterred potential recruits from joining the MLN-T. Two observations form the basis of this judgment.

The first of these is the demonstrated efficacy of the FFAA's anti-Tupamaro campaign. In contrast with the police, which unsuccessfully struggled for six years to check Tupamaro violence, and, in the process, earned themselves a reputation for incompetence;[229] the armed forces had essentially destroyed the MLN-T within five months of the declaration of a 'state of internal war' – capturing and killing approximately 1,000 Tupamaros over this period.[230] It is likely that such a prompt and potent display of government power would have dramatically increased the perceived riskiness of joining the MLN-T.

The second observation is the brutality of the FFAA's anti-Tupamaro campaign. Generally speaking, the armed forces conducted its operations against the MLN-T with unrestrained aggression, employing the full weight of its coercive power and freely resorting to lethal violence when required. Furthermore, as already discussed, the FFAA submitted basically all of its captives to physical and psychological abuse; a phenomenon which (thanks to MLN-T propaganda) was widely-publicised. Of course, the PN was also brutal in its pursuit of the MLN-T, engaging in extensive and heavy-handed search operations, and using torture against suspected Tupamaros. The police' brutality, however, appears to have been merely *detested*, while the FFAA's was genuinely *feared*. For example, whereas Porzecanski describes the police' search of 20,000 homes in August 1970 as having 'created great resentment among Montevideo's population', SERPAJ portrays the military's similar raids and mass arrests after April 1972 as having spread 'fear and terror'.[231] Weinstein suggests that this difference in perceptions was possibly linked to the 'systematic' and 'sustained manner' in which the FFAA employed its repressive techniques, compared to the generally haphazard nature of the PN's repression.[232]

Like the FLQ case, while it is possible to draw a tentative link between the Uruguayan Government's repression from mid-April 1972 onwards and the MLN-T's declining recruitment, it is much more difficult to describe this repression as having been *selective*. Rather, those knowingly and directly connected with the MLN-T formed only a minority of those targeted by the FFAA's repressive actions. For instance, from mid-April to December 1972, the armed forces detained approximately 5,000 Uruguayans as part of its anti-Tupamaro campaign.[233] However, only one-fifth of these detainees were MLN-T members.[234] The remainder were students, union members, politicians (the most notable of which was Luis Batalla, a Christian Democrat labor leader, who was 'found dead after four days in an army camp'), and ordinary citizens – the majority of whom 'had no connection with the Tupamaros'.[235] Further examples of the FFAA's indiscrimination include: the routine use of 'extensive house searches';[236] and the harassment of the political opposition.[237] This latter campaign reached its nadir on 17 April 1972 when the armed forces killed seven civilian members of the *Partido Comunista* (PC). An officer at the scene summed up the FFAA's approach when he stated: 'So long as my comrades are being killed, I am not making fancy distinctions between leftists'.[238]

Discrediting the insurgent actor's ideology

A dearth of adequate data regarding Uruguayan attitudes towards the MLN-T's goal of establishing a socialist socio-economic system and its strategy of violence during 1972 and 1973 prevents this book from reaching a definitive judgment about whether the MLN-T's recruitment declined because the organisation's ideology was discredited. However, two pieces of information suggest that it is unlikely that the latter factor contributed to the former outcome. The first of these is the 18.3 per cent of the vote that the *Frente Amplio* (FA) received at the November 1971 general election. This tally is significant because: (1) the FA campaign on a clear socialist platform (e.g. the coalition called for the expropriation and redistribution of large-landed estates, the nationalisation of Uruguay's banking and export systems, and 'active government participation in the industrial sector');[239] and (2) it was nearly double what the member parties of the FA had collectively received at the previous election in 1966.[240] This increase suggests that public approval for the MLN-T's goal of a socialist socio-economic system was trending upwards immediately before the organisation's recruitment problems began.

The second piece of information is the Gallup polling data measuring Uruguayan opinions about whether 'there was some justification for the MLN-T's campaign'. Given that the proportion of people who agreed with this statement rose from 1970 to 1972 (from a low of 17 per cent to a high of 51 per cent), it is unlikely that public approval of the MLN-T's strategy of violence would have contracted over the same period.[241]

Conclusion

The primary objective of this chapter has been to shed greater light on why the MLN-T's previously robust capacity for regeneration began to weaken from April 1972 onwards.

It sought to achieve this by first examining a variety of contextual information relevant to the emergence and persistence of the Tupamaros.

Second, this chapter examined the MLN-T's regenerative experience from the organisation's inception in 1965 to its eventual demise in 1973. It is clear from this investigation that an increase in attrition played at least an equal, and arguably greater, role than that of a decrease in recruitment in weakening the MLN-T's capacity to regenerate. This finding is seemingly at odds with the prevailing view in the literature that a declining intake of recruits is more important than a burgeoning loss of personnel in bringing about the deterioration of an insurgent actor's capacity to regenerate.

Third, this chapter examined whether the MLN-T's attrition increased because of the improvement of the government's intelligence collection capabilities and/or the restriction of civil liberties. Regarding the former, this chapter found that the Uruguayan Government's ability to collect information about the Tupamaros did improve during 1972 and 1973, and this improvement does appear to have significantly contributed to the MLN-T's burgeoning loss of personnel. These results support the literature's emphasis on enhancing intelligence collection capabilities as a means of increasing an insurgent actor's attrition. With regard to the latter, this chapter observed that, while the MLN-T's burgeoning loss of personnel from April 1972 onwards did coincide with the Uruguayan Government's declaration of a 'state of internal war', earlier legislative measures which restricted civil liberties (some to the same extent as the 'state of internal war') did not have a noticeable impact on the MLN-T's rate of attrition. These findings suggest that: (1) in the Tupamaro case, the relationship between restricting civil liberties and increasing an insurgent actor's loss of personnel was coincidental, rather than causative; and (2) broadly speaking, restricting civil liberties is not a necessary condition for increasing an insurgent actor's rate of attrition.

Finally, this chapter examined whether the MLN-T's recruitment declined because of the amelioration of grievances, the use of selective government repression, and/or the discrediting of the insurgent actor's ideology. Regarding the first, this chapter found that the grievances which lay at the heart of the MLN-T's collective action frame remained more or less unchanged during the period when the organisation's recruitment declined. This supports the conclusion from the previous chapter that ameliorating grievances is not a necessary condition for reducing an insurgent actor's intake of recruits.

With regard to selective government repression, this chapter observed that, while it is possible the Uruguayan Government's repression following the declaration of a 'state of internal war' deterred aspiring revolutionaries from joining the MLN-T, the authorities' use of repression during this period was not selective. These results support the implications from the previous case that: (1) a negative and conditional relationship may exist between government repression and insurgent recruitment; and (2) selectiveness is not necessarily an indicator of whether a government's use of repression will have a deterrent effect.

Last of all, in reference to discrediting the insurgent actor's ideology, this chapter found that, although a lack of direct evidence hinders attempts to discern the exact nature of the relationship between the MLN-T's recruitment and public approval of the organisation's goal and strategy of violence, it is unlikely that the latter contracted while the former declined. This suggests that it is possible for an insurgent actor's intake of recruits to decline, even though public support for its ideology remains unchanged.

5 Provisional Irish Republican Army

At first glance, the Provisional Irish Republican Army (PIRA) may appear an odd choice for a book examining why the regenerative capacities of insurgent actors weaken. After all, the PIRA is generally portrayed as having been resistant to any and all security force pressure. As Bell states: 'A grand sweep of all the active [Volunteers], the introduction of internment, all the panaceas to destroy the Provos would only have opened the way for the generation in waiting to become operational.'[1] However, it is important to recognise that the PIRA's regenerative capacity was not static for the entire 28 years of its campaign. Rather, during the period from roughly mid-1972 to 1977, the PIRA not only experienced a significant deterioration in its ability to replace lost personnel with new recruits, but the organisation also came the 'closest' in its history to 'collapse and defeat'.[2]

The central purpose of this chapter is to illuminate why the PIRA's capacity to regenerate weakened during the mid-1970s. To assist this undertaking, this chapter is divided into six sections. The first three of these are contextual in nature, outlining: (1) the history of the Northern Ireland conflict; (2) characteristics of the PIRA itself (such as the group's operational history and collective action frame); and (3) the security forces with which the Provisionals were confronted. The fourth and fifth sections, meanwhile, will focus on the PIRA's capacity to regenerate; describing the organisation's fluctuating regenerative experience, and analysing the relative strength of an increase in attrition and a decrease in recruitment as catalysts of regenerative decay, and the dynamics of these factors. Finally, the sixth section will provide a summary of the chapter and its key findings.

The roots of the Northern Irish conflict

As Fay, Morrissey and Smyth note, it is possible to trace the antecedents of 'The Troubles' back into the deep 'recesses of Irish, European and British history'.[3] For the sake of brevity, however, this book will begin its account on Easter Monday, the 24th of April, 1916. On this day, approximately 1,300 Irish Volunteers (a nationalist militia) and 220 members of the Irish Citizen Army (a socialist vanguard) occupied key points throughout Dublin and proclaimed the birth of the Irish Republic.[4] Although this rebellion lasted for only six days, it – or, more specifically, the British Government's handling of the crisis – triggered a wave of nationalist sympathy across Ireland.[5] The primary benefactor of this awakening was the separatist party Sinn Féin; which was thrown from virtual obscurity to a position of political dominance when it won 73 of Ireland's 105 seats in Westminster at the 1918 general election.[6] One month later, these Members of Parliament (MPs) assembled at Mansion House in Dublin, convened the first Irish Parliament (*Dáil Éireann*), declared Ireland's formal independence from the United Kingdom, and called on the Irish Volunteers (now widely known as the Irish Republican Army, or IRA) to defend the *Dáil* and repel the British 'occupation'.[7] Soon after, the IRA, under the leadership of Michael Collins and Richard Mulcahy, launched a bloody guerrilla war against the Crown Forces in Ireland. The British Government, loathe to see any part of the United Kingdom rise in rebellion, responded with both force and vigour.

As the months and years passed, however, it gradually became clear that neither side could secure a favourable outcome through the force of arms alone.[8] Thus, in July 1921, the British Government and Sinn Féin agreed to a truce and the commencement of negotiations to end the conflict. The result of these deliberations was the Anglo-Irish Treaty of 1921. This agreement established the Irish Free State – a self-governing dominion of the British Empire (equal in status to that of Canada and Australia). Despite the Treaty's ratification in January 1922, however, the movement for an independent Ireland soon suffered two setbacks. The first of these was the splitting of its ranks. The primary source of dissension was the perceived merit of the Treaty. Specifically, whether it was the best possible deal under the circumstances or a betrayal of the principles for which the War of Independence had been fought.[9] By 23 June 1922, this split had descended from personal acrimony to civil war. The next 11 months witnessed an intensity of fighting that surpassed the War of Independence only one year earlier. This conflict eventually came to an end on 24 May 1923, when Frank Airken, Chief of Staff of the anti-Treaty IRA, called on his members to 'dump arms'. Nevertheless, the legacy of the Civil War – approximately 800 deaths and 10,000 internees[10] – embittered the politics of the Irish Free State well into the twentieth century.

The second setback was the refusal of Ireland's six northeastern counties to remove themselves from the Union and join the Irish Free State. The origins of this development stretch back to the nineteenth century. It was during this period that Ireland's Protestants began to grow increasingly anxious about their status and security. The primary source of concern was the rise of Irish nationalism. While to Ireland's Catholic-majority, the concept of self-government promised a more representative and just governing system;[11] to Ireland's Protestant-minority, it 'threatened a Catholic Nationalist hegemony in all aspects of Irish society'.[12] The Protestants were mainly concerned that a Catholic-dominated Irish Parliament would embrace ultramontanism and, given the agrarian background of most Irish Catholics, undermine the economic and political interests of Protestant-owned industry.[13] Thus, as Ireland's Catholics increasingly embraced nationalism, their Protestant compatriots did likewise with *unionism*. That is, the belief in the desirability of Ireland remaining as an undifferentiated part of the United Kingdom.[14]

Though 'numerically weak' in both Ireland and Westminster, the unionists did have 'important political weapons'.[15] These included: 'close personal and economic ties' with Britain's aristocracy (which allowed the unionists to exert significant influence over the House of Lords); and, from 1912 onwards, the existence of the Ulster Volunteer Force – a 100,000 strong armed militia dedicated to resisting Irish Home Rule.[16] Wielding these various instruments of power, the unionists were able to frustrate three attempts (in 1886, 1893 and 1914) to establish a devolved Irish Parliament in the United Kingdom. It was because of this history of (successful) opposition that the British Government's fourth attempt at introducing Home Rule (the Government of Ireland Act 1920) included a new feature. Specifically, it partitioned Ireland into two parliamentary jurisdictions: 'Northern Ireland', which was to consist of six counties in Ireland's northeast, centred on the industrial city of Belfast; and 'Southern Ireland', which was to comprise Ireland's remaining 26 counties. The significance of this decision (in particular, its uneven distribution of counties) lay in Ireland's demography. While unionists were a minority in Ireland as a whole, they nonetheless constituted a majority (roughly two-to-one) in the area of Northern Ireland. Thus, by partitioning Ireland, the British Government was essentially trying to temper unionist opposition in the six counties by guaranteeing them that they would not be subject to 'Rome Rule'.[17]

Given the timing of its enactment, the ongoing war between the IRA and the Crown Forces quickly consumed the Government of Ireland Act 1920. Although the unionists in the six counties (begrudgingly) acceded to London's measure, with King George V opening the first Parliament of Northern Ireland in June 1921; virtually every MP elected to the Parliament of Southern Ireland refused to attend its inauguration, resulting in the assembly's suspension. Despite this rejection by the nationalists, the Government of Ireland Act 1920 did form the basis of the eventual negotiations between the British Governments and Sinn Féin. Consequently, the Anglo-Irish Treaty, rather than automatically including Northern Ireland in the agreement, gave Belfast the option of either joining the newly-created Irish Free State or remaining as part of the United Kingdom. Not surprisingly, the parliament of Northern Ireland voted for the latter.

Initially, most nationalists in the north were relatively unconcerned about this development. After all, in the event of Northern Ireland choosing to preserve the Union, the Treaty called for the establishment of a Boundary Commission – the remit of which was to 'determine in accordance with the wishes of the inhabitants ... the boundaries between Northern Ireland and the rest of Ireland'.[18] Given that much of Northern Ireland's border areas contained significant Catholic majorities, many nationalists believed that the Boundary Commission would eventually transfer swathes of Northern Ireland's territory to the Irish Free State – shrinking the former to such an extent that it would no longer be able to continue as a viable political entity. In August 1925, however, the British and Irish

Governments, due largely to unionist intransigence and Dublin's war debt to the United Kingdom, revoked the Boundary Commission and ratified the border established by the Government of Ireland Act 1920. The partition of Ireland was thus, more or less, finalised.

Two factors would come to define Northern Ireland as it progressed through the twentieth century. The first of these was unionist insecurity.[19] In essence, the Protestant-majority in the six counties were anxious that Dublin and London's acceptance of Northern Ireland as a constituent part of the United Kingdom was only temporary and vulnerable to political expediency.[20] As Townshend states, these fears of Catholic irredentism and British abandonment were both 'quite well founded'.[21] For instance, Éamon de Valera, a leading figure in the Easter Rebellion and Prime Minister[22] from 1932 to 1948, rewrote the constitution of the Irish Free State in 1937 to explicitly declare that 'the national territory consists of the whole island of Ireland';[23] effectively repudiating the entire legal basis of Northern Ireland's existence as a distinct political entity.[24] The British Prime Minister Winston Churchill, meanwhile, offered de Valera London's support for Irish unification 'in return for Eire's entry into the [Second World War] on the side of the British and its allies'; a proposal that outraged unionist opinion when it eventually became public.[25]

The second factor which characterised Northern Ireland was a consequence of the first: namely, institutionalised unionist discrimination against northern Catholics (who constituted approximately one third of the six counties' population). Apprehensive about the possibility of being subject to Dublin control (either by nationalist scheming or British betrayal), most unionists believed that the 'only safe course was for Protestants to stand firmly together in order that they might keep a tight grip on all the organs of political power and, as far as possible, on all the means of economic and social influence'.[26] Thus, successive unionist administrations introduced numerous measures to strengthen Protestant control over Northern Ireland. These included: the abolition in the 1920s of the province's proportional representation electoral system, in favour of a first-past-the-post system and a property-based franchise (two measures that benefited the numerically superior and wealthier Protestant community);[27] the gerrymandering of electorates (most notably in Derry, where unionist councillors received only one third of the total vote in 1967, yet won 60 per cent of the available seats);[28] employment discrimination, especially in the public sector ('justified ... on the grounds that [Catholics] were a disloyal "enemy within" who could not be trusted in positions of power');[29] and favouritism in the allocation of public housing, with Catholics restricted to government accommodation in existing Catholic-majority areas.[30]

The initial response of northern Catholics to the growing sectarian and discriminatory nature of Northern Ireland was to withhold their recognition of Ireland's partition and to exclude themselves from Northern Irish institutions. For example, Catholic teachers 'refused to accept their salaries from the Northern Ireland administration' (drawing funds from the Irish Free State instead);[31] while nationalist politicians either abstained from elections, or participated and then, once elected, refused to acknowledge the existence of the Northern Irish Parliament (leading to their speedy dismissal).[32] However, as it became increasingly clear that Dublin lacked both the means and the will to induce Ireland's reunification, and the commitment of the British Government remained (relatively) steadfast, northern Catholic attitudes gradually shifted from non-participation to limited acceptance, matched by a strong desire for reform.[33] This conversion culminated in the 1960s with the emergence of the Northern Ireland civil rights movement. Organised under such groups as the Campaign for Social Justice, the Derry Housing Action Committee (DHAC), and the Northern Ireland Civil Rights Association (NICRA), this movement sought to stimulate the pace of reform through the use of non-violent protest (a method inspired by the civil rights campaign in America). As the 1960s progressed, the civil rights movement drew increasing support from northern Catholics, and protest marches become more frequent.[34]

As the size and number of the protests grew, however, so did Protestant suspicion. To many unionists, the civil rights movement was less a genuine attempt to secure reform, and more Catholic irredentism in disguise. During the late-1960s, tensions between unionists and protestors began to mount. These came to a head on 5 October 1968, when the Royal Ulster Constabulary (RUC) baton-charged a civil rights march in Derry that the Home Affairs Minister had earlier banned.[35] Televised around the world, the RUC's actions triggered two days of rioting in Derry.[36] However, it was not until 12 August 1969 that Northern Ireland reached its true tipping point. A march by the Apprentice Boys (a militant unionist group) provoked nationalist rioting in the Bogside area of Derry. The RUC's attempt to impose order soon escalated into a two-day pitched battle (romantically known as the 'Battle of the Bogside').[37] Violence soon spread to the rest of the province, as Protestant mobs attacked Catholic enclaves throughout Belfast. On the 14th of August, with the RUC stretched thin and exhausted, the Northern Ireland Government called on London for assistance. The latter responded by deploying British troops to help secure the six counties. Two days later, a degree of calm finally descended on Northern Ireland. By this stage, however, five Catholics and two Protestants had been killed, '[h]undreds had been injured', and 3,500 families – the majority of them Catholic – had been forced from their homes.[38] The scar from these events would prove a long time to heal.

The PIRA

It was soon after the rioting of August 1969 that the PIRA emerged. Its birth marked the second major split in the IRA since the latter's inception in 1919. The first split occurred during the Irish Civil War, with pro-Treaty Volunteers joining the National Army and anti-Treaty Volunteers waging a campaign against the Irish Free State. Despite its surrender in May 1923, however, the anti-Treaty IRA (henceforth referred to as simply the IRA) did not fade from existence. After adopting an amended constitution in 1925, the organisation was able to regroup and continue agitating for its desired goal of an independent, 32-county repub-lic.[39] Although persistent pressure from governments in both Belfast and Dublin constrained the IRA's ability to conduct operations, it was, nevertheless, respons-ible for a number of significant actions. These included: the Bombing (or Sabo-tage) Campaign of 1939–40 (primarily targeted against economic and military infrastructure in Britain); and the Border Campaign of 1956–62. This latter under-taking was an attempt to 'break down the enemy's administration until he is forced to withdraw' through the use of guerrilla warfare in Northern Ireland (particularly in the nationalist areas along the border).[40] However, the IRA made little effort to win over northern Catholic opinion and, after both the Republic of Ireland and Northern Ireland Government introduced Internment in 1957, the Border Campaign petered out until the IRA Army Council was forced to call on its Volunteers to 'dump arms' on 26 February 1962.[41]

This failure was a serious blow to the IRA's morale.[42] Consequently, the organisation underwent a leadership change, with Cathal Goulding assuming the position of Chief of Staff. His major proposal for reversing the IRA's fortunes was for the organisation to shift its emphasis away from physical force to more political means (such as grassroots campaigning and contesting elections).[43] Goulding's prescription did generate some dissension in the IRA. It was not until the rioting of August 1969, however, that this discord became destabilising.

Traditionally, the IRA had portrayed itself as the defender of Catholics living in Northern Ireland; the ultimate guarantee against unionist excess. However, in line with Goulding's policy, the IRA had sold off most of its weaponry and neglected military training.[44] The organisation was thus unable to adequately protect Catholic communities during the trauma of August 1969.[45] This incapac-ity shamed many Volunteers (especially those in the north); a feeling com-pounded by the increasingly prevalent belief amongst northern Catholics that the IRA was cowardly (famously represented by the Belfast graffiti, '**I Ran Away**').[46] After it became clear that the Gouldingites, despite the events of August 1969, would not alter their political focus, a number of dissident republi-cans, led by the likes of Seán MacStiofáin, Seamus Twomey and Gerry Adams, began to discuss the possibilities of forming a breakaway organisation. These moves culminated on 18 December 1969, when 26 dissidents met and elected a 'Provisional' IRA Executive, who in turn elected a 'Provisional' Army Council.[47] The Provisionals' split with the IRA (later known as the Official Irish Republican Army, or OIRA) was finalised on 11 January 1970 when MacStiofáin led a walkout at Sinn Féin's *ard fheis* (annual convention); forming the Provi-sional Sinn Féin (PSF) and announcing that a Provisional Army Council had been established to capture the true spirit of the IRA.

Over the next 28 years, the PIRA first regrouped, then concentrated on protect-ing Catholic communities in Northern Ireland (particularly in Derry and Belfast), before engaging in a full-scale uprising against the Northern Ireland Government and, eventually, British security forces. By the time the Belfast (or 'Good Friday') Agreement was signed on 10 April 1998,[48] 3,440 people had been killed and over 40,000 injured as a result of paramilitary and security force violence (see Table 5.1).[49] As Hayes and McAllister note, these figures suggest that 'in its duration and intensity relative to population size, the conflict [in Northern Ireland] approaches that of a war rather than a local insurgency'.[50] The PIRA was unquestionably the dominant actor of The Troubles; responsible for approximately 50 per cent of the total conflict-related deaths. As Table 5.1 illustrates, the primary target of Provisional violence was British security personnel, followed by civilians. Though specific statistics about the PIRA's activities do not exist, the organisation appears to have most commonly engaged in hit-and-run assaults and bombings.

In line with its insistence that the Provisionals represented the 'real' IRA, the PIRA initially adopted the IRA's historic organisational structure (first devised in July 1923).[51] As Bell states:

> This inheritance was never seen as a matter of choice, sometimes as a responsibility, but mostly as desirable. With it came the right to wage war, even to claim the right to govern in the name of the Irish people.[52]

At the apex of this structure lay the Army Council. Comprised of seven Volunteers, the Army Council was the PIRA's supreme decision-making body. A 16-man Executive determined the composition of the Army Council; while a General Convention, consisting of delegates from the entire organisation, was endowed with the responsibility of electing the Executive. As well as deciding military strategy and policy, the Army Council also chose a commanding officer, or Chief of Staff, to conduct the PIRA's campaign.[53] A General Headquarters Staff (GHQ) assisted both the Army Council and the Chief of Staff. Below the GHQ, the PIRA was organised 'along British Army lines into brigades, battalions, and companies'.[54] While elements of this structure were in place for the length of the PIRA's campaign, the Provisionals did undergo a significant reorganisation during the late-1970s. This will be discussed in greater detail below.

Table 5.1 PIRA and total conflict-related deaths, Northern Ireland, 5 October 1968 to 10 April 1998

Victim's status	Total deaths	PIRA-inflicted deaths	
		Number	As % of total
British security personnel	1,110	1,011	91.1
Civilians	1,799	516	28.7
Republican paramilitaries	389	140	36.0
Loyalist paramilitaries	132	32	24.2
Irish security personnel	10	7	70.0
Total	3,440	1,706	49.6

Source: M. Sutton 'An index of deaths from the conflict in Ireland', Conflict Archive on the Internet (CAIN) www.cain.ulst.ac.uk/sutton/index.html (accessed on 1 August 2005), 2004.

Collective action frame

The central tenet underlying the PIRA's diagnosis was that the English presence in Ireland had 'been the root cause of Ireland's ills'.[55] In this respect, the PIRA was echoing centuries of republican thought, which, since the time (the late-eighteenth century) of Theobald Wolfe Tone, had 'regarded the connection between Ireland and Great Britain as the curse of the Irish nation, and felt convinced, that whilst it lasted, this country would never be free or happy'.[56] Like their republican forefathers, the Provisionals based their condemnation of the British presence in Ireland on a colonial perspective.[57] From this point of view, Ireland had been '[f]or centuries … an exploited dependency of England, remaining underdeveloped and a source of cheap food and cheap labour for her growing industry. The results were depopulation and poverty for us'.[58] Prior to the Anglo-Irish War, Britain was able to subjugate Ireland directly through its agents in Dublin Castle and sympathetic Protestant settlers. After 1922, however, London's primary instrument of maintaining its imperial control was the 'artificial' partition of Ireland. Through its occupation of the six counties, Britain kept the Irish 'divided and weak';[59] retarded Ireland's progress as a political, economic, and cultural unit;[60] and allowed 'the British in the North, and their neo-colonial business allies in the South, to carry on making their mint out of the exploitation of the Irish people'.[61]

A related theme in the PIRA's diagnosis was that the British Army were not neutral peacekeepers (as many Catholics initially perceived them to be);[62] but rather, anti-nationalist agents like the RUC, willing to engage in all forms of indiscriminate repression to maintain the status quo. To support this charge, the PIRA highlighted: the British Army's tendency to conduct massive 'search and seal' operations (such as the 'mass intimidation reminiscent of the Nazi regime in Europe' that the residents of Ballymurphy were subjected to in January 1971);[63] British Army killings of innocent Catholics (e.g. after the death of Daniel O'Hagan on 31 July 1970, the PIRA angrily claimed that 'HE HAD NOT A PETROL BOMB in his hand, as alleged; but was deliberately SHOT down in cold blood');[64] and the seemingly random and prejudiced nature of British Army actions, with soldiers assaulting, arresting, and jailing Catholics for simply

> walking down a street and being unfortunate enough to be in the path of an army patrol, to be standing on a street corner, to be talking to a girlfriend. Homes wrecked, wives and mothers shattered: torn, sad hearts hurt by blatant injustices and positive discrimination.[65]

The Provisionals also heavily exploited the introduction of Internment in August 1971 and 'Bloody Sunday' in March 1972 – two events which will be discussed in greater detail below.[66]

Interestingly, the PIRA's diagnosis (at least during the 1970s) focused relatively little on unionist-related problems. Of course, the Provisionals did agitate for the fall of the unionist-dominated government in Stormont, and the PIRA's Dublin-based publication *An Phoblacht* did highlight the inequities of the unionist regime (such as gerrymandering, the lack of 'political and civil rights', and discrimination in the 'allocation of housing, employment, and political representation').[67] Generally speaking, however, the PIRA tended to downplay unionist issues, even going so far as to attribute deaths caused by loyalist paramilitaries to British 'murder gangs'.[68] This minimising of the unionist threat (which was considerable during the mid-1970s) was a result of not only the PIRA's avowed nonsectarianism, but also the organisation's simplistic comprehension of unionist motives. In essence, the Provisionals believed that the unionists were as Irish as the nationalists and (if justly compensated) 'would not strenuously object to some form of united or federally united Ireland'.[69] The PIRA explained away the history of unionism and contemporary unionist actions and attitudes by blaming partition. Specifically, Britain's division of Ireland and continued occupation of the six counties had 'served to blind unionists ... to their true nationality'.[70] Thus, once Ireland was reunited, the Provisionals believed that unionist-nationalist tensions would dissipate.

The PIRA's proposed solutions to the aforementioned problems were, unsurprisingly, the expulsion of the British presence from Ireland, the annulment of the Government of Ireland Act 1920 and the creation of a 32-county republic. In September 1971, the Provisionals detailed the type of republic they sought when they unveiled their Éire Nua ('New Ireland') policy. This prescription proposed a federal system, 'based on the four ancient Provinces of Ireland: Ulster, Munster, Leinster and Connaught'.[71] The PIRA envisaged that the regional parliaments would be responsible for the vast majority of governance and administrative duties, with the central government restricted to the realms of defence and diplomacy. Éire Nua was intended to address two concerns. First, by establishing strong regional parliaments, the PIRA hoped to allay unionist concerns about 'Dublin-rule'. Second, by expanding the Ulster of Northern Ireland (with its six counties) to traditional Ulster (with its nine), the PIRA sought to balance the province's ratio of Catholics to Protestants and thus hopefully prevent the discrimination and excesses of the past. Furthermore, despite the fact that concerns over the avowed Marxism of the Gouldingites was often cited as one of the principal factors behind the split of 1969,[72] the PIRA often framed its desired 32-county republic in socialist terms.[73] For instance, the organisation stated during the early-1970s that it wanted to create a system of government which would 'give everyone a joint share of the nation's wealth' and ensure 'social and economic justice for all'.[74]

The PIRA sought to achieve these various goals through armed struggle. As the organisation stated in 1971: 'THEY [the British] HAVE NO RIGHT TO BE HERE, OUT WITH THEM! RESIST THEM! DRIVE THEM FROM OUR SHORES!'[75] To facilitate the accomplishment of its goals through the application of violence, the PIRA originally adopted a three-phase guerrilla strategy devised by the organisation's first Chief of Staff, Seán MacStiofáin. The first phase of this approach was for the Provisionals to recapture the IRA's traditional reputation as the guardian of northern Catholics.[76] Thanks largely to such laudable defensive actions as the 'Battle of St. Matthews', the PIRA had, more or less, recovered its standing amongst the Catholic community by mid-1970.[77] MacStiofáin's second phase entailed the PIRA moving 'from a purely defensive position' to 'combined defence and retaliation'.[78] That is, the Provisionals would not only seek to prevent attacks against northern Catholics, but also to retaliate against British Army and RUC actions that 'brutalised' Irish people.[79]

By the end of 1970, the PIRA was strong enough, both in terms of manpower and weaponry, to advance to MacStiofáin's third phase. That is, engaging in a 'war of psychological attrition'; the 'proto-typ[ical] anti-colonial campaign of the twentieth century'.[80] The principal goal of psychological attrition is to undermine an adversary's confidence in their chosen course of action (ideally to a state of hopelessness). Whereas the strategy of 'shock and awe' (heavily publicised during the early stages of the Iraq War in 2003) seeks to achieve this cognitive effect through the demonstration of sudden and devastating destruction and/or dominance;[81] psychological attrition attempts to accomplish the same affect gradually, through the sustained application of small-scale military operations.[82]

The PIRA justified its armed struggle using a mix of utilitarian and normative arguments. With regard to the former, the organisation's first justificatory argument was that Ireland's history had proved how ineffective constitutional (broadly defined as non-violent) methods were as instruments of political change. As the Provisionals stated in 1972, for the past 50 years, nationalists had relied on 'constitutional agitation' to remedy Northern Ireland's 'undisguised discrimination and repression ... It achieved nothing'.[83] This point was stressed again in 1973, when the PIRA asserted that, in response to those who questioned whether the organisation's use of violence was justified,

> [t]his viewpoint ignores the fact that we have gone through most phases of passive resistance and political activity which have only provided limited success. Even party politicians who had attended Stormont for many years, eventually admitted that the exercise had been a waste of time as the Unionist regime treated them with contempt.[84]

The PIRA even reached back deep into Ireland's history to demonstrate the limited efficacy of constitutional approaches. For example, after noting that '[b]oth constitutional and violent methods were used' over the previous two centuries to secure Irish's independence, the organisation claimed '[i]t is a historical fact that, although initial gains were often made, the constitutional movements were invariably crushed by military strength'.[85] 'Of course', as the Provisionals were quick to note: 'it can be argued that most of the revolutionary movements failed as well. However, the reason for their failure is different ... The revolutionary movements failed because of incompetence in practice rather than in theory.'[86]

The PIRA's second utilitarian justificatory argument was deeply intertwined with the first; specifically, that 'English rule in Ireland can only be ended by force'.[87] This line of reasoning was essentially an offshoot of the organisation's colonial analysis. The Provisionals contended that, since Britain had such strong economic and strategic interests to maintain its occupation of the six counties, only the use of force could compel the British authorities to disengage from Ireland. As evidence of this, the PIRA highlighted such instances in Irish history as the Irish Republican Brotherhood's (IRB) uprising in 1867 (which resulted in heightened British concern about the 'Irish Question', the 'disestablishment of the Protestant Church of Ireland and the beginnings of the Home Rule movement'),[88] and the IRA's actions during the Anglo-Irish War, to illustrate that 'England never yields to right, reason or justice, only to force'.[89] The Provisionals also pointed to the success of guerrilla campaigns in Aden and Cyprus as confirmation of the utility of violence in forcing the British Government to abandon its colonial possessions.[90] The PIRA even went so far as to claim that the broader human experience demonstrated the utility of violence. As the organisation stated in 1973: 'almost all civilisations on earth owe their continued existence during conflicts on the success of violence. I don't think the fact that the use of violence can bring success is an issue.'[91]

The PIRA's third utilitarian justificatory argument was that the organisation's track record demonstrated the efficacy of violence. For example, the Provisionals maintained that, prior to 1970, 'a united Ireland was never even considered or mentioned by either London or Stormont'.[92] Then came the PIRA and its campaign of resistance, 'a resistance which has been so successful as to seem incredible ... Today [1972], the leader of the opposition in Britain ... as well as many Tories and even unionists recognise the inevitability of a united Ireland'.[93] Two years later, the Provisionals claimed that there were only two groups in Northern Ireland 'who [were] making the pace, calling the tune'.[94] That is, the PIRA and the Ulster Workers' Council (UWC); the latter being responsible for a two-week strike in May 1974 that brought down the power-sharing Northern Ireland Executive. The PIRA attributed the success and importance of itself and the UWC to both group's reliance on guerrilla warfare; a tactic which was '*shown* to be effective'.[95] Indeed, the PIRA was so confident in the efficacy of its violence that it habitually declared the organisation's imminent victory. For instance, in 1971, the Provisionals announced that victory was 'in sight'.[96] Twelve months later, the PIRA was ready to affirm 1972 as 'the year of victory';[97] an appellation that the organisation would also attribute to 1974.[98] The Provisionals confidence in 'victory' was still evident three years later when they pronounced they were in 'the final phase of [their] war with England'.[99]

Generally speaking, the PIRA employed two normative arguments to justify its use of violence. The first of these was one of retributive justice.[100] As aforementioned, the Provisionals accused the British Army of conducting sectarian repression against Catholics in Northern Ireland. As a result, northern Catholics 'have seen their young men and women murdered. They have seen their old men and women assaulted'.[101] Furthermore, this state of affairs was unlikely to change in the foreseeable future. As the organisation stated in 1971:

When Cardinal Conway says that violence has been rejected by all responsible political parties, does he not realise that Mr Heath and Mr Wilson are both regarded as 'responsible' but they are the people who maintain partition by violence. And all thinking people must admit that partition is the problem. What responsible political leader on the British or Unionist side has ever put forward any solution to the problem other than British military force?[102]

Thus, if 'the British will not rule out the use of force to maintain' partition and the subjugation of the Irish people, 'logic decrees – meet force with force!'[103]

The PIRA's second normative argument was that the Irish nation's right of self-determination justified the organisation's recourse to violence.[104] According to the Provisionals: (1) every nation has an undeniable right to freely determine their political status and government structures (a prerogative enshrined in Woodrow Wilson's 14 Points and the United Nations International Covenant on Civil and Political Rights); and (2) the Irish people exercised this right at the general election of 1918, when a majority of the Irish people (approximately 53 per cent)[105] endorsed a political party (Sinn Féin) whose platform explicitly demanded the 'complete independence for the unitary state of Ireland'.[106] In the eyes of the Provisionals, however, the British Government had prevented the Irish people from truly and fully implementing their desired right for a unified, independent Ireland: through the introduction of the Government or Ireland Act in 1920; and its continued military presence (or 'occupation' as the PIRA termed it) across the six counties. Thus, because of the perceived unjust violation of the Irish nation's will and the unquestionable importance of the right involved, the PIRA maintained that it was justified in engaging in any necessary act to free Northern Ireland from its 'imperialist yoke'.

Recruitment process

Traditionally, familial ties underpinned recruitment into the IRA. Strong Republican families (such as the Adams) tended to dominate the organisation, with membership being 'passed from father to son, mother to daughter'.[107] White provides an example of this when he quotes a Donegal Republican who joined the IRA in the 1940s:

I was involved with the Republican Movement at a very early age because of my father being a member of the Republican Movement as well. From 1916 'til the Civil War my home was a place for anybody who came on the run, or to seek help. It was always given to them. So I was sought of brought up, you know what I mean, within Republican circles, my father being a Republican. And uh, I supposed it rubbed off on me.[108]

With the emergence of The Troubles in the late-1960s, the recruitment dynamics of the Republican movement changed. Although traditional Volunteers would continue to join the PIRA, the majority of the organisation's recruits after 1969 were neither from Republican families, nor extensively versed in Republican ideology.[109] Instead, their motivation for joining the Provisionals stemmed from the continuing violence in Northern Ireland. Not surprisingly, most of these new Volunteers came from the six counties. Known as the Sixty-niners, they were driven by 'an atavistic fear of loyalist violence', seething rage over state repression, and an 'overwhelming need' to defend their community and 'strike back'.[110] Due to a number of 'barriers' (e.g. 'time, social and political change, and state censorship') that made the 'Northern war less immediate for Southern Irish people', the PIRA's recruitment in the 26 counties was relatively paltry.[111] Nevertheless, new Volunteers did emerge in the Republic of Ireland; primarily driven by anger at the perceived injustice of British actions (most notably, 'Bloody Sunday' of 1972 and the Hunger Strikes of the early-1980s) against their fellow Irish people.[112]

Generally speaking, the PIRA had two recruitment networks to accommodate the influx of new Volunteers. In Northern Ireland, Sixty-niners typically sought to join the PIRA by approaching a known Republican in their area and 'drop[ping] a word in his ear'.[113] This was a relatively easy undertaking, given the PIRA's broad and established presence in the working-class neighbourhoods of Belfast and Derry (the main recruitment centres). For the new Volunteers in the Republic of Ireland, establishing such an interpersonal relationship with an existing-member of the PIRA was a more difficult task; primarily because the 'Dublin Government actively work[ed] to limit the organizational abilities of Republicans' and the relative dearth of Provisionals in the 26 counties.[114] Thus, according to White, contacts between new Volunteers and the PIRA were generally made at events (like 'marches and protest rallies' against British actions in Northern Ireland) where potential and existing members would be concentrated in the same area.[115]

The British and Northern Ireland Governments and their security forces

For the 50 years after the British Government introduced the Government of Ireland Act in 1920, the Northern Ireland Parliament (also known as Stormont) was the six counties' principal legislative body. Although London theoretically retained significant control over Northern Ireland during this period, thanks to a convention which restricted MPs in Westminster from raising 'any issue within the direct responsibility of a Stormont minister', the British Government's authority was effectively 'limited to such issues as foreign trade, defence, major taxation, customs and excise, and the High Court'.[116] The British administration of Edward Heath, however, terminated this constitutional arrangement in March 1972. After becoming convinced that Stormont lacked both the capacity and legitimacy to address Northern Ireland's spiralling crisis, Heath suspended the Northern Ireland Parliament and introduced Direct Rule. For the next two-and-a-half decades, Northern Ireland was governed by London through a Secretary of State for Northern Ireland (SSNI) and a handful of junior ministers.[117] Direct

Rule was only brought to an end in 1998, when a devolved Assembly was created as part of the Belfast Agreement.[118]

The British and Stormont Governments maintained three principal security forces in Northern Ireland: the British Army, the RUC, and the Ulster Defence Regiment (UDR). The British Army was arguably the most important of these. Prior to The Troubles, the army garrison in the six counties was approximately 2,000 strong and a 'popular posting'.[119] However, after London's decision to deploy troops in mid-August 1969 – a move which essentially made the British Army the lead actor for law and order in Northern Ireland – the army garrison began to swell. By the end of 1970, 6,300 soldiers were deployed in the province (see Figure 5.1). Over the next decade, the British Army's presence in Northern Ireland would average at 14,000 troops per year; peaking at 16,900 in 1973 (though approximately 22,000 British troops were involved in Operation Motorman in mid-1972).[120] During this period, the army garrison in the six counties largely consisted of personnel from Britain's various infantry and support units.[121] Prominent regiments included the Special Air Service (SAS) regiment (first publicly deployed in January 1976) and 14 Intelligence Company ('the Det').[122]

Established in June 1922, the RUC was a descendant of the Royal Irish Constabulary (RIC); the British regime's chief police force in Ireland during the nineteenth and early-twentieth centuries. Like its predecessor, the RUC was structured as a paramilitary force and was tasked with the dual functions of curtailing crime and maintaining the 'existing socio-political order' (i.e. the unionist domination of the six counties).[123] After the breakdown in security during the late-1960s, the British Home Secretary, James Callaghan, reorganised the RUC;

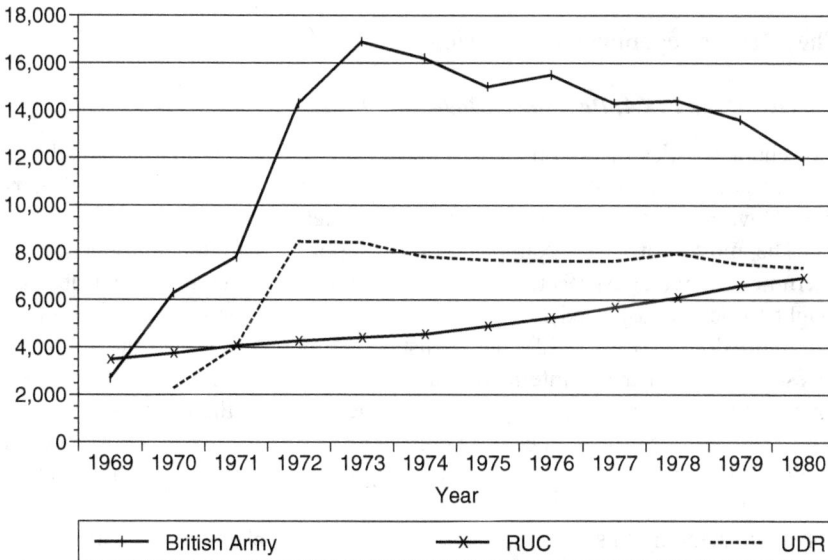

Figure 5.1 Numerical strength of security forces, Northern Ireland, 1969–80.

bringing the force in line with traditional police practices used throughout the rest of the United Kingdom.[124] After the imposition of Direct Rule, the British Government sought to professionalise the RUC further, primarily by increasing its full-time component and seeking to boost its number of Catholic recruits.[125] Driving these efforts was London's desire to shift responsibility for law and order from the British Army back to the RUC. The British Government initiated this policy of 'police primacy' in September 1974, and it was eventually final-ised by June 1977.[126] As Figure 5.1 illustrates, the RUC's strength gradually expanded during the 1970s, effectively doubling from 1969 to 1980. One of the most important units of the RUC was the Special Branch; responsible for the force's intelligence collection and analysis.

A major support element of the RUC during The Troubles was the UDR. A (largely part-time) infantry regiment of the British Army, the UDR can trace its origins to the Ulster Special Constabulary (USC; more popularly known as the 'B' Specials). Formed in November 1920, the USC was a part-time paramilitary organisation that acted as a reserve force for the police in Northern Ireland.[127] Over the next 50 years, the 'B' Specials would play a significant role in Stormont's various campaigns against the IRA. Due largely to its overt sectarianism, however, the Home Secretary abolished the USC in 1969; replacing it with a locally-raised and professional army regiment. Though the UDR actively sought recruits from both denominations, it was never able to fully earn the trust of northern Catho-lics.[128] At its peak in 1972, the UDR had 8,476 full- and part-time troops. However, from 1972 onwards, the UDR's strength slowly declined (see Figure 5.1). It is important to note that, in 1992, the British Government amalgamated the UDR with the Royal Irish Rangers, forming the Royal Irish Regiment (RIR).

The PIRA's regenerative experience

The rise of the PIRA, December 1969–June 1972

Two characteristics marked the PIRA's campaign during the first 30 months of its existence. The first of these was the general inefficacy of the British and Stor-mont Governments in their attempts to contain (let alone defeat) the Provision-als. The most prominent example of this ineptitude was the introduction of Internment on 9 August 1971. This was not the first time that the authorities had sought to detain suspected insurgents without trial. Under the Special Powers Act (ratified on 7 April 1922), the Minister of Home Affairs had the ability to 'arrest without warrant or intern without trial' any person s/he deemed to pose a threat to the province's security.[129] Prior to The Troubles, the most recent large-scale exercise of this power occurred during the late-1950s, when Stormont (and Dublin) interned hundreds of Volunteers;[130] greatly contributing to the eventual defeat of the IRA's Border Campaign.[131]

Notwithstanding this seeming familiarity with its application, the British and Stormont Governments' introduction of Internment in August 1971 was largely (and startlingly) ineffective. Specifically, while the authorities were able to apprehend and intern some members of the PIRA, the vast majority of those detained 'were not members of that organisation'.[132] For instance, within 24 hours of internment's introduction, the RUC and the British Army had detained 342 people. Of these, 116 were released almost immediately (their alleged relationship with Republican paramilitaries having been unable to withstand even the most basic scrutiny). Of the 226 that remained, '[f]ewer than a hundred' were connected with the IRA; the majority of whom were members of the more pacific OIRA (the membership of which tended to be better known by the police).[133] Unfortunately for the security forces, as the months progressed, their ability to intern significant numbers of actual Provisionals did not. Indeed, of the 1,179 people who were interned between August 1971 and June 1972, 239 were released by the Stormont Government, and a further 700 were released by the British Government during the first five months of Direct Rule.[134]

The second characteristic of the PIRA's campaign was the organisation's dramatic influx of recruits. Due to a lack of data, it is impossible to ascertain when and how many Volunteers joined the PIRA during this period.[135] Nevertheless, the literature does highlight a number of key episodes that stimulated the Provisionals' recruitment. These episodes included: (1) the 'Battle of St. Matthew's' on 27 June 1970, during which a handful of Provisionals repulsed a Protestant mob in the Catholic enclave of the Short Strand in East Belfast ('It was very significant ... A lot of people joined the Republican Movement after St. Matthew's. It finished the business of IRA equals "I Ran Away."');[136] (2) the 'Rape of the Falls' in early-July 1970, during which British troops battled with residents and Republican paramilitaries on the Lower Falls road in Belfast, resulting in the widespread use of CS gas, the imposition of a curfew, and the death of four civilians ('[a]fter that', according to Gerry Adams, 'recruitment to the IRA was massive');[137] (3) the introduction of Internment on 9 August 1971, which, due to its seeming bias against nationalists (no unionists were interned until February 1973) and targeting of innocent people, 'enraged Catholics in the north' and 'provided [the] PIRA with an enormous propaganda victory [that] boosted recruitment';[138] and (4) 'Bloody Sunday' on 30 January 1972, during which soldiers from the British Parachute Regiment opened fire on a civil rights march in Derry, killing 14 and injuring many more. This last act had arguably the greatest impact on the PIRA's recruitment. As Taylor states:

> As a result [of 'Bloody Sunday'], hundreds joined the Provisional IRA, eager to seek revenge for the murders they believed the British army had committed and the cover-up they were convinced had been perpetrated by Lord Widgery. If any young men had previously held back because they felt morally uncomfortable about killing, 'Bloody Sunday' removed any lingering restraint ... 'Bloody Sunday' had given the Provisional IRA the biggest boost in its history.[139]

As a consequence of these two characteristics, the PIRA experienced a significant expansion in its membership. From an initial core of '40 to 50 volunteers' at its inception, the PIRA grew to approximately 100 members in mid-1970;

increasing again to 'several hundred volunteers by the end of the first year'.[140] As 1971 progressed, the Provisionals' strength ballooned to between 1,000 and 1,500 members.[141] By 1972, Jeffrey estimates that the PIRA had grown to 2,000 Volunteers, the peak of the organisation's strength.[142] The Provisionals' rate of operations reflected this dramatic growth. As Table 5.2 illustrates, the number of conflict-related incidents recorded by the RUC increased by over 600 per cent from 1970 to 1971, and increased again (exponentially with regard to shooting incidents) from 1971 to 1972. The number of people killed by the PIRA also exhibited this expansive nature, with 15 people falling to Provisional violence in 1970 (out of a total of 26 conflict-related deaths), 85 in 1971 (out of 171 deaths), and a remarkable 234 in 1972 (out of 479 deaths).[143]

The deterioration of the PIRA's regenerative capacity, mid-1972–77

Unbeknown to the Provisionals at the time, 1972 would later prove to be the peak of their campaign. Never again would the PIRA be able to inflict so much damage upon Northern Ireland society and the British security forces. Furthermore, and partly because of this, the PIRA would never again enjoy so much potential power to influence the political situation in Northern Ireland.[144] After all, the first seven months of 1972 had witnessed the abolition of Stormont and the imposition of Direct Rule (a political and strategic triumph for the Provisionals) and the British Government agreeing to secret talks with the insurgent actor. These talks, held in London on 8 July between seven Volunteers (including MacStiofáin and Adams) and the SSNI, William Whitelaw, achieved little. Nevertheless, they were an indication of the seriousness with which the British Government viewed the Provisionals and their coercive capability.

The tipping-point for the PIRA came during the last ten days of July 1972. On the 21st of that month, in an attempt to intensify their pressure on London and to overshadow recent Loyalist activity, the Provisionals detonated 21 bombs in the Belfast city centre within the space of an hour. In the resulting pandemonium, nine people were killed and 130 were injured;[145] earning 21 July 1972 the epithet of 'Bloody Friday'. There were two consequences of this outrage. The first was that the Provisionals became 'politically untouchable. There was no

Table 5.2 Conflict-related incidents, Northern Ireland, 1970–72

Year	Shooting incidents	Bombings		
		Bomb explosions	Devices neutralised	Total devices used
1970	213	153	17	170
1971	1,756	1,022	483	1,515
1972	10,631	1,382	471	1,853

Source: PSNI, 'Security-related incidents, 1969–2005', Statistics Branch, www.psni.police.uk/security_related_incidents_cy-18.doc (accessed 1 August 2005), 2005.

way back to the negotiating process'.[146] The second was that 'Bloody Friday' gave the British Government the pretext it had been looking for to remove the 'no-go' areas. Beginning in August 1969, Catholic residents in Derry had instinctively sought to protect themselves from incursions by Loyalist mobs by erecting a series of barricades around their communities. As the conflict in Northern Ireland escalated, this practice soon spread to other Catholic districts in Belfast. Given London's desire not to offend either the nationalist or unionist populations, the British Army left the barricades in place and generally refrained from patrolling in the neighbourhoods behind them.[147] As this practice became institutionalised, the PIRA increasingly established itself in these no-go areas. Not only did the Provisionals assume responsibility for maintaining law and order, but they also exploited the no-go areas as operational bases. As Smith states: '[t]hese areas were a considerable military asset. They provided the Provisionals with safe havens from where they could mount operations and remain effectively immune from the security forces.'[148]

As the years progressed, London maintained its reluctance about moving against the no-go areas; even in the face of opposition from both the unionist community (who constructed their own barricades in protest) and the British Army. As Neumann states: 'Westminster believed that employing the military instrument was harmful to the prospect of regaining the trust of the Catholic community and persuading its political leaders to participate in negotiations over power-sharing.'[149] However, 'Bloody Friday' transformed the 'political and military calculus within which British strategy operated'.[150] On hearing the Provisionals had just killed nine civilians, 'Whitelaw reportedly turned to Minister of Defence, Peter Carrington, and said, "Right, now they've given it to us. We can go into the no-go areas"'.[151] Ten days later, the security forces launched Operation Motorman. Within 24 hours, 31,000 British Army and UDR troops (the largest British military operation since the Suez Crisis of 1956) had reoccupied all the no-go areas throughout Northern Ireland. Eager to limit potential bloodshed, the authorities had broadcast their intention to move against the no-go zones. Because of this, and the PIRA's realisation that to stand and fight would have been 'suicidal', casualties were minimal.[152]

It was at this point that the PIRA's capacity to regenerate began to weaken. This degeneration was the function of two factors. The first of these was the Provisionals' declining ability to attract new recruits. As previously acknowledged, there is a general absence of precise information about the PIRA's recruitment. This deficiency is even starker for the mid-1970s, due to the literature's typical refrain from commenting on either the organisation's strength or recruitment during this period. Nevertheless, it is possible to deduce that, while the PIRA never lost its ability to attract new recruits, its rate of recruitment from 1972 to the late-1970s was less than during the initial years of the organisation's campaign, and was (if only slightly) declining.

Three observations form the basis of this deduction. The first of these is that, as Bell notes, the Provisionals' 'influx of volunteers peaked in 1972'.[153] The PIRA was never again to experience the flood of recruits that beset the organisation during the early-1970s. The second observation is that, as the 1970s progressed, a feeling of war-weariness emerged amongst northern Catholics;[154] an environment that was likely to have depressed the PIRA's recruitment. The third observation is that the 1975 Ceasefire between the PIRA and the British Government had a disastrous impact on the morale of many Volunteers; an effect which was also likely to have been felt by the organisation's potential members. The Provisionals agreed to a ceasefire with London in February 1975 after they believed they had secured a commitment from Merlyn Rees (the then-SSNI) that the British would gradually begin to withdraw their forces from the six counties. However, as 1975 progressed, it became increasingly clear that the British Army was not leaving Northern Ireland. This dawning comprehension, as well as the forced inactivity of the ceasefire, slowly chipped away at the PIRA's 'morale and numbers'.[155] Martin McGuiness, on his return to Derry from prison during 1975, alluded to the impact this 'atrophy' was having on the PIRA's recruitment when he stated that 'good operations are the best recruiting sergeant'.[156] Tommy McKearney, another senior Provisional, also hints at the debilitating effect the ceasefire had on the organisation's recruitment, when he notes that the results of the 1975 ceasefire prompted a debate within the ranks of the PIRA about:

'how do we make progress from here?' ... It wasn't just a question of getting more recruits for the IRA. It was a much wider debate than that. It was how to bring the struggle forward in every sense. But more recruits for the Republican Army was part of the debate. One couldn't be separated from the other. It was a question of how to involve the population, the republican population, in the struggle.[157]

The second factor that led to the deterioration of the PIRA's regenerative capacity was the organisation's burgeoning rate of attrition. It is important to note that deaths of Volunteers, while substantial, played only a minor role in this upsurge. Although 105 Provisionals were killed between 31 July 1972 and 31 December 1977, the rate at which they were killed was (more or less) equal to what the PIRA experienced during the first 30 months of its campaign.[158] Rather, the increase in the Provisionals' rate of attrition was primarily due to a gradual, yet relentless, rise in the number of Volunteers who were arrested and convicted on terrorism-related charges. Operation Motorman was the trigger for this escalation of arrests; exposing the PIRA to greater contact with the security forces. By December 1972, the British Army claimed that it had detained 200 Volunteers since Motorman.[159] The Provisionals' vulnerability to security force pressure even extended across the border. During the final two months of 1972, the Irish Gárdái arrested such PIRA luminaries as: MacStiofáin, Ruairí Ó'Brádaigh and Máire Drumm (the President and Vice-President of Sinn Féin, respectively), and Martin McGuiness and Joe McCallion (the commander and deputy commander of the Derry Brigade).

The arrests of Volunteers continued through 1973. In July, the Northern Ireland Office (NIO) declared that 500 Provisionals had been convicted and sentenced over the past year; 'eight of whom had been given life sentences, the rest an average of four years in jail apiece'.[160] Not counted in the NIO's figure was Joe Cahill, MacStiofáin's successor as Chief of Staff. The Irish Navy arrested Cahill on 28 March 1973 aboard the *Claudia*, a West German-registered cargo ship loaded with five tonnes of Libyan arms.[161] 1974 was also a difficult year for the PIRA. As Bishop and Mallie state: Volunteers were 'being increasingly hard-pressed by the Army ... The more experienced of them now ran considerable risks with every operation they carried out. They either persisted and courted arrest and a long prison sentence or they stopped active service.'[162] Brendan Hughes and Billy McKee, two prominent Provisionals, confirmed this analysis, declaring that: 'for the first time since the early-1970s, the police and the military machine were actually working and the IRA was under severe pressure'; and that the Belfast Brigade was 'in a very poor state, a very poor state indeed ... There were only a handful of men in each area and weaponry was very poor'.[163]

Arrests of Volunteers declined slightly during the 1975 Ceasefire. However, the Provisionals' loss of personnel continued when the truce dissolved in late-1975. In December 1976, the newly-appointed SSNI, Roy Mason, claimed that '690 members of the PIRA had been charged since the start of the year, that is, more than twice the total (320) in 1975'.[164] Jackie McMullan, a former Provisional, supports Mason's statement, stating that a 'very large number of volunteers [were] arrested in 1976–77, many of them experienced volunteers'; consequently, 'a large gap had been left in structures that lasted several years'.[165] By the end of 1977, it was clear that the 'type of campaign' the PIRA 'had deemed necessary to achieve [its goals] quickly had proved costly in terms of volunteers killed and imprisoned'.[166] The result: the PIRA was 'left ... in a situation where we found that numbers were smaller, and a smaller number of men were carrying more and more responsibility on their shoulders'.[167] Circumstances were so dire that, according to Kelley, '[s]ome Provos today admit that there were fewer than 250 active guerrillas at the end of 1977'.[168]

The PIRA's operational activity reflected the organisation's increased rate of attrition and shrinking membership. As Table 5.3 illustrates, paramilitary violence exhibited a clear downward trend during the mid-1970s. Indeed, by

Table 5.3 Conflict-related incidents, Northern Ireland, 1972–77

Year	Shooting incidents	Bombings		
		Bomb explosions	Devices neutralised	Total devices used
1972	10,631	1,382	471	1,853
1973	5,019	978	542	1,520
1974	3,208	685	428	1,113
1975	1,803	399	236	635
1976	1,908	766	426	1,192
1977	1,081	366	169	535

Source: PSNI, 'Security-related incidents, 1969–2005', Statistics Branch, www.psni.police.uk/ security_related_incidents_cy-18.doc (accessed 1 August 2005), 2005.

1977, the number of shooting incidents, bombings, and attempting bombings in Northern Ireland had dropped by 89.8 per cent, 73.5 per cent, and 64.1 per cent, respectively, from 1972.[169] Deaths attributed to the PIRA also fell over this period. From a high of 234 in 1972, the Provisionals killed 126 people in 1973 (out of a total of 253), 134 in 1974 (out of 294), 79 in 1975 (out of 260), 112 in 1976 (out of 295), and 67 in 1977 (out of 111).[170]

The PIRA regains its composure, 1978 onwards

The disastrous state of the PIRA's campaign was not lost on its membership. Consequently, as the organisation approached the end of the decade, there was growing dissent within its ranks. The most notable source of this discord was Her Majesty's Prison Maze (colloquially known as 'the Maze' or 'Long Kesh'). Beginning in 1975, a number of Provisional inmates, following the tradition of such Republican luminaries as Michael Collins, sought to use the 'time, leisure, and opportunity' provided by their imprisonment to reflect on the problems besieging the Republican movement.[171] Moloney describes how 'cages' nine and 11 in the Maze, under the guidance of Adams, Ivor Bell and Brendan Hughes, 'became think tanks devoted to planning new structures and policies designed to rescue the [P]IRA from what every activist, inside and outside the jail, could see was imminent defeat'.[172] These debates and discussions eventually formed the intellectual foundations of a 'blueprint' for reforming the PIRA. From late-1975 to late-1977, the 'dissident' Provisionals began to trial balloon some aspects of this blueprint; primarily through a semi-regular column in the *Republican News* (authored by Adams under the pseudonym 'Brownie') and selected proxies that had avoided imprisonment (e.g. Danny Morrison and Jimmy Drumm).[173] Later, as Adams and his allies were released from Long Kesh and took over key positions within the PIRA, the organisation gradually adopted elements of the proposed reforms. This process was largely completed by late-1978 and early-1979.

The reforms implemented by the PIRA were organisational, educational, and strategic in nature. With regard to the first, the Provisionals adopted a cellular structure, as well as creating a 'Northern Command' – that is, a body, separate from the GHQ in Dublin, in charge of all operations in Northern Ireland and the five border counties of the Republic. Educationally, the PIRA devised a new training manual, the *Green Book*, which sought to improve security discipline within Provisional ranks. Lastly, the PIRA introduced two major strategic reforms. The first of these was the concept of 'politicisation'; the essence of which was that the PIRA would abandon its 'mono-military approach' and instead utilise both political and military means to beget the organisation's goals.[174] The Provisionals' chief political instrument was Sinn Fein, which was unleashed and tasked with the duty of 'agitat[ing] about social and economic issues which attack the welfare of the people'.[175] The second strategic reform, meanwhile, was that of the 'Long War'. The central assumption of this concept was that, due to their imperial interests in maintaining a presence in Ireland, the British were in 'for a long haul against the IRA'.[176] Thus, it was necessary for the PIRA to prepare for a 'long term armed struggle' if it wanted to achieve its goal of a sovereign, united Ireland.[177]

It was during the implementation of these reforms that the PIRA's capacity to regenerate regained its previous vigour. This rejuvenation was the function of two factors. The first of these was that, as Smith notes, the PIRA's previously 'haemorrhage[ing]' loss of personnel began to subside.[178] As Figure 5.2 illustrates, the number of people charged in Northern Ireland with terrorism-related offences dropped by 35.5 per cent from 1977 to 1978, and continued to trend downwards (notwithstanding a brief upsurge in 1981) for the remainder of the PIRA's campaign. The second factor, meanwhile, was that the Provisionals' rate of recruitment stabilised. As Brigadier James M. Glover noted in his renowned 1978 intelligence assessment, while the Provisionals were still unable to 'attract the large number of active terrorists they had in 1972/73', they, nevertheless, were able to recruit enough new members to replace their losses and, as a result, 'sustain' their 'manpower' and 'violence'.[179] The likes of Bell, Drake and Reilly share Glover's assessment, indicating that, after the late-1970s, the PIRA's pool of potential members consistently outstripped the organisation's recruitment needs.[180] From this period onwards, the organisation's membership would remain at approximately 300 Volunteers until the Belfast Agreement of 1998.[181]

Analysis

From the above account of the PIRA's regenerative experience, it appears that an increase in attrition played at least an equal, and arguably greater, role than a

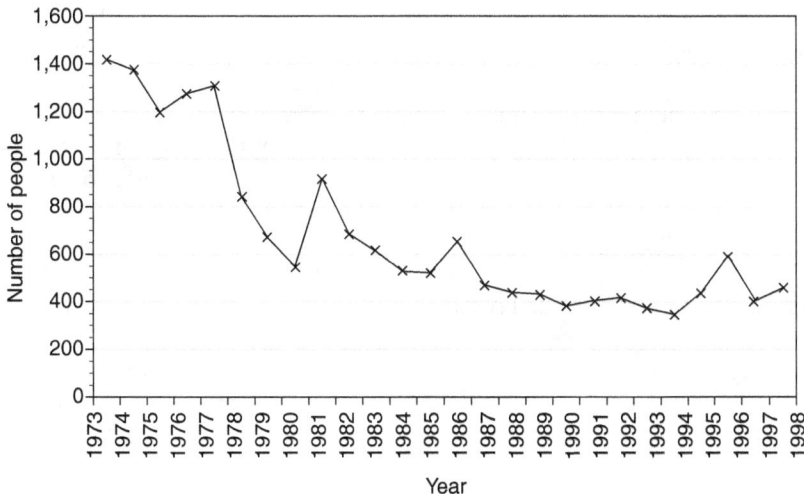

Figure 5.2 People charged with terrorism-related offences, 1973–98 (source: PSNI, *Number of Persons Charged with Terrorist and Serious Public Order Offences, 1972–2005*, Statistics Branch, available from www.psni.police.uk/ persons_charged_cvy-19doc, accessed: 1 August 2005, 2005).

decrease in recruitment in weakening the organisation's capacity to regenerate. Three observations form the basis of this judgment.

The first of these is that the deterioration of the PIRA's regenerative capacity coincided with both an increase in attrition and a decrease in recruitment.

The second observation, meanwhile, is that, while this book is unable to quantify the rates at which the PIRA's loss of personnel increased and intake of recruits decreased, the language used by the literature to describe the organisation's attrition and recruitment during the mid-1970s suggests that the former grew at a rate greater than at which the latter declined. For instance, Bell, in one of the few analyses of Provisional recruitment, implies that, while the PIRA had 'fewer recruits' after 1972, this reduction was not an overly-pressing issue, since the organisation was still able to attract aspiring Volunteers ('recruits still came').[182] In contrast, scholars tend to depict the PIRA's loss of personnel during the mid-1970s in much more expansionary and consequential terms. For example: (1) according to Bishop and Mallie, '[a]s the [1970s] progressed it became increasingly hazardous to be in the IRA';[183] (2) Smith describes the PIRA's rate of arrests during the mid-1970s as 'haemorrhaging';[184] (3) Kelley notes that, in 1976 and 1977, the security forces were 'sending more and more volunteers off to prison';[185] and (4) a host of authors have highlighted how, due to the efforts of the security forces during the mid-1970s, the PIRA came the closest in its history to 'collapse and defeat'.[186]

The final observation is that the PIRA's burgeoning loss of personnel appears to have generated greater concern within the organisation than its declining intake of recruits. The infamous 'Staff Report' arguably provides the best evidence of this seeming contrast. Commissioned by the PIRA's GHQ in 1977 to assess the organisation's current position and 'long-term military plans', the 'Staff Report' was seized by the Irish *Gárdái*, along with the PIRA's then-chief of staff, Seamus Twomey, in December of the same year.[187] The 'Staff Report' is notable not only for the 'dramatic insight' it offers 'into the Provisional IRA after the setback of the truce';[188] but also for its overwhelming emphasis on attrition-related issues. Opening with the observation that the success of the security forces in 'breaking volunteers' during interrogations, and the 'inefficient' nature of the organisation's structure were 'contributing to [the PIRA's] defeat', the vast remainder of the 'Staff Report' set out in detail how the PIRA could: (1) 'return to secrecy and strict discipline'; (2) endow Volunteers with the psychological strength to resist interrogations; and (3) restructure the organisation (along cellular lines) to limit the amount of information Volunteers could willing and unwillingly provide the security forces.[189] Only a fraction of the 'Staff Report' was concerned with recruitment-related issues; specifically, its recommendation that Sinn Féin become more active in winning 'support for, and sympathy to, the movement'.[190]

In light of the above findings, the remainder of this chapter will thus seek to provide greater insight into why the above shifts in Provisional recruitment and attrition occurred. Specifically, this section will examine: (1) whether the PIRA's increase in attrition was the result of the improvement in the government's intelligence collection capabilities and/or restricting civil liberties; and (2) whether the PIRA's decrease in recruitment was the result of the amelioration of grievances, selective government repression, and/or the discrediting of the insurgent actor's ideology.

The improvement of the Government's intelligence collection capabilities

The PIRA case provides strong support for the notion that an insurgent actor's loss of personnel will increase if the opposing government's ability to collect information about the insurgent actor improves. According to a host of scholars, at the outset of The Troubles, the British and Northern Ireland Governments' intelligence capability was generally defective.[191] This was partly due to the relative speed of the emergence of both sectarian violence and the Provisional threat in the six counties. As Jeffrey observes, '[b]efore 1969 there had been very little [British] "intelligence" involvement in Northern Ireland at all, for the very good reason that the sort of threats to the state against which such personnel might be employed were virtually non-existent'.[192] The deficiency of the security forces' intelligence capability was also due to negligence on behalf of the RUC. As Charters notes, owing to a lack of funds, personnel and 'foresight', the RUC's 'files were out of date, and their intelligence network in the Catholic areas badly neglected'.[193] A lack of coordination between the British Army and the RUC soon exacerbated these initial problems. This was primarily the result of the British Army's general contempt for, and distrust of, the RUC; which many officers saw as a 'shambles' and a 'busted, discredited force'.[194]

Given this unwillingness to work with the RUC and its intelligence arm (Special Branch), and the paucity of London's initial intelligence infrastructure in Northern Ireland (comprising of 'one Intelligence Corps captain and one sergeant'), the British Army set out to dramatically expand its ability to collect and process information.[195] The ensuing months and years witnessed an 'intelligence "gold rush"' as the army 'poured in huge sums of money, men and effort' into its intelligence system.[196] Establishing an intelligence presence from scratch is a difficult undertaking, however, especially in a hostile environment like the Nationalist areas of Northern Ireland, where the British Army was 'a "foreign force", unfamiliar with the area, the people, and the sources of information'.[197] Thus, it took the British Army some time to find its intelligence 'feet'. The best example of this learning process was the brief experience of the Mobile Reconnaissance Force (MRF; also known as the Military Reconnaissance Force). The British Army created this covert surveillance unit in late-1971 with a desire to obtain a stream of ready-to-use contact intelligence. The MRF did partly achieve this goal, as well as display a flair for innovation. For example, one of the unit's more infamous operations involved the establishment of a laundry service (the 'Four Courts') in West Belfast. The MRF used this conventionally-run business as a cover to forensically analyse the clothing of suspected Provisionals, and run high-tech and mobile surveillance equipment (disguised as a delivery van) around sensitive Republican areas.[198] However, the MRF had a tendency to engage in 'piratical ventures';[199] seemingly driven more by an impulse to action and a desire to 'get at' the enemy, rather than tactical, strategic, or propagandistic concerns. Consequently, after the Provisionals launched a surprise attack on the Four Courts on 2 October 1972 (resulting in the death of one British soldier) and a series of controversial shootings involving MRF agents, the British Army shut the unit down.

Nevertheless, it was from this point onwards that the security forces' intelligence capability gradually began to improve. This was especially evident with regard to the security forces' ability to collect actionable intelligence. This improvement had four sources. The first of these was Operation Motorman, which allowed the British Army to expand its surveillance of the no-go areas – previously intelligence 'black spots'.[200] This expansion consisted of both increased patrolling – the routine, but necessary, chore of intelligence collection – and the construction of a fixed-base surveillance infrastructure. This was comprised largely of observation posts 'equipped with newly-designed night-vision equipment, large telescopes fitted with cameras, and swift communications'.[201] The British Army erected these observation posts extensively in nationalist areas. Adams, for instance, claims that, after Motorman, the security forces constructed nine in the Andersontown area of Belfast alone.[202]

The second source was the influence of Brigadier Frank Kitson. After writing *Low Intensity Operations* during a fellowship at Oxford University, Kitson was deployed to Belfast in September 1970. He immediately set about challenging the army's prevailing approach to managing the conflict in Northern Ireland – particularly the seemingly common belief amongst commanders that 'intelligence' was a task best left to the 'spooks'. Kitson's contrary view was that the only way the British Army could maximise its intake of timely and accurate information was if every soldier and unit became actively involved in the collection of intelligence. As Bishop and Mallie and Hamill note, due to the successes he enjoyed with 39 Brigade in Belfast, Kitson's approach to intelligence collection soon spread to most other British Army units in Northern Ireland, and was enthusiastically embraced by General Frank King, General Officer Commanding in Northern Ireland from 1973 to 1975.[203]

The third source was the MRF's replacement, 14 Intelligence Company (commonly known as the 'Det'). Formed in early-1973, the Det's mission was 'to infiltrate republican and loyalist areas and become part of the landscape in order to watch and track the enemy'.[204] The Det soon developed a reputation for secrecy and professionalism; pointedly avoiding the 'piratical ventures' and controversies that had plagued the MRF.[205] More importantly, the Det was also highly effective. As Taylor states:

> In terms of results, a single 'operator' was said to be worth a Company of a hundred regular soldiers. As the years went by … the 'Det' became an even more lethal weapon in the counter-terrorist armoury of the 'Brits' and played a huge part in the war of attrition against the IRA.[206]

The final source was the Provisionals' own security deficiencies. The first of these was the PIRA's tendency to base its brigades and companies in the cities and neighbourhoods from which its members came. This not only meant that most Volunteers were well-known to their local communities; but also that the security forces had an easier time linking Provisional units with their violent acts.[207] The second PIRA weakness was the average Provisionals' seeming disdain for security. As Coogan states:

> One only had to stroll into an IRA haunt like the Prisoners Defence Fund Club in Andersontown and listen to the audience join in a rousing rebel chorus to the music of the Wolfehounds or some other group ... to tell where the spectators came from – they used to raise their aims in the air, swaying in time to the music, holding up one, two or three fingers on each hand to show which battalion they belonged to, supported, or lived under the aegis of. In either case a useful starting point for any police agent present.[208]

The PIRA's most pressing security deficiency, however, was the organisation's structure.[209] As aforementioned, at this inception in December 1969, the Provisionals adopted the IRA's long-standing hierarchical pyramid structure, which was formed along traditional military lines. Although this organisational framework had provided the dissident Republicans with a sense of continuity, it had also proved to heighten their susceptibility to penetration by spies and informers. Specifically, by organising Volunteers into large groups (i.e. companies and brigades), the PIRA's military structure increased the potential amount of information that a 'tout' could supply the authorities. As the mid-1970s progressed, the security forces were able to take increasing advantage of this vulnerability. Both the Det and Special Branch expanded their efforts to recruit informers within the PIRA; an undertaking that accelerated during the 1975 ceasefire.[210] In addition to this, the RUC became progressively more adept at obtaining information from captured Volunteers. Although its interrogation methods attracted growing criticism during the mid- and late-1970s,[211] the RUC's cross-examination centre at Castlereagh was, nevertheless, 'the engine room of the Government's "criminalization" policy, churning out the confessions that put scores of IRA men (and loyalists) behind bars'.[212] This judgment was shared by a number of Provisionals. For instance, the PIRA's *Staff Report* (famously seized along with the capture of Seamus Twomey in 1977) acknowledged that Volunteers were being 'broken' while serving either three- or seven-day detention orders.[213] Similarly, a Volunteer quoted by Moloney stated that: 'Men were breaking in the police stations. We'd hear of people handing over 25 to 30 names at a time. In the first 12 to 18 months of Castlereagh we suffered great damage'.[214]

Further support for the notion that the PIRA's attrition increased during the mid-1970s because the authorities' intelligence collection capabilities improved is derived from the twin observations that: (1) a number of the Provisionals' reforms of the late-1970s were implemented with the intention of hampering the British Government's ability to collect intelligence; and (2) these reforms appear to be linked to the decline and eventual stabilisation of the PIRA's loss of personnel from 1978 onwards. The seemingly most consequential of these reforms was the PIRA's adoption of a cellular structure in 1977. This modification primarily involved the PIRA channelling its 'active' Volunteers (i.e. those responsible for conducting violent operations) into Active Service Units (ASUs). Ideally, each ASU was to comprise four Volunteers; one of which was the cell's Officer in Command (OC).[215] These ASUs were also intended to be autonomous (i.e. responsible for arranging their own finances, safe houses and transport) and specialise in a particular type of action (e.g. intelligence work, 'sniping...', executions, bombings, robberies, etc.').[216] Furthermore, each ASU was to function under the principle of compartmentalisation; with operational information restricted to a 'need-to-know' basis, identities limited to pseudonyms, and the cell's contact with the broader organisation confined to a link between the OC and a Brigade Adjutant. As the last condition implies, the Provisionals' new cellular structure did not replace their 'old system of organisation'; but rather, was 'superimposed upon it'.[217] Nevertheless, the PIRA's reorganisation did transform its companies and brigades, with the former now responsible for various support and policing duties, and the latter for organising and directing the companies and ASUs.[218] The apex of the PIRA's traditional structure (i.e. the Army Council, Executive and General Convention), meanwhile, remained more or less unaffected by the reorganisation.

The primary objective of the PIRA's adoption of a cellular structure was 'to improve security by limiting the amount of information known by individual volunteers'; which would, as a consequence, restrict the amount of information an individual Volunteer could willingly or unwillingly provide the security forces.[219] Of course, the PIRA's ASUs 'were not watertight'; as attested by the 'supergrass' trials of the early-1980s – during which scores of Provisionals were imprisoned on the word of a small number of informers who divulged the identities of their compatriots in exchange for immunity from prosecution.[220] Nevertheless, it does appear that 'after the reorganisation the average member's detailed knowledge of the membership and activities of the rest of the organisation was severely constrained' and this, in turn, helped the PIRA reduce the 'damaging losses' it had been suffering through informants and interrogations over the previous five years.[221]

The PIRA's second 'intelligence-hampering' reform was the development of a training manual, the *Green Book*. A 'cunningly thought out mixture of philosophy and guide to action',[222] the *Green Book* not only contained extensive tracts about the history, ideology and strategy of the Republican movement; but it also sought to improve security discipline within the PIRA and 'indoctrinat[e] volunteers with the psychological strength to resist interrogation'.[223] The *Green Book* attempted to achieve the former objective by providing Volunteers with a series of basic regulations about how they should conduct themselves. For instance, the manual states:

The most important thing is security, that means you:

DON'T TALK IN PUBLIC PLACES:

YOU DON'T TELL YOUR FAMILY, FRIENDS, GIRL-FRIENDS OR WORK-MATES THAT YOU ARE A MEMBER OF THE IRA. DON'T EXPRESS VIEWS ABOUT MILITARY MATTERS, IN OTHER WORDS YOU SAY NOTHING to any person. Don't be seen in public marches, demonstrations or protests. Don't be seen in the company of known Republicans, don't frequent known Republican houses, Your prime duty is to remain unknown to the enemy forces and the public at large.[224]

The *Green Book* sought to help Volunteers withstand interrogations in two respects. First, the *Green Book* informed aspiring Provisionals about the trials associated with membership in the PIRA. For example: 'It [the PIRA] enters into every aspect of your life. It invades the privacy of your home life, it fragments your family and friends, in other words claims your total allegiance'; and 'all people wishing to join the Army must fully realize that when life is being taken, that very well could mean their own'.[225] The *Green Book* also stressed the need for members to adhere to Republican and Socialist principles ('[b]efore any potential volunteers decides to join the Irish Republican Army ... he should examine his political motives bearing in mind that the Army are intent on creating a Socialist Republic') and accept the necessity of using violence to achieve the organisation's objectives.[226] The intention here was that, by providing such information, the *Green Book* would deter all but the truly committed; in other words, those who were thought (amongst other things) to be less likely to 'crack' if caught and interrogated.

Second, the *Green Book* supplied Volunteers with a comprehensive account of what they could expect if they were caught by the security forces. Specifically, the *Green Book* focused on: (1) the likely actions of the police and the interrogators (with particular emphasis on possible forms of physical and psychological torture to which a Volunteer may be subjected); and (2) the motives and strategies behind the interrogators' actions ('[t]he best defence in anti-interrogation techniques is to understand the techniques as practiced by the police force').[227] The purpose of this information was to minimise 'the surprise element that interrogators used, and thus place activists in a more confident and secure footing'.[228] The *Green Book* also provided its readers with a stream of advice on how to endure interrogations. For example:

The most important thing to bear in mind when arrested is that you are a volunteer of a revolutionary army, that you have been captured by an enemy force, that your cause is a just one, that you are right and that the enemy is wrong and that as a soldier you have taken the change expected of a soldier and that there is nothing to be ashamed of in being captured....

This cannot be overstressed: when arrested SAY NOTHING...

Another important point to be remembered and one which is extremely important, DON'T GET INVOLVED IN A POLITICAL CONVERSATION.[229]

By late-1978 and early-1979, the *Green Book* had become a fixture of the PIRA's recruitment process, and required reading for new and current members alike.[230] As Sarma notes, '[i]t is difficult to estimate the importance of [the *Green Book*]', especially its impact on the PIRA's rate of attrition.[231] However, the training manual does appear to have: (1) 'strengthened' internal discipline 'a great deal';[232] and (2) 'minimised the surprise element that interrogators utilised, and thus placed activists in a more confident and secure footing'.[233] Consequently, it is likely that the *Green Book* contributed to the PIRA's declining loss of personnel from the late-1970s onwards.

In summary, the relationship between the British Government's intelligence collection capabilities and the PIRA's attrition appears strong; given that when the former improved, the latter increased, and that when the Provisionals sought to hinder the former, the latter decreased.

Restricting civil liberties

Unlike both the Canadian and Uruguayan authorities during their respective campaigns against the FLQ and MLN-T, the British and Northern Ireland Governments restricted civil liberties for essentially the entirety of their 28-year struggle with the PIRA.

Three legislative measures formed the basis of this near-permanent curtailment of freedoms and protections. The first of these was the *Civil Authorities (Special Powers) Act (Northern Ireland)*. Enacted by the recently inaugurated Northern Ireland Parliament on 7 April 1922 in response to growing sectarian violence in the six counties (a by-product of the ongoing Irish Civil War), the Special Powers Act: provided the 'minister for home affairs, and members of the police force acting at his discretion ... virtually unlimited power to search for and seize contraband and to detain those suspected of subversive behaviour';[234] empowered the civil authority to 'prohibit the circulation of any newspaper for any specified period'; and authorised the government 'to take all such steps and issue all such orders as may be necessary for preserving the peace and maintaining order'.[235] Although the duration of the act was initially limited to one year, Stormont repeatedly renewed it before eventually making it permanent in 1933. It was under the Special Powers Act that the security forces introduced Internment in August 1971.

The second legislative measure was the *Northern Ireland (Emergency Provisions) Act*. Ratified on 8 August 1973, this statute was born out of an attempt by the British Government to reform the Special Powers Act; primarily from a utilitarian perspective.[236] Thus, the Emergency Provisions Act retained many aspects of the Special Powers Act – such as allowing indefinite internment (though only at the request of the SSNI and subject to limited judicial review) and search for and seizure of proscribed goods without a warrant – while also introducing a range of new regulations.[237] These included: suspending the 'right to trial by jury'; allowing the security forces to detain individuals for up to three days before deciding whether 'to bring them to trial, release them, or intern them'; and relaxing the 'evidentiary requirements to allow confessions obtained under interrogations to be sufficient for conviction'.[238]

The third legislative measure was the *Prevention of Terrorism (Temporary Provisions) Act*. Enacted on 29 November 1974, this statute was Westminster's response to a series of OIRA and PIRA bombings that rocked Great Britain during the early-1970s – culminating with the Birmingham pub bombings of 21 November 1974 that killed 21 people.[239] Unlike the Emergency Provisions Act, with which it was in force alongside, the Prevention of Terrorism Act applied to the entire United Kingdom and not just Northern Ireland. The Act's primary regulations included: allowing the police to detain 'suspected terrorists' for up to seven days for questioning; empowering the civil authority to exclude 'suspected terrorists', even if they were British citizens, from entering Great Britain; and permitting the police to 'search and make arrests without warrant'.[240]

There is little support for the notion that the PIRA's attrition increased during the mid-1970s because the British and Northern Ireland Governments' restricted civil liberties. On the one hand, the timing of the enactment of both the Emergency Provisions and Prevention of Terrorism Acts (i.e. near the beginning of the PIRA's attritional problems) suggests that a relationship may have existed between the authorities' restriction of civil liberties and the Provisionals' burgeoning loss of personnel. This linkage, however, is undercut by two observations. The first of these is that, prior to mid-1972, the authorities' restriction of civil liberties under the Special Powers Act did not have a discernible impact on the PIRA's attrition. For instance, even though the security forces detained over 1,100 people during the first 11 months of Internment (August 1971 – June 1972), the vast majority of these (over 80 per cent) 'were not members of' the PIRA and were eventually released without charge.[241] The second observation is that, as discussed above (and demonstrated in Figure 5.2), from 1978 onwards, the PIRA's loss of personnel first abated, before eventually stabilising – despite the continued presence of the Emergency Provisions and Prevention of Terrorism Acts and their respective curtailments of individual freedoms. The apparent weakness of the relationship between the restriction of civil liberties and the PIRA's attrition *before* mid-1972 and *after* 1977 suggests that the relationship between the restriction of civil liberties and the PIRA's burgeoning loss of personnel from mid-1972 to 1977 was similarly weak.

The amelioration of grievances

There is mixed support for the notion that the PIRA's intake of recruits declined during the mid-1970s because the organisation's grievances were ameliorated.

On the one hand, the PIRA's recruitment problems were preceded by the rectification of one of the organisation's highlighted grievances. Specifically, the British Government's decision to impose Direct Rule in March 1972 brought an end to the unionist-dominated government in Stormont and its perceived institutionalised discrimination against the Catholic minority. The apparent link between the amelioration of this grievance and the PIRA's declining recruitment is further strengthened (though not beyond doubt) by the observation that the fall of Stormont brought about a noticeable change in Catholic opinion. As authors like Moloney and Smith note, while '[m]ost Catholics, moderate as well as militant', celebrated Stormont's abolition, this celebration came with 'an important qualification. Many Catholics believed that, having achieved this success, the IRA should then at least review its options', such as calling a ceasefire.[242] This attitudinal shift would not likely have been conducive for the PIRA's ability to attract new recruits.

However, while it is possible to draw a tentative link between the fall of Stormont and the PIRA's declining recruitment, it is important to note that the PIRA's other highlighted grievances remained more or less unchanged as the 1970s progressed.

Consider, first of all, the Provisionals' overarching grievance, the British presence in, and control over, Northern Ireland. This condition not only persisted, but arguably intensified, during the mid-1970s. This is evident from three perspectives.

Politically, the mid-1970s witnessed the apparent solidification of Northern Ireland's position within the United Kingdom, as: (1) the British Government, in an attempt to mollify unionists after the abolition of Stormont, frequently reaffirmed its commitment to the 'consent principle' (i.e. 'that there would be no change to the constitutional status of Northern Ireland without the consent of the majority of its people');[243] and (2) the 'Border Poll' of March 1973, which saw 57.5 per cent of the electorate vote in favour of Northern Ireland remaining as part of the United Kingdom, demonstrated that such consent would unlikely be forthcoming well into the foreseeable future.[244]

Militarily, as Figure 5.3 illustrates, the mid-1970s represented the peak of British Army troop levels in the six counties. It was also during this period – specifically, in January 1976 – that the British Government formally announced the deployment of the SAS to Northern Ireland to assist the local security forces manage the PIRA threat.

Last of all, from an economic perspective, the mid-1970s witnessed 'a major expansion in the British state's role in the [Northern Irish] economy'.[245] For instance, in the 1969–70 financial year, the British Government paid £612 million[246] to cover the difference between public revenue and expenditure in the six counties; a figure which represented roughly 5 per cent of Northern Ireland's Gross Domestic Product (GDP).[247] However, by the 1976–77 financial year, London's subvention to Northern Ireland had essentially quadrupled to £2,279 million, and now represented over 20 per cent of the six counties' GDP.[248]

Another of the PIRA's identified grievances which remained more or less unchanged during the mid-1970s was the British Army and RUC's use of indiscriminate repression. Although the pattern of the security forces' repression did change from 1969–72 to 1972–77, the British Army and RUC nevertheless per-

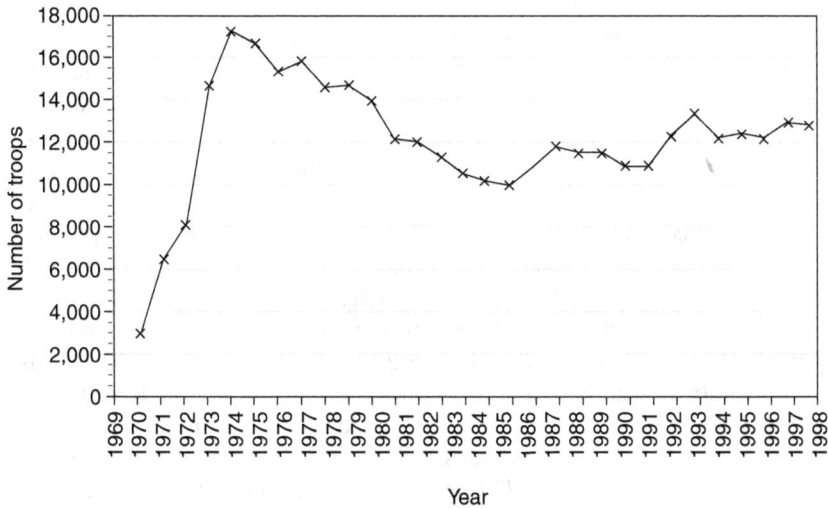

Figure 5.3 British Army strength in Northern Ireland, 1969–98 (source: P.R. Neumann, *Britain's Long War: British Strategy in the Northern Ireland Conflict, 1969–98*. Houndmills and New York: Palgrave Macmillan 2003, 190).

sisted in targeting large numbers of people who were not directly connected with the PIRA or any other paramilitary group. This is evident from three sources.

The first of these is Sluka's contention that, while the period following Operation Motorman did not witness a repeat of such defining provocations as the 'Rape of the Falls' or 'Bloody Sunday', the security forces still continued to subject the inhabitants of working-class Catholic districts to more mundane forms of indiscriminate repression. These included: 'the constant presence of heavily armed and sometimes overly aggressive troops and policemen'; 'constant surveillance, identity checks, census taking, and other forms of intelligence gathering activities'; and 'petty and not so petty acts of harassment, verbal abuse, vandalism, and brutality by policeman and British soldiers on patrol and at checkpoints'.[249] According to Sluka, the accumulation of these 'everyday' acts of repression did 'as much in the long run to alienate public opinion' as the security forces' 'larger and more systematic actions did'.[250]

The second source is that Internment, despite the best intentions of the British Government, continued to detain 'many innocent people' until the program was eventually phased out in 1975.[251] When London assumed direct control over Northern Irish affairs in March 1972, it was quick to realise that, under the Stormont Government, Internment had not been a surgical instrument.[252] Thus, the British Government introduced a number of safeguards in an attempt to ensure that only those individuals who posed a genuine threat to security in the six counties would be interned. These safeguards included: entrusting the initial decision to detain a person without charge to the SSNI; and guaranteeing all internees a review of their detention by a relatively independent Commissioner after 28 days.[253] However, while these reforms undoubtedly represented an improvement over the excesses witnessed during 1971, they nevertheless failed to make Internment 'sufficiently discerning'.[254] As Spjut highlights, over 30 per cent of internees whose detention came before a Commissioner for review in 1973 were summarily released; indicating that their relationship to the PIRA or other paramilitary groups was minimal.[255] Lowry even suggests that this 30 per cent rate of release was possibly *deflated*, given the low evidentiary requirements for Commissioners to recommend continued detention, and that the ability of internees to 'present a defense' was hamstrung by their lack of rights to know 'the precise nature of the charge against [them]', or 'the facts upon which the charge [was] based'.[256]

The final source is the seeming abuse by the security forces of their powers to detain people for up to seven days for questioning without a warrant. The British Government bestowed these powers on the British Army and the RUC through section 14 of the Emergency Provisions Act and section 12 of the Prevention of Terrorism Act. As Table 5.4 illustrates, the security forces detained people under these sections from 1975 to 1978 (the first years for which statistics are available) at a level that greatly exceeded the number of people who were eventually charged with terrorism-related offences.

Selective government repression

There is little support for the notion that the PIRA's recruitment declined during the mid-1970s because of selective government repression. Two observations form the basis of this judgment. The first of these is, as discussed in detail above, that the authorities' use of repression from mid-1972 to 1977 was not selective. The second observation is that, during the 1970s and early-1980s (if not the entire 28 years of The Troubles), the use of repression by the British Army, the RUC, and the UDR appears to have facilitated (rather than hindered) recruitment into the PIRA. Support for this observation is drawn from two sources.

First, Provisionals, in discussing why they joined the PIRA, tend to highlight the role played by security force repression. For instance, after interviewing 27

Table 5.4 Number of detainees under the Emergency Provisions and Prevention of Terrorism Acts and persons charged with terrorism-related offences, 1975–78

Year	s.14 (EPA)	s.12 (PTA)	Persons charged with terrorism-related offences
1975	4,141	8	1,197
1976	8,321	246	1,276
1977	5,878	162	1,308
1978	3,692	155	843

Source: G. Hogan and C. Walker, *Political Violence and the Law in Ireland*, Manchester and New York: Manchester University Press, 1989, 55–56; PSNI, 'Number of persons charged with terrorist and serious public order offences, 1972–2005', Statistics Branch, www.psni.police.uk/persons_charged_cy-19.doc (accessed on 1 August 2005), 2005.

republicans who joined either the PIRA or PSF between 1969 and 1984, White concludes that the 'common experience ... of state violence' – either against 'their families, neighbours, friends, ... or themselves' – was 'the essential catalyst in the collective recruitment of post-1969 Republicans'.[257] Likewise, English quotes a recruit from the early-1970s who states: 'Why did I become involved in the IRA? It was because of a process of British state repression as clearly distinct from any sort of attachment to republican ideology'.[258]

Second, ethnographies conducted in working-class areas of Belfast (one of the PIRA's primary recruiting grounds) reveal that security force repression was an important driver of support for the PIRA. For example, Burton, who lived in and studied the Short Strand between September 1972 and April 1973, observed that: (1) 'community support for the IRA' was not static, but rather, fluctuated in reaction to external events; and (2) '[o]ffensive and aggressive British activity, whether or not in response to IRA activity, had the effect in the community of tilting the balance of allegiance towards the Provisionals'.[259] Similarly, Sluka, who undertook fieldwork in the Divis Flats during 1981, noted that '[t]he actions of the Security Forces in Northern Ireland' – ranging from Bloody Sunday to the 'everyday acts of harassment and abuse by individual soldiers' – 'have done as much, if not more, to sway public support towards the IRA and [Irish National Liberation Army] as anything done by the guerrillas themselves'.[260]

Discrediting the insurgent actor's ideology

The PIRA case provides some support for the notion that an insurgent actor's recruitment will decline if its ideology is discredited. First of all, there is evidence that the PIRA's recruitment problems during the mid-1970s did coincide with a contraction in public approval for the organisation's goal of establishing a sovereign, 32-county republic. For instance, in his examination of the link between terrorism and public opinion, Hewitt collated a series of surveys that measured Northern Irish attitudes towards the prospect of a united Ireland. The results from these polls reveal an apparent collapse in Catholic support for Irish unity – dropping from approximately 60 per cent in early 1973 to 23 per cent in 1974 and 1976. Hewitt links this plunge to the attempts at constitutional reform (such as the creation of a new Northern Irish Assembly, a 'power-sharing' executive, and a Council of Ireland) which dominated the politics of the six counties during the mid-1970s, and the seeming favourable opportunities these reforms offered the nationalist community.[261] Likewise, the partial recovery of northern Catholic support for a united Ireland that is evident during the late-1970s can be interpreted as a reaction to the forceful rejection of the aforementioned reforms by both the PIRA and, more importantly, a seeming majority of northern Protestants. The epitome of this Protestant rejectionism was the Ulster Workers' Council (UWC) strike of May 1974, which brought the six counties to an economic standstill, and led to the eventual demise of the Assembly established in 1973 and its power-sharing executive.

Furthermore, it appears that the PIRA's recruitment problems also coincided with a contraction in northern Catholic acceptance of the utility of the PIRA's armed struggle. According to authors like Kelley and Smith, as the 1970s progressed and the 'British gave no sign that they were preparing to pull out', it became increasingly clear to the Catholic community that, despite the PIRA's frequent claims of imminent victory, the organisation's strategy of violence was 'completely fail[ing] to secure its objectives'.[262] As a consequence of this and such factors as the continued threat posed by loyalist killers and the oppressive nature of the PIRA's policing of the ghettoes, a sense of 'war-weariness' emerged amongst northern Catholics. The most prominent manifestation of this despondency was the emergence of the 'Peace People' in August 1976.[263] Formed by two Catholic women from Belfast in the wake of the tragic death of three children, the Peace People sought the end of paramilitary violence in the six counties.[264] During August and September of 1976, marches in Belfast and Dublin organised by the group attracted approximately 40,000 people from across the sectarian divide.[265]

The seeming popularity of the Peace People amongst northern Catholics, and the growing war-weariness that the group represented, alarmed the PIRA.[266] The organisation's response, beyond public criticism and denigration of the Peace People, was to introduce the two strategic reforms of 'politicisation' and the 'Long War'. Regarding the former, the PIRA hoped that, by unleashing Sinn Féin, the organisation would not only become more responsive to the needs of the Catholic community, but also be able to educate 'the people' about the importance of its campaign, and how Provisional violence was a 'direct outgrowth' of Catholic suffering in the six counties.[267] With regard to the latter, the PIRA sought to reframe how northern Catholics judged the effectiveness of the organisation's armed struggle. Previously, the PIRA had claimed that its campaign of violence would be able to achieve the organisation's goals rapidly; promising victory 'just around the corner'. However, the problem with this assertion was that when the PIRA's goals were *not* achieved rapidly – or, for that matter, did not even appear close to realisation – the efficacy of the organisation's violence was called into question. The Provisionals thus sought to redress this issue by linking their armed struggle not to 'imminent victory'; but rather, a long haul of indeterminate duration. This new frame allowed the PIRA to persist with its contention that violence was the most efficient means of begetting Ireland's reunification, while excusing for the fact that the organisation's armed struggle had not yet achieved this goal.

Conclusion

The primary objective of this chapter has been to uncover why the PIRA's previously robust capacity for regeneration weakened during the mid-1970s. It sought to achieve this by first examining the political and strategic environments in which the Provisionals arose and pursued their campaign.

Second, this chapter examined the PIRA's regenerative experience from the organisation's inception in late-1969 to the late-1970s and beyond. It is clear from this investigation that an increase in attrition played at least an equal, and arguably greater, role than a decrease in recruitment in weakening the PIRA's capacity to regenerate. This finding is at odds with the prevailing view in the conflict studies literature that a declining intake of recruits is more important than a burgeoning loss of personnel in bringing about the deterioration of an insurgent actor's regenerative capacity.

Third, this chapter examined whether the PIRA's attrition increased during the mid-1970s because of the improvement of the government's intelligence collection capabilities and/or the restriction of civil liberties. Regarding the former, this chapter found that: (1) the British authorities' ability to collect information about the Provisionals improved from mid-1972 to 1977; (2) this enhancement seems to have contributed to the PIRA's burgeoning loss of personnel over the same period; and (3) the Provisionals appear to have reduced their attrition from the late-1970s onwards by, in part, hampering the British Government's ability to collect intelligence about the insurgent actor. These findings support the literature's emphasis on enhancing intelligence collection capabilities as a means of increasing insurgent attrition; but also suggest that, due to the interdependent nature of insurgencies, any improvement in a government's intelligence collection capabilities is likely to be only temporary in nature.

With regard to the latter, this chapter observed that, since the British and Northern Ireland Governments' restriction of civil liberties prior to mid-1972 and after 1977 had seemingly no impact on the PIRA's rate of attrition, it is likely that the relationship between the authorities' restriction of civil liberties and the Provisionals' burgeoning loss of personnel from mid-1972 to 1977 was similarly weak. These results call into question the validity of the notion that a government can improve its ability to arrest and kill members of an insurgent actor by restricting civil liberties.

Finally, this chapter examined whether the PIRA's recruitment declined because of the amelioration of grievances, the use of selective government repression, and/or the discrediting of the insurgent actor's ideology. Regarding the first, this chapter found that, while the PIRA's recruitment problems did coincide with the rectification of one of the organisation's grievances (i.e. the fall of Stormont), the PIRA's other major grievances remained more or less unchanged during the period when the organisation's recruitment declined. This supports the conclusion from the previous chapters that ameliorating grievances is not a necessary condition for reducing an insurgent actor's intake of recruits.

With regard to selective government repression, this chapter observed that the British and Northern Ireland Governments' use of repression: (1) was not selective; and (2) appears to have facilitated, rather than deterred, recruitment into the PIRA. These results call into question the validity of 'selectiveness' as an indicator of whether a government's use of repression will or will not have a deterrent effect.

Last of all, in reference to discrediting the insurgent actor's ideology, this chapter found that there is some evidence the PIRA's recruitment declined during the mid-1970s because public approval for the insurgent actor's goal of a united Ireland, and the utility of the actor's armed struggle contracted. This finding suggests that a link does exist between public approval for an insurgent actor's ideology and the strength of the actor's intake of recruits.

6   Conclusion

For an insurgent actor like al-Qaeda, Jemaah Islamiah, or Lashkar-e-Taiba, there are many factors which can affect the likely intensity and success of its campaign. These include: the group's access to resources; the proficiency of its leadership; and the extent of its territorial control. Perhaps one of the most important factors, however, is the strength of the insurgent actor's *capacity to regenerate* (i.e. its ability to replace lost personnel with new recruits). While a strong regenerative capacity will allow the group to withstand opposing security force pressure and (at the very least) persist with its armed struggle; a weak regenerative capacity will trigger a contraction in the group's membership – threatening its ability to conduct operations and, eventually, the very existence of the group itself. Thus, from a government perspective, attempting to weaken an insurgent actor's capacity to regenerate is a seemingly intuitive and attractive means of managing, if not outright defeating, the insurgent actor. However, being able to affect insurgent regeneration is far from a simple undertaking; one that a number of governments – including, most notably, the Bush Administration in relation to al-Qaeda – have struggled to realise.

The primary objective of this book is to provide scholars and officials with a greater understanding of how governments can favourably influence the capacity to regenerate of an insurgent actor. It sought to achieve this by exploring: *why do the regenerative capacities of insurgent actors weaken?* The exploration of this question took the form of a two-tier examination of three insurgent actors whose capacity to regenerate weakened in the past – namely, the *Front de libération du Québec* (FLQ) of Canada, the *Movimiento de Liberación Nacional – Tupamaros* (MLN-T) of Uruguay, and the Provisional Irish Republican Army (PIRA) of Northern Ireland. The findings and implications of this examination will be discussed below. This will include general deductions for academics and policy-makers, followed by specific recommendations for liberal democratic governments to improve their ability to manage jihadi insurgent actors.

An increase in attrition versus a decrease in recruitment

At the first level of its examination, this study investigated the extent to which the regenerative capacities of the FLQ, MLN-T, and PIRA weakened because of an increase in attrition and a decrease in recruitment. The primary objectives of this analysis are: (1) to uncover whether a declining intake of recruits played a lesser, equal, or greater role than a burgeoning loss of personnel in weakening the capacities to regenerate of the three insurgent actors; and (2) to shed greater light on the broader validity of the prevailing view in the conflict studies literature that a decrease in recruitment is more important than an increase in attrition in effecting the corrosion of an insurgent actor's capacity to regenerate.

The relative strength of a burgeoning loss of personnel and a declining intake of recruits as catalysts of regenerative decay varied between the FLQ case, on the one hand, and the MLN-T and PIRA cases, on the other. With regard to the former, a decrease in recruitment clearly played the greater role in weakening the movement's capacity to regenerate. Although the FLQ's attrition in the wake of the 'October Crisis' of 1970 was considerable, it was no more considerable than what the movement had experienced prior to the kidnappings of Cross and Laporte. The only real difference was that, while aspiring *felquistes* repeatedly stepped forward to replace lost members and networks before October 1970, they gradually stopped doing so afterwards – leading to the movement's eventual demise by the end of 1972.

Conversely, an increase in attrition appears to have played at least an equal, and arguably greater, role than a decrease in recruitment in weakening the MLN-T's capacity to regenerate. Three observations form the basis of this judgment. The first of these is that the deterioration of the MLN-T's regenerative capacity coincided with both an increase in attrition and a decrease in recruitment. For instance, although the MLN-T suffered a steadily increasing rate of attrition prior to April 1972 (with the number of arrested Tupamaros rising from an average of three a month in 1968 to 13 in early-1972), it was easily able to offset these losses through the organisation's bountiful intake of new recruits. However, following the Tupamaro assassinations of 14 April 1972 and the Uruguayan Government's declaration of a 'state of internal war' the following day, the MLN-T experienced not only a contraction in its recruitment, but also a dramatic increase in the number of arrested and killed Tupamaros that it had to replace. Buffeted between these two trends, the MLN-T first began to shrink, before disappearing entirely from the Uruguayan scene.

The second observation is that the MLN-T's loss of personnel seemingly increased at a rate greater than that at which the organisation's intake of recruits declined. This is largely evident from the contrast between the apparent lack of urgency with which the MLN-T framed its recruitment problems during 1972, and the unbridled ferocity of the organisation's losses following the 'state of internal war' – with the average number of arrested Tupamaros rising from four a week over the six months before April 1972, to an average of 39 a week over the six months after. The third observation, meanwhile, is that the MLN-T's burgeoning loss of personnel appears to have had a greater impact on the organisation's decision-making process than its declining intake of recruits. This is evident from the utter disorientation seemingly engendered by the MLN-T's mounting losses from April 1972 onwards (as Arraras states, the 'Tupamaros experienced internal chaos as the Armed Forces dismantled their organization');[1] compared to the relative apathy generated by the organisation's recruitment problems over the same period.

Similar to the MLN-T, an increase in attrition appears to have played at least an equal, and arguably greater, role than a decrease in recruitment in weakening the PIRA's capacity to regenerate. Three observations underlie this assessment. The first of these is that the deterioration of the PIRA's regenerative capacity coincided with both a burgeoning loss of personnel and a declining intake of recruits. For instance, during the first 30 months of its campaign, the PIRA was virtually impervious to security force pressure. Yet, in the months and years following Operation Motorman in July 1972, the Provisionals suffered both a reduction in their intake of recruits (which had peaked after Bloody Sunday in January 1972), and a surge in their loss of personnel. As Bishop and Mallie state: 'As the decade progressed it became increasingly hazardous to be in the IRA.'[2] Accordingly, the PIRA's membership strength began to contract, and the organisation looked destined to follow in the footsteps of its predecessor during the Border Campaign of the early-1960s. Unlike the Tupamaros, however, the Provisionals were able to reverse their regenerative fortunes. After introducing a series of reforms, the PIRA witnessed the reduction of its attrition, and the stabilisation of its recruitment. This state of affairs would remain unchanged until the signing of the Good Friday Agreement in April 1998.

The second observation is that the PIRA's loss of personnel appears to have increased at a rate greater than that at which the organisation's intake of recruits declined. This is apparent from the contrast between the lack of urgency in which the literature frames the PIRA's reduction in recruitment following 1972, and the more expansionary and consequential language the literature uses to describe the organisation's attritional problems over the same period.

The third observation, meanwhile, is that the PIRA's burgeoning loss of personnel appears to have generated greater concern within the organisation than its declining intake of recruits. This is evident from the contrasting emphasis in which Provisional documents, such as the Staff Report, discussed and proposed remedies for the PIRA's increasing attrition and decreasing recruitment during the mid-1970s.

These findings provide mixed support for the prevailing view in the conflict studies literature that a decrease in recruitment is more important than an increase in attrition in bringing about the deterioration of an insurgent actor's capacity to regenerate. On the one hand, it is clear from the FLQ (and, as briefly outlined in the Introduction, the Malayan Races' Liberation Army and the Viet Cong) that the above notion is a valid explanation for why the regenerative capacities of *some* insurgent actors weaken. However, it is also clear from the MLN-T and PIRA that the literature's tendency to emphasise a decrease in recruitment, and disregard an increase in attrition, as likely sources of regenerative capacity deterioration is *not* an accurate representation of the regenerative experiences of *all* insurgent actors. Indeed, the Tupamaro and Provisional cases suggest that the prevailing view in the literature: (1) underestimates the role a burgeoning loss of personnel can play, either as an equal or primary source, in weakening an insurgent actor's capacity to regenerate; and (2) mistakenly universalises a declining intake of recruits as the most important catalyst of regenerative decay.

In light of these conclusions, the conflict studies literature should refashion how it conceptualises the relationships between a declining intake of recruits, a burgeoning loss of personnel, and regenerative decay. A more appropriate approach, from this study's perspective, is for scholars and officials to assume not that the relative strength of an increase in attrition and a decrease in recruitment is static; but rather, that it varies across insurgent actors. Such an approach would not only better reflect the broader regenerative experience of insurgent actors, but also encourage the examination of perhaps the more important and intriguing question: *why does the relative strength of the two factors vary?* Why, for instance, did a burgeoning loss of personnel play a significant role in weakening the MLN-T's capacity to regenerate, but not the FLQ's? The exploration of questions like this would both give scholars a richer understanding of regenerative decay, as well as provide policymakers with greater guidance about how they should manage the insurgent threat.

Two further policy implications emerge from the above findings. The first of these is that a government seeking to weaken an insurgent actor's capacity to regenerate should focus at least part of its efforts on reducing the actor's intake of recruits. Although the relative strength of a decrease in recruitment varied between the cases, it nevertheless played a role in weakening the regenerative capacities of all three insurgent actors. Indeed, the FLQ, MLN-T, and PIRA cases raise the possibility that a declining intake of recruits is a *necessary condition* for regenerative decay. More testing is required, however, before this relationship can be asserted with any certainty.

The second policy implication is that governments should not automatically assume that the only way they can beget the decay of an insurgent actor's capacity to regenerate is by focusing on the actor's intake of recruits. Rather, policymakers should be aware that: (1) a burgeoning loss of personnel can play a significant role in weakening the regenerative capacities of some insurgent actors; and (2) trying to increase insurgent attrition may thus offer further, and possibly even better, options to weaken an insurgent actor's capacity to regenerate than simply trying to reduce insurgent recruitment. The key for governments is to be able to identify those insurgent actors whose capacities to regenerate are vulnerable to a burgeoning loss of personnel (like the MLN-T and the PIRA during the mid-1970s) from those whose are not (such as the FLQ). Such wisdom will hopefully emerge with greater scholarly exploration of the variation between an increase of attrition and a decrease of recruitment as catalysts of regenerative decay.

The dynamics of insurgent recruitment and attrition

At the second level of its examination, this book investigated whether: (1) the decrease in recruitment that the FLQ, MLN-T, and PIRA experienced was the result of the amelioration of grievances, the use of selective government repression, and/or the discrediting of the insurgent actor's ideology; and (2) the increase in attrition that the MLN-T and PIRA experienced was the result of the improvement of the government's intelligence collection capabilities, and/or the restriction of civil liberties. The central purpose of this analysis is to strengthen the empirical foundations of the literature's understanding of the best ways in which a government can favourably influence an insurgent actor's loss of personnel and intake of recruits. Each of the five prescriptions will be discussed in turn below.

The amelioration of grievances

The FLQ, MLN-T, and PIRA cases provided little or no support for the notion that an insurgent actor's intake of recruits will decline because the grievances which are driving the actor's recruitment are ameliorated. Rather, in all three cases, the insurgent actor's intake of recruits fell (and with regard to the FLQ and MLN-T, ultimately evaporated), even though the grievances which formed the basis of their collective action frames remained more or less unchanged. For instance, during the period when the FLQ's recruitment declined: (1) the structural basis of Quebec's perceived political colonisation (i.e. the power differential between English- and French-Canada) had not been rectified; (2) French-Canada's relative economic deprivation and the 'Anglo-Saxon' domination of Quebec's economy continued largely unabated; and (3) concern over the precarious state of the French language in Quebec remained high. Likewise, the primary grievance identified by the MLN-T – the state of Uruguay's economy – appeared to exhibit a positive relationship with the organisation's intake of recruits from the late-1960s onwards (i.e. the MLN-T's recruitment declined as Uruguay's economy worsened, and vice versa). In addition, the Uruguayan military's actions following 15 April 1972 were unlikely to have changed many opinions that the authorities acted in defence of the 'established order'. Lastly, while the fall of Stormont in March 1972 did address one of the PIRA's grievances; the organisation's other major grievances – i.e. the British presence in, and control over, Northern Ireland, and the British Army's use of 'indiscriminate repression' – either remained unchanged or, in the case of the former, arguably intensified during the mid-1970s.

While these results do not support the notion that ameliorating grievances will reduce an insurgent actor's recruitment, they do not disprove it either. Further research on the recruitment patterns of insurgent actors whose identified grievances were ameliorated is required before a judgment in this regard can be made. Nevertheless, the *felquiste*, Tupamaro, and Provisional cases do suggest that: (1) ameliorating grievances is not a necessary condition for reducing an insurgent actor's recruitment; (2) the role of grievances in influencing an individual's decision to join, or not to join, an insurgent actor may be relatively minor, or at least smaller than other factors, such as the perceived efficacy of violence, the threat of possible harm, and the accessibility of recruitment networks; and (3) while decision-makers should not desist from attempting to ameliorate grievances as part of their counterinsurgent efforts, scholars and officials should not regard the amelioration of grievances as the 'be-all and end-all' of counterinsurgent policy.

Selective government repression

This study provided mixed support for the notion that an insurgent actor's intake of recruits will decline if the opposing government employs selective repression. On the one hand, in the cases of the FLQ and MLN-T, there is some evidence that the use of government repression did have a deterrent effect on insurgent recruitment. Regarding the former, this evidence is comprised of judgments drawn from the secondary literature, and the observation that the movement's recruitment problems coincided with the expansion and intensification of the Canadian authorities' anti-FLQ campaign. With regard to the latter, the evidence is primarily composed of the contrast between the fear generated by, and the perceived proficiency of, the Uruguayan military's counterinsurgent efforts from April 1972 onwards, and the resentment generated by, and the perceived incompetence of, the police's anti-Tupamaro campaign prior to September 1971. On the other hand, however, interviews with Volunteers and ethnographies conducted in Catholic, working-class ghettoes in Belfast indicate that, in the PIRA case, government repression during the mid-1970s (if not the entire Troubles) was more likely to have facilitated an individual's recruitment into the PIRA, rather than have discouraged it.

Nevertheless, while it is possible to discern contrasting relationships between the Canadian, Uruguayan, and British Governments' use of repression and the FLQ, MLN-T, and PIRA's intake of recruits; it is not possible, in any of the cases, to describe the relevant government's use of repression as having been selective. For instance, the vast majority of the 468 people detained by the Canadian authorities under the War Measures Act during late-1970 had no connection with the FLQ; approximately two-thirds to four-fifths of the 5,000 people imprisoned by the Uruguayan military following the declaration of a 'state of internal war' were not Tupamaros; and, during the mid-1970s, the British Government continued to intern 'many innocent people', killed more or an equal number of civilians than Volunteers, and detained suspects for up to seven days for questioning at a rate that greatly exceeded the number of people eventually charged with terrorism-related offences.[3]

A number of implications emerge from these findings. The first of these is that a *conditional* relationship does appear to exist between government repression and insurgent recruitment. That is, under different conditions, a government's use of repression can either have a deterring or radicalising effect on an insurgent actor's intake of recruits. This conclusion is in accordance with Leites and Wolf's writings on insurgent recruitment and government repression; as well as the broader literature on political protest, which has long noted the existence of a conditional relationship between repression and protest participation.[4]

A second implication is that, while a conditional relationship may exist between government repression and insurgent recruitment, 'selectiveness' is a seemingly poor indicator of whether a government's use of repression will have a deterring or radicalising effect on an insurgent actor's intake of recruits. As aforementioned, each of the opposing governments in the three cases employed indiscriminate repression. Yet, while the British Government's repression appears to have facilitated recruitment into the PIRA, the Canadian and Uruguayan Governments' repression seems to have tempered recruitment into the FLQ and MLN-T. These results undermine the claim by Leites and Wolf and others that the more selective government repression is, the more likely it will discourage, rather than encourage, people from joining an insurgent actor.

A final implication is that policymakers should be wary about attempting to use repression as a means of influencing an insurgent actor's recruitment. As the FLQ, MLN-T, and PIRA cases demonstrate, while it is possible that repression may, under some conditions, deter people from joining an insurgent actor, identifying these conditions is a difficult exercise. Until the conflict studies literature is able to address its own ignorance in this regard, governments should temper their expectations about the possibilities of using repression to 'control' an insurgent actor's intake of recruits.

Discrediting the insurgent actor's ideology

The three cases provide mixed support for the notion that an insurgent actor's intake of recruits will decline if its ideology is discredited. On the one hand, the MLN-T's waning recruitment during 1972 and 1973 does not appear to have coincided with a contraction in public approval for either the organisation's goal of a socialist Uruguay or its strategy of revolutionary violence. Underlying this judgment are the observed upswings in: (1) support for political parties that advocated socialist ideals between the 1966 and 1971 elections; and (2) the number of respondents who told the Gallup Organisation during 1970–72 that they believed there was 'some justification' for the Tupamaros' campaign.

On the other hand, while public approval for the FLQ's goal of an independent, socialist Quebec remained steady during the early-1970s, the FLQ's declining recruitment did appear to coincide with a contraction in public support for the movement's strategy of violence. This latter shift was driven by two factors: (1) the October Crisis, and its repudiation of the notion that violence was an effective instrument of change; and (2) the rise of the *Parti Québécois* (a separatist political party) in 1968, which, through its convincing performance at the 1970 provincial election, demonstrated the possibilities of electoralism as a means of achieving *le Québec libre*.

Likewise, the Provisionals' recruitment problems during the mid-1970s did appear to coincide with a transitory contraction in northern Catholic approval for both the PIRA's overarching goal of a united Ireland, and the utility of the PIRA's armed struggle. The former of these shifts was linked to: (1) the various attempts at constitutional reform that dominated Northern Irish politics during the mid-1970s (which sought, amongst other things, to share executive power between the warring communities, and to create a pan-Ireland body to facilitate harmonisation and cooperation between the six and 26 counties); and (2) the eventual and forceful rejection of these reforms by an apparent majority of northern Protestants. The latter shift, meanwhile, was linked to: (1) the seeming lack of progress achieved by the PIRA's campaign – especially given the organisation's frequent claims of imminent victory; and (2) the PIRA's eventual embrace of two strategic reforms that increased the PIRA's political activity, and reframed the timescale by which northern Catholics judged the efficacy of the organisation's use of violence.

These results suggest that discrediting an insurgent actor's ideology has both promise and limitations as a means of reducing insurgent recruitment. On the one hand, it is clear from the FLQ and PIRA cases that contracting public approval for an insurgent actor's ideology can have a significant impact on the strength of the actor's intake of recruits. Indeed, in the former case, waning support for the FLQ's strategy of violence appears to have played the leading role – particularly in the medium- to long-term – in reducing the movement's recruitment. Conversely, the MLN-T case demonstrates that discrediting an insurgent actor's ideology is not a necessary condition for reducing the actor's intake of recruits. Furthermore, the above findings also raise questions about the extent to which governments can exert control over public approval for an insurgent actor's ideology. For instance, while contracting support for the FLQ's strategy of violence did play a key role in weakening the movement's recruitment; this contraction was primarily driven by factors (such as the *Parti Québécois'* impressive results at the May 1970 election, and the discernible revulsion triggered by Laporte's murder) which were not the consequence of direct or deliberate action by the Canadian authorities. Similarly, but from a different perspective, although the British Government's efforts in pushing constitutional reform and frustrating the PIRA's campaign arguably influenced northern Catholic perceptions about the desirability of a united Ireland and the utility of violence; these efforts eventually came to naught due to the actions of parties beyond London's control – namely the Ulster Workers' Council (UWC) and the PIRA. This is not to suggest that governments should not seek to discredit an insurgent actor's ideology as a means of reducing its recruitment; but rather, that they should be aware that their ability to influence public approval for an insurgent actor's ideology may be limited, and possibly held hostage to the whims of other parties, including the insurgent actor itself.

Improving the Government's intelligence collection capabilities

The MLN-T and PIRA provide strong support for the notion that an insurgent actor's loss of personnel will increase if the opposing government enhances its intelligence collection capabilities. For example, prior to September 1971, the Uruguayan Government's ability to gather information about the Tupamaros was generally defective. However, the period from early-1972 onwards witnessed a dramatic improvement in the authorities' intelligence collection capabilities. This improvement was the function of three factors. Namely: (1) a breakdown in the MLN-T's internal security (a consequence of the breakout of 100 imprisoned Tupamaros and their reintegration back into the organisation); (2) a series of high-profile, Tupamaro defections; and (3) the Uruguayan military's expanded and systematic use of torture as a method of interrogation.

Likewise, at the outbreak of The Troubles, the British and Northern Ireland Governments' ability to collect information about the Provisionals was lacking; largely due to the absence of a Republican threat in the six counties prior to 1970; the incompetence of the Royal Ulster Constabulary (RUC); and a lack of cooperation between the RUC and British Army. However, the mid-1970s witnessed the gradual improvement of the authorities' intelligence collection capabilities. This was driven by: (1) Operation Motorman, which opened up 'intelligence blackspots' in Belfast and Derry; (2) the influence of Brigadier Frank Kitson; (3) the growing professionalism of 'The Det' (the British Army's covert intelligence unit); and (4) the security forces' increasing exploitation of the PIRA's security deficiencies. Further evidence of the link between improving a government's intelligence collection capabilities and insurgent attrition is provided by the observation that the PIRA was able to reduce its loss of personnel during the late-1970s by, in part, implementing various reforms which hampered the authorities' ability to collect intelligence. These reforms included: the adoption of a cellular organisational structure; and the creation of a system to educate new Volunteers about how to resist interrogations and maintain proper security etiquette.

These findings suggest that the literature's faith in the relationship between improving a government's intelligence collection capabilities and insurgent attrition is warranted, and that, for a government seeking to increase an insurgent actor's loss of personnel, enhancing its ability to gather information about the insurgent actor should be a priority, or, at the very least, part of its counterinsurgent efforts. It is important to note, however, that, as the PIRA case highlights, an insurgency is an *interdependent* relationship. While a government can improve its intelligence collection capabilities and, consequently, increase an insurgent actor's attrition; the insurgent actor is also capable of undertaking its own measures to frustrate the government's ability to gather information and, as a result, minimise its loss of personnel. Thus, while improving a government's intelligence collection capabilities is important as a means of increasing an insurgent actor's attrition, it does have its limits. Policymakers should both be aware of these and prepared to act within them – perhaps by exploiting any information collection advantage as quickly and strenuously as possible.

Restricting civil liberties

The Tupamaro and Provisional cases provide little support for the notion that an insurgent actor's loss of personnel will increase if the opposing government restricts civil liberties. For instance, at first glance, the link between curtailing individual rights and Tupamaro attrition appears strong; given that the MLN-T's skyrocketing loss of personnel did coincide with the Uruguayan Government's declaration of a 'state of internal war'. Two observations suggest, however, that the authorities' restriction of civil liberties and the MLN-T's burgeoning attrition from April 1972 onwards was more coincidental than causative. These observations include: (1) that the Uruguayan Government had restricted civil liberties on three occasions prior to April 1972 (for a combined period of 12 months); and (2) that these efforts – which, at times, matched the 'state of internal war' in terms of severity – had no impact on the MLN-T's rate of attrition. Likewise, given that the British and Northern Ireland Governments' curtailed individual freedoms and protections for essentially the entirety of The Troubles, and that the authorities' restriction of civil liberties prior to mid-1972 and after 1977 had seemingly no impact on the PIRA's rate of attrition, it is likely that the relationship between the British Government's restriction of civil liberties and the Provisionals' burgeoning loss of personnel from mid-1972 to 1977 was similarly weak.

These results call into question the validity of two related concepts. First, that constitutionally- and legislatively-enshrined individual rights hamper the ability of governments to arrest and kill members of an insurgent actor. Second, that restricting said civil liberties (either fully or in part) will enhance the capacity of governments to increase an insurgent actor's loss of personnel. The repudiation of these concepts is in accordance with the broader literature's general scepticism about the relationship between restricting civil liberties and improving the efficacy of a government's counterinsurgent response. The above findings also suggest that: (1) governments seeking to favourably influence an insurgent actor's rate of attrition, rather than curtailing individual freedoms and protections, would be better served by concentrating their resources on other measures, such as improving their intelligence collection capabilities; and (2) greater testing of the alleged utilitarian benefits of restricting civil liberties is required. For example, researchers should examine whether curtailing individual freedoms and protections actually improves a government's ability to manage the rate and intensity of insurgent violence, or to influence public support for an insurgent actor.

Recommendations for liberal democracies

Jihadi insurgent actors (such as al-Qaeda, Jemaah Islamiah and Lashkar-e-Taiba) pose a growing threat to many liberal democratic governments. The past decade has witnessed: (1) devastating bombings in key liberal democratic countries (the United States, Spain and the United Kingdom); (2) attacks against citizens of liberal democracies in other parts of the world (for example, in Bali and North Africa); and (3) the apparent expansion of jihadi networks in Europe.[5] As its final act, this book, drawing on its research and findings, will offer liberal democratic governments three recommendations. These seek to improve the ability of liberal democracies to manage the threat posed by the broader jihadi insurgency.

The first recommendation is that liberal democratic governments should recognise that they may have a wider range of policy options to weaken a jihadi group's capacity to regenerate than simply trying to reduce the group's recruitment. At least in terms of framing their counterinsurgency strategy, officials should not assume that a declining intake of recruits will be the primary driver of jihadi regenerative decay. This being said, however, it is possible that al-Qaeda – a leading, albeit unique, element of the jihadi insurgency – may be more susceptible to measures that seek to decrease its recruitment rather than expand its attrition. Underlying this prospect is the observation that al-Qaeda and the FLQ share a number of pertinent similarities. For instance, both insurgent actors seem less like a centralised, 'coherent and tight-knit organisation' (along the lines of the PIRA), and more like a 'loose association' of networks, which share a common desire to beget their goals through the application of violence.[6] Furthermore, recruitment into the FLQ and al-Qaeda (at least after 11 September 2001) appears less a 'top down' phenomenon than an organic process based around familial and friendship ties.[7] Last of all, the regenerative experience of al-Qaeda over the last eight years resembles that of the FLQ prior to the October Crisis. Specifically, although al-Qaeda has suffered considerable losses since the 9/11 attacks, aspiring jihadists have repeatedly stepped forward to either join existing networks or, with the assistance of like-minded associates, form their own.[8] Similarities such as these raise the possibility that, as with the FLQ, a decrease in recruitment will play the greater (indeed, solitary) role in weakening al-Qaeda's capacity to regenerate.

The second recommendation is that if a liberal democratic government is planning to weaken a jihadi group's capacity to regenerate by attempting to increase its loss of personnel, officials should concentrate their efforts on improving their intelligence collection capabilities. This book can suggest three specific prescriptions to achieve this goal. First, enhance the government's human intelligence capabilities. This could involve expanding the use of frontline security personnel to collect operational intelligence (similar to Frank Kitson's advice to British Army troops) and the use of more covert and innovative human intelligence units (such as 'the Det' in Northern Ireland). Second, if relevant, reduce or eliminate safe-havens. As the 'no-go' areas in Belfast and Derry demonstrate, safe-havens can significantly hinder the ability of security forces to collect intelligence about an insurgent actor. Third, encourage insurgent informers and defectors. These were valuable sources of intelligence in both the Tupamaro and Provisional cases. Encouraging insurgents to inform or defect could involve exacerbating internal power struggles (as occurred after previously incarcerated leaders were re-integrated into the MLN-T) and targeting the less than ideologically committed.

Despite the role that it seemingly played in the Uruguayan armed forces' campaign against the MLN-T, this book would not prescribe the use of torture to improve the intelligence collection capabilities of a liberal democratic government. The reasons for this are twofold. First, in the author's personal view, torture is a moral wrong and runs counter to the norms and ideals underpinning the liberal democratic form of governance. Second, the apparent utility of torture as a means of acquiring intelligence about the MLN-T was largely a function of the unrestricted nature of the Uruguayan armed forces' campaign. As observed both in the Tupamaro case and more broadly, one of the many limiting factors of torture is that it can produce unreliable information. As Bufacchi and Arrigo state, those being tortured 'may say anything for the sake of temporarily stopping the torture, but the information they reveal may be the wrong information'.[9] This can confuse decision-making and lead to inefficient outcomes (as innocent people are pursued and detained, while insurgents remain unidentified). The Uruguayan armed forces' solution to this problem was essentially to overwhelm it. That is, they detained and tortured people (ultimately in the thousands) at levels deemed sufficient to compensate for any unreliable information they obtained. Concerns about arresting and harming innocent civilians were subsumed to the greater goal of destroying the MLN-T. Unless a liberal democratic government is prepared to wage a similarly unrestricted campaign against the jihadi insurgency (an unlikely and undesirable prospect), the problem of unreliable information is likely to limit the utility of torture as a means of acquiring intelligence.

The third recommendation is that if a liberal democratic government intends to weaken a jihadi group's capacity to regenerate by attempting to decrease its intake of recruits, officials should focus their efforts on discrediting the group's ideology. Different aspects of jihadi ideology are likely to have greater promise in this regard. On the one hand, discrediting the *goal* of jihadi ideology (roughly, the end of Western influence in Muslim countries, the imposition of Sharia and the establishment of a pan-Islamic caliphate)[10] is likely to be a difficult undertaking. As the FLQ, MLN-T and PIRA cases highlight, the proposed solution underpinning an insurgent ideology can be highly resilient, able to withstand concerted government attempts to undermine it, and even survive the defeat of an insurgent campaign. The FLQ example is particularly illuminating. The movement's goal of an independent Quebec not only survived Ottawa's attempts to diminish its appeal (primarily through increased Federal spending) and the eventual discrediting of the FLQ's broader ideology of violent separatism, but also managed to grow in popularity, becoming the subject of referenda in 1980 and 1995. This is not to say that liberal democratic governments should not attempt to discredit the goal of jihadi ideology. But officials should realise that undermining the notion of a pan-Islamic caliphate (for instance) may be a complex and protracted undertaking; one that may ultimately be determined by factors outside of their immediate control.

Discrediting the *utilitarian justifications* of jihadi ideology, in contrast, is likely to be a more fruitful endeavour for liberal democratic governments. For the majority of insurgent actors, there is a considerable distance between their identified goals and their ability to realise these goals through the application of violence. The arguments insurgent actors employ to justify the utility of violence are thus susceptible to events that expose or highlight this gap. For instance, the relative success of the *Parti Québécois* at the provincial elections in May 1970, the public outpouring of revulsion towards the killing of Pierre Laporte, and the Federal Government's far reaching crackdown following the October Crisis emphasised the inability of the FLQ to effect *la Québec libre* through the use of violence (as well as highlighting the possibilities offered by democratic politics). Likewise, the ongoing British presence in Northern Ireland during the mid-1970s – in the face of the repeated Provisional claim of 'imminent victory' – called into question the PIRA's arguments about the utility of its armed struggle.

Consequently, liberal democratic governments should seek to discredit the utilitarian justifications of a jihadi group's ideology by responding in a manner that will most likely expose or highlight the gap between the group's capacity to affect change through violence and its desired goals. In some cases, this may simply involve waiting a jihadi group out – allowing the passage of time to accentuate the futility of the group's strategy of violence. In other cases, it may require a concerted and overwhelming government response to emphasise the government's strength and resolve and, in turn, the limits of jihadi violence. It is also important for liberal democratic governments to recognise that utilitarian justifications are, in essence, relative arguments. That is, they general frame the utility of violence in comparison with the alleged ineffectiveness of other approaches (such as contesting elections and non-violent protest). Discrediting the utilitarian justifications of jihadi ideology should thus also involve attempts to bolster the perceived efficacy of alternative instruments of change. This could include reducing structural and cultural barriers to political participation by domestic Muslim communities, and recognising (and potentially supporting) Islamist groups in Muslim countries that advocate non-violence and democratic action.

Hopefully, by pursuing such policies to discredit the utilitarian justifications of insurgent ideology, as well as improving intelligence collection capabilities and recognising the wide range of policy options that may be available to affect regenerative decay, future Defence Secretaries can avoid asking their key lieutenants: 'Are we winning or losing the Global War on Terror?'

Notes

1 Introduction

1 Richard J. Goss, *Principles of Regeneration* (New York and London: Academic Press, 1969), 1.
2 These were: Deputy-Secretary of Defence, Paul Wolfowitz; Under-Secretary of Defence for Policy, Douglas Feith; Chairman of the Joint Chiefs of Staff, General Richard Myers; and Vice-Chairman of the Joint Chiefs of Staff, General Peter Pace.
3 Bradley Graham, 'Rumsfeld Questions Anti-Terrorism Efforts', *Washington Post*, 23 October 2003, 1A; Dave Moniz and Tom Squitieri, 'Rumsfeld Memo Prompts Praise and Told-You-So's', *USA Today*, 23 October 2003, 6A; Thom Shanker, 'Rumsfeld Sees Need to Realign Military Fight against Terror', *New York Times*, 23 October 2003, 12.
4 Donald H. Rumsfeld, 'Town Hall Meeting: Remarks as Delivered by Secretary of Defense Donald H. Rumsfeld, Soto Cano Air Base, Honduras', www.defenselink.mil/speeches/2003/sp20030920-secdef2075.html.
5 ——, 'Global War on Terrorism', GlobalSecurity.org, www.globalsecurity.org/military/library/policy/dod/d20031016sdmemo.pdf.
6 Ibid.
7 Ibid.
8 National Intelligence Council, 'Declassified Key Judgments of the National Intelligence Estimate "Trends in Global Terrorism: Implications for the United States" Dated April 2006', (Washington, D.C. 2006).
9 ——, 'National Intelligence Estimate: The Terrorist Threat to the US Homeland', (Washington, D.C. 2007).
10 Daniel Benjamin and Steven Simon, *The Next Attack: The Failure of the War on Terror and a Strategy for Getting It Right* (New York: Owls Books, 2006), 126. See also: Mark Danner, 'Taking Stock of the Forever War', *New York Times Magazine*, 11 September 2005, 47; James Fallows, 'Bush's Lost Year', *The Atlantic Monthly*, October 2004, 72; Peter R. Neumann, 'Europe's Jihadist Dilemma', *Survival* 48, no. 2 (2006): 76–78.
11 Allan Bäck, 'Thinking Clearly About Violence', *Philosophical Studies* 117, no. 1–2 (2004): 224.
12 An 'insurgency', in this sense, is seen as a conflictual relationship between a 'nonruling group and the ruling authorities'; in which the former seeks to overturn, and the latter maintain, the political status quo. See: David J. Kilcullen, 'Countering Global Insurgency', *The Journal of Strategic Studies* 28, no. 4 (2005): 603; Frank Kitson, *Low Intensity Operations: Subversion, Insurgency, Peacekeeping* (London: Faber, 1973), 3; Thomas A. Marks, *Maoist Insurgency since Vietnam* (New York: Frank Cass, 1996), 4; Ariel Merari, 'Terrorism as a Strategy of Insurgency', *Terrorism and Political Violence* 5, no. 4 (1993): 219; Steven Metz and Raymond Millen, *Insurgency*

and Counterinsurgency in the 21st Century: Reconceptualizing Threat and Response (Carlisle: Strategic Studies Institute, 2004), 2; Bard E. O'Neill, *Insurgency and Terrorism: Inside Modern Revolutionary Warfare* (Washington, D.C.: Brassey's Incorporated, 1990), 13; Julian Paget, *Counter-Insurgency Campaigning* (London: Faber and Faber Limited, 1967), 14; Robert Thompson, *Defeating Communist Insurgency: Experiences from Malaya and Vietnam* (London: Chatto & Windus, 1966), 28.

13 Vittorfranco S. Pisano, 'The Red Brigades: A Challenge to Italian Democracy', *Conflict Studies*, no. 120 (1980): 10; Xavier Raufer, 'Al Qaeda: A Different Diagnosis', *Studies in Conflict and Terrorism* 26 (2003): 394.

14 Christopher C Harmon, *Terrorism Today* (London and Portland: Frank Cass, 2000), 31. For an examination of the differences between pro-state and anti-state violent non-state actors, see: Steve Bruce, *The Red Hand: Protestant Paramilitaries in Northern Ireland* (Oxford: Oxford University Press, 1992), 269–280.

15 Bruce Hoffman, *Inside Terrorism* (New York: Columbia University Press, 1998), 31. See also: Martha Crenshaw, 'Thoughts on Relating Terrorism to Historical Contexts', in *Terrorism in Context*, ed. Martha Crenshaw (University Park: The Pennsylvania State University Press, 1995), 8; Grant Wardlaw, *Political Terrorism: Theory, Tactics and Counter-Measures* (Cambridge: Cambridge University Press, 1989), 4–5.

16 Brian Michael Jenkins, *The Study of Terrorism: Definitional Problems* (Santa Monica: RAND, 1980), 10.

17 Leonard Weinberg, Ami Pedahzur, and Sivan Hirsch-Hoefler, 'The Challenges of Conceptualizing Terrorism', *Terrorism and Political Violence* 16, no. 4 (2004): 778.

18 Saint Thomas Aquinas, *Summa Theologica*, vol. 3 (New York: Benziger Brothers, 1981), 2382 (Q. 66, Art. 9, Part III).

19 Jeremy P. Brockes, Anoop Kumar, and Cristiana P. Velloso, 'Regeneration as an Evolutionary Variable', *Journal of Anatomy* 199, no. 1–2 (2001): 3–4; Richard J. Goss, 'The Natural History (and Mystery) of Regeneration', in *A History of Regeneration Research: Milestones in the Evolution of a Science*, ed. Charles E. Dinsmore (Cambridge: Cambridge University Press, 1991), 17–18; Anthony J. Schmidt, *Cellular Biology of Vertebrate Regeneration and Repair* (Chicago and London: The University of Chicago Press, 1968), 4.

20 Zachary Abuza, 'Balik-Terrorism: The Return of the Abu Sayyaf', (Carlisle: Strategic Studies Institute, 2005), 10–44.

21 Foreign Affairs Committee, 'Tenth Report of Session 2002–03, Foreign Policy Aspects of the War against Terrorism', (London: House of Commons, 2003), 51.

22 Commonwealth of Australia, *Transnational Terrorism: The Threat to Australia* (Canberra 2004), 76. Jones shares this perspective of the Australian Government, stating that Jemaah Islamiah has been able to survive the 'massive arrests of its members' over the past four years because of its 'capacity for regeneration, made possible by deep roots in Indonesia that go back long before JI officially came into being'. Sidney Jones, 'The Changing Nature of Jemaah Islamiyah', *Australian Journal of International Affairs* 59, no. 2 (2005): 177.

23 Cited in: Bryan Bender, 'US Military Worried over Change in Iraq Attacks', *Boston Globe*, 24 April 2005, 1.

24 This meaning of 'attrition' differs slightly from its usage in the strategic studies literature, where the term generally denotes the 'gradual and piecemeal process of destroying an enemy's military capability'. Carter Malkasian, *A History of Modern Wars of Attrition* (Westport: Praeger, 2002), 1.

25 Jeremy Varon, *Bringing the War Home: The Weather Underground, the Red Army Faction, and Revolutionary Violence in the Sixties and Seventies* (Berkeley, Los Angeles and London: University of California Press, 2003), 215; Joanne Wright, *Terrorist Propaganda: The Red Army Faction and the Provisional IRA, 1968–86* (Basingstoke and London: Macmillan, 1991), 190.

26 Stefan Aust, *The Baader-Meinhof Group: The inside Story of a Phenomenon*, trans. Anthea Bell (London: The Bodley Head, 1987), 213.

27 Dennis A. Pluchinsky, 'An Organizational and Operational Analysis of Germany's Red Army Faction Terrorist Group (1972–91)', in *European Terrorism: Today & Tomorrow*, ed. Yonah Alexander and Dennis A. Pluchinsky (McLean, VA.: Brassey's (US), Inc., 1992), 46.

28 Christoph Rojahn, 'Left-Wing Terrorism in Germany: The Aftermath of Ideological Violence', *Conflict Studies*, no. 313 (1998): 7.

29 Peter H. Merkl, 'West German Left-Wing Terrorism', in *Terrorism in Context*, ed. Martha Crenshaw (University Park, PA.: Pennsylvania State University Press, 1995), 185.

30 Rojahn, 'Left-Wing Terrorism in Germany'; Silke Maier-Witt, a former member of the second generation, provides a similar figure, estimating the groups strength in 1977 at over 25 members. Cited in: Harriet Rubin, 'Terrorism, Trauma, and the Search for Redemption', *Fast Company*, no. 52 (2001): 162.

31 These events are known collectively as the *Deutscher Herbst* ('German Autumn'), and involved: Schleyer's initial kidnapping (during which his driver and three body-guards were killed); the hijacking of a Lufthansa flight by the Popular Front for the Liberation of Palestine (PFLP) in support of the RAF; the eventual storming of the hijacked flight by West German Commandos in Mogadishu; and Schleyer's murder. For more information, see: Margit Mayer, 'The German October of 1977', *New German Critique*, no. 13 (1978); Hans Josef Horchem, 'Terrorism and Government Response: The German Experience', *The Jerusalem Journal of International Relations* 4, no. 3 (1980): 50–51.

32 For an overview of the origins of the conflict, see: Gurharpal Singh, 'Understanding the "Punjab Problem"', *Asian Survey* 27, no. 12 (1987): 1268–1277; Gurpreet Singh, *Terrorism: Punjab's Recurring Nightmare* (New Dehli: Sehgal Book Distributors, 1996), 1–2, 10–16.

33 Sanjoy Hazarika, 'Sikh's Mood: Insulted, Hurt and out for Revenge', *New York Times*, 6 July 1984, 2; Paramjit S. Judge, *Religion, Identity and Nationhood: The Sikh Militant Movement* (Jaipur: Rawat Publications, 2005), 94.

34 Steven R. Weisman, 'In Punjab, the Young Are Particularly Restless', *New York Times*, 29 June 1986, 3.

35 V.N. Narayanan, *Tryst with Terror: Punjab's Turbulent Decade* (New Dehli: Ajanta Publications, 1996), 60; South Asia Terrorism Portal, 'Annual Casualties in Terrorist Related Violence', www.satp.org/satporgtp/countries/india/states/punjab/data_sheets/annual_casualties.htm.

36 Paul Wallace, 'Political Violence and Terrorism in India: The Crisis of Identity', in *Terrorism in Context*, ed. Martha Crenshaw (University Park: The Pennsylvania State University Press, 1995), 357–358.

37 Gurharpal Singh, 'Punjab since 1984: Disorder, Order, and Legitimacy', *Asian Survey* 36, no. 4 (1996): 413–414; South Asia Terrorism Portal, 'Annual Casualties in Terrorist Related Violence'.

38 K.P.S. Gill, 'Endgame in Punjab: 1988–1993', *Faultlines: Writings on Conflict & Resolution* 1, no. 1 (1999): 66.

39 Gurharpal Singh, 'India's Akali-BJP Alliance: The 1997 Legislative Assembly Elections', *Asian Survey* 38, no. 4 (1998): 401.

40 Anthony Short, *The Communist Insurrection in Malaya 1948–1960* (London: Frederick Muller, 1975), 231–253; Richard Stubbs, *Hearts and Minds in Guerrilla Warfare: The Malayan Emergency 1948–1960* (Singapore: Eastern Universities Press, 2004), 150–151; Eric M. McFadden, 'Contemporary Counterinsurgency Operations: History as a Guide to Assist in the Development of the Joint Interagency Task Force', *Comparative Strategy* 24, no. 4 (2005): 363–365.

41 'U.S. Ground Strategy and Force Deployments, 1965–1968; Section 3', in *The*

Pentagon Papers: The Defense Department History of United States Decisionmaking on Vietnam (Boston: Beacon Press, 1971), 385–447; Lyndon B. Johnson, *The Vantage Point: Perspectives of the Presidency, 1963–1969* (New York: Holt, Rinehart and Winston, 1971), 259; William C. Westmoreland, *A Soldier Reports* (New York: Doubleday & Company, 1976), 149–153. The MACV also intended its attritional strategy to push the Viet Cong and the North Vietnamese towards their 'breaking point'. That is, the point at which the level of past losses would seem so intolerable that continued military action would seem undesirable, if not unthinkable. See: John E. Mueller, 'The Search for the "Breaking Point" in Vietnam', *International Studies Quarterly* 24, no. 4 (1980).

42 Thompson, *Defeating Communist Insurgency*, 116.

43 Stubbs, *Hearts and Minds in Guerrilla Warfare*, 263–264.

44 Stephen D. Biddle, 'American Grand Strategy after 9/11: An Assessment', (Carlisle: Strategic Studies Institute, 2005), 22. See also: R.G. Coyle, 'A System Description of Counter Insurgency Warfare', *Policy Sciences* 18, no. 1 (1985): 73–75; Brian Michael Jenkins, 'Countering Al Qaeda: An Appreciation of the Situation and Suggestions for Strategy', (Santa Monica: RAND, 2002), 24.

45 Robert Jackson, *The Malayan Emergency: The Commonwealth's Wars 1948–1966* (London and New York: Routledge, 1991), 14; Short, *The Communist Insurrection in Malaya*, 350, 505–506; Stubbs, *Hearts and Minds in Guerrilla Warfare*, 258.

46 Hirschman, Preston, and Loi contend that, despite the horrific casualties they had suffered, the Viet Cong had access to 'more potential military recruits every years … than in each previous year'. Charles Hirschman, Samuel Preston, and Vu Manh Loi, 'Vietnamese Casualties During the American War: A New Estimate', *Population and Development Review* 21, no. 4 (1995): 809.

47 Richard A. Hunt, 'Strategies at War: Pacification and Attrition in Vietnam', in *Lessons from an Unconventional War: Reassessing U.S. Strategies for Future Conflicts*, ed. Richard A. Hunt and Richard Shultz (New York: Pergamon Press, 1982), 28. Record notes, for instance, that the communist forces initiated 75–80 per cent of all firefights during the Vietnam War. Jeffrey Record, *The Wrong War: Why We Lost in Vietnam* (Annapolis: Naval Institute Press, 1998), 73–85.

48 Douglas S. Blaufarb, *The Counterinsurgency Era: U.S. Doctrine and Performance, 1950 to the Present* (New York: Free Press, 1977), 252.

49 Richard Gillespie, 'Political Violence in Argentina: Guerrillas, Terrorists, and *Carapintadas*', in *Terrorism in Context*, ed. Martha Crenshaw (University Park: The Pennsylvania State University Press, 1995), 212. Though, as Lewis notes, 'no exact membership figures were ever made public' and estimates range from as low as 3,000 to as high as 30,000. Paul H Lewis, *Guerrillas and Generals: The Dirty War in Argentina* (Westport: Praeger, 2002), 47–48.

50 Approximately 300–400 Montoneros were arrested during the 24 months prior to the March 1976 coup, compared to 4,500 during the 24 months after. See: Richard Gillespie, *Soldiers of Peron: Argentina's Montoneros* (Oxford: Clarendon Press, 1982), 217–218, 38; Patricia Marchak, *God's Assassins: State Terrorism in Argentina in the 1970s* (Montreal: McGill-Queen's University Press, 1999), 126.

51 Gillespie, *Soldiers of Peron*, 251.

52 Steven Metz, 'The Future of Insurgency', (Carlisle: Strategic Studies Institute, 1993), 21.

53 Merom states, '[a]fter nine months of an intense and brutal campaign [the French Army] virtually destroyed the FLN terror network in Algiers'. Gil Merom, *How Democracies Lose Small Wars: State, Society, and the Failures of France in Algeria, Israel in Lebanon, and the United States in Vietnam* (Cambridge: Cambridge University Press, 2003), 84.

54 Ian F.W. Beckett, *Modern Insurgencies and Counter-Insurgencies: Guerrillas and Their Opponents since 1750* (London and New York: Routledge, 2001), 151–180.

55 Walter Laqueur, *A History of Terrorism* (New Brunswick and London: Transaction Publishers, 2002), 86.

56 Nathan Leites and Charles Wolf, *Rebellion and Authority: An Analytical Essay on Insurgent Conflicts* (Chicago: Markham Publishing Company, 1970), 108–109; William Rosenau, 'Waging the "War of Ideas"', in *The McGraw-Hill Homeland Security Handbook*, ed. David Kamien (New York: McGraw-Hill, 2006), 1132; James B. Steinberg, 'Counterterrorism: A New Organizing Principle for American National Security?', *The Brookings Review* 20, no. 3 (2002): 7.

57 Paget, *Counter-Insurgency Campaigning*, 163–164.

58 Richard A. Posner, 'Security Versus Civil Liberties', *The Atlantic Monthly*, December 2001, 46.

59 Kim Cragin and Peter Chalk, *Terrorism & Development: Using Social and Economic Development to Inhibit a Resurgence of Terrorism* (Santa Monica: RAND, 2003).

60 Michael Freeman, *Freedom or Security: The Consequences for Democracies Using Emergency Powers to Fight Terror* (Westport and London: Praeger, 2003).

61 Arend Lijphart, 'Comparative Politics and the Comparative Method', *The American Political Science Review* 65, no. 3 (1971): 683.

62 Ibid.: 683–684, Arend Lijphart, 'The Comparable-Cases Strategy in Comparative Research', *Comparative Political Studies* 8, no. 2 (1975): 164.

63 Ernest Gellner, *Nations and Nationalism* (Ithaca: Cornell University Press, 1983), 1.

64 'Socialism' is an incredibly difficult concept to define, largely due to the heterogeneity of socialist thought since the nineteenth century. As Geoghegan highlights, different strands of socialism disagree over such fundamental issues as 'their conceptualisations of the state' and the role of private property. The above definition is derived from both Geoghegan's discussion, as well as from a similar summary written by Heywood. See: Vincent Geoghegan, 'Socialism', in *Political Ideologies: An Introduction*, ed. Robert Eccleshall *et al.* (New York: Routledge, 2003), 73–80; Andrew Heywood, *Political Ideologies: An Introduction*, Third ed. (Basingstoke: Palgrave Macmillan, 2003), 107–117.

65 Henry Patterson, *The Politics of Illusion: Republicanism and Socialism in Modern Ireland* (London: Hutchinson Radius, 1989).

66 Arturo C. Porzecanski, *Uruguay's Tupamaros: The Urban Guerrilla* (New York, Washington and London: Praeger Publishers, 1973), 7–8.

67 Polity IV Project, 'Polity IV Annual Time-Series Dataset', Integrated Network for Societal Conflict Research, www.cidcm.umd.edu/inscr/polity/index.htm.

68 Ibid.

69 This estimate is limited to the 1970s.

2 Concepts, relationships and measurement

1 Sidney Tarrow, *Power in Movement: Social Movements, Collective Action and Politics* (Cambridge: Cambridge University Press, 1994), 3–4.

2 Robert W. White, *Provisional Irish Republicans: An Oral and Interpretive History* (Westport and London: Greenwood Press, 1993); Donatella della Porta, *Social Movements, Political Violence, and the State: A Comparative Analysis of Italy and Germany* (Cambridge and New York: Cambridge University Press, 1995).

3 Erving Goffman, *Frame Analysis: An Essay on the Organization of Experience* (Harmondsworth: Penguin Books, 1974), 21.

4 Robert D. Benford and David A. Snow, 'Framing Processes and Social Movements: An Overview and Assessment', *Annual Review of Sociology*, no. 26 (2000): 614; David A. Snow and Robert D. Benford, 'Ideology, Frame Resonance, and Participant Mobilization', in *International Social Movement Research: A Research Annual*, ed. Bert Klandermans, Hanspeter Kriesi, and Sidney Tarrow (Greenwich and London: JAI Press, 1988), 198.

5 Benford and Snow, 'Framing Processes and Social Movements', 514; Bert Klander-mans, *The Social Psychology of Protest* (Oxford and Cambridge MA.: Blackwell Publishers, 1997), 16–18; William A. Gamson, *Talking Politics* (Cambridge: Cambridge University Press, 1992), 6–8.

6 Snow and Benford, 'Ideology, Frame Resonance and Participant Mobilization', 199.

7 Benford and Snow, 'Framing Processes and Social Movements', 615–616.

8 Michael Y. Dartnell, *Action Directe: Ultra-Left Terrorism in France, 1979–1987* (London: Frank Cass, 1995), 109. In the early-1980s, *Action Directe* split into two factions: one based in Paris (ADi), and the other based in Lyon (*Action Directe nationale*, or ADn).

9 Benford and Snow, 'Framing Processes and Social Movements', 615.

10 Gamson, *Talking Politics*, 32.

11 Ibid.

12 Snow and Benford, 'Ideology, Frame Resonance and Participant Mobilization', 199.

13 Benford and Snow, 'Framing Processes and Social Movements', 616.

14 Ernesto (Che) Guevara, *Guerrilla Warfare* (Middlesex: Penguin, 1969); Jose A. Moreno, 'Che Guevara on Guerrilla Warfare: Doctrine, Practice, and Evaluation', *Comparative studies in society and history* 12, no. 2 (1970).

15 Snow and Benford, 'Ideology, Frame Resonance and Participant Mobilization', 199.

16 Robert D. Benford, 'You Could Be the Hundredth Monkey: Collective Action Frames and Vocabularies of Motive within the Nuclear Disarmament Movement', *Sociological Quarterly* 34, no. 2 (1993): 196.

17 Ted Robert Gurr, *Why Men Rebel* (Princeton: Princeton University Press, 1970), 155–156; Garrett O'Boyle, 'Theories of Justification and Political Violence: Examples from Four Groups', *Terrorism and Political Violence* 14, no. 2 (2002): 23–28.

18 Judy M. Torrance, *Public Violence in Canada, 1867–1982* (Kingston and Montreal: McGill-Queen's University Press, 1986), 85.

19 Cited in: Catharine Munro, 'Amrozi Says Bomb Was to Get White People out of Bali', *Australian Associated Press*, 13 June 2003.

20 Osama bin Laden, 'Fatwa against Americans, February 23, 1998', in *Osama Bin Laden: America's Enemy in His Own Words*, ed. Randall B. Hamud (San Diego: Nadeem Publishing, 2005), 61.

21 Ibid.

22 Ibid., 62.

23 Ibid.

24 Ibid.

25 Ibid., 61–62.

26 Earl Conteh-Morgan, *Collective Political Violence: An Introduction to the Theories and Cases of Violent Conflicts* (London and New York: Routledge, 2004), 257; Martha Crenshaw, 'The Causes of Terrorism', *Comparative Politics* 13, no. 4 (1981): 383; Jeffrey Ian Ross, 'Structural Causes of Oppositional Political Terrorism: Towards a Causal Model', *Journal of Peace Research* 30, no. 3 (1993): 325.

27 Chalmers Johnson, 'Civilian Loyalties and Guerrilla Conflict', *World Politics* 14, no. 4 (1962): 657–658; Frank Kitson, *Low Intensity Operations: Subversion, Insurgency, Peacekeeping* (London: Faber, 1973), 50–51; Bard E. O'Neill, *Insurgency and Terrorism: Inside Modern Revolutionary Warfare* (Washington, D.C.: Brassey's Incorporated, 1990), 77–79.

28 D. Michael Shafer, 'The Unlearned Lessons of Counterinsurgency', *Political Science Quarterly* 103, no. 1 (1988): 62.

29 Gareth Evans, 'Where Are We in the War on Terrorism?', *Australian Book Review*, no. 261 (2004): 14.

30 Jessica Stern, *Terror in the Name of God: Why Religious Militants Kill* (New York: HarperCollins, 2003), 59.

31 Gurr, *Why Men Rebel*, 22–37.

32 For excellent summaries of the literature surrounding relative deprivation theory, see Stephen G. Brush, 'Dynamics of Theory Change in the Social Sciences: Relative Deprivation and Collective Violence', *The Journal of Conflict Resolution* 40, no. 4 (1996); Steven E. Barkan and Lynne L. Snowden, *Collective Violence* (Boston: Allyn and Bacon, 2001), 17–19.

33 Scott Atran, 'Mishandling Suicide Terrorism', *The Washington Quarterly* 27, no. 3 (2004): 67–68.

34 For more on the origins of the hearts-and-minds approach, see: Richard Stubbs, *Hearts and Minds in Guerrilla Warfare: The Malayan Emergency 1948–1960* (Singapore: Eastern Universities Press, 2004).

35 Austin Long, *On 'Other War': Lessons from Five Decades of RAND Counterinsurgency Research* (Santa Monica: RAND, 2006), 21–23; Shafer, 'The Unlearned Lessons of Counterinsurgency', 62–71; Richard Shultz, 'Breaking the Will of the Enemy During the Vietnam War: The Operationalization of the Cost-Benefit Model of Counterinsurgency Warfare', *Journal of Peace Research* 15, no. 2 (1978): 109–110.

36 Stubbs, *Hearts and Minds in Guerrilla Warfare*, 258.

37 Jeffrey Ian Ross and Ted Robert Gurr, 'Why Terrorism Subsides: A Comparative Study of Canada and the United States', *Comparative Politics* 21, no. 4 (1989): 422.

38 Ibid.

39 Kim Cragin and Peter Chalk, *Terrorism & Development: Using Social and Economic Development to Inhibit a Resurgence of Terrorism* (Santa Monica: RAND, 2003), 34–35.

40 Bert Klandermans, Marlene Roefs, and Rohan Olivier, 'Grievance Formation in a Country in Transition: South Africa, 1994–1998', *Social Psychology Quarterly* 64, no. 1 (2001): 42.

41 Ross, 'Structural Causes of Oppositional Political Terrorism', 325.

42 Richard Shultz, 'Coercive Force and Military Strategy: Deterrence Logic and the Cost–Benefit Model of Counterinsurgency Warfare', *The Western Political Quarterly* 32, no. 4 (1979): 444–445. Though, as Stubbs notes, what was known as 'hearts-and-minds' in Vietnam differed greatly from the 'original Malayan strategy. For some, winning the "hearts-and-minds" [of the Vietnamese] simply entailed a massive propaganda, or psychological warfare, assault on the general population'. Stubbs, *Hearts and Minds in Guerrilla Warfare*, 3.

43 Long, *On 'Other War'*, 25.

44 Nathan Leites and Charles Wolf, *Rebellion and Authority: An Analytical Essay on Insurgent Conflicts* (Chicago: Markham Publishing Company, 1970), 11–14, 42–44.

45 Ibid., 36, 76–78.

46 Ibid., 155.

47 See Leites and Wolf's lengthy discussion about 'inflicting damage', and the differences between 'hot violence' and 'coercion'. Ibid., 90–131.

48 This statement derives from Opp and Roehl's famous article about how the literature on political protest should, in light of the growing evidence that repression could both stimulate and deter participation in political protest, refocus its empirical inquiries. Karl-Dieter Opp and Wolfgang Roehl, 'Repression, Micromobilization, and Political Protest', *Social Forces* 69, no. 2 (1990): 523. This book maintains that the quote accurately characterises Leites and Wolf's understanding of the relationship between repression and insurgent participation.

49 Leites and Wolf, *Rebellion and Authority*, 107.

50 Mohammed M. Hafez and Quintan Wiktorowicz, 'Violence as Contention in the Egyptian Islamic Movement', in *Islamic Activism: A Social Movement Theory Approach*, ed. Quintan Wiktorowicz (Bloomington: Indiana University Press, 2004), 70; Leites and Wolf, *Rebellion and Authority*, 108; T. David Mason, 'Insurgency, Counterinsurgency, and the Rational Peasant', *Public Choice* 86, no. 1–2 (1996): 76.

51 Leites and Wolf, *Rebellion and Authority*, 108–109.
52 John A. Nevin, 'Retaliating against Terrorists', *Behavior and Social Issues* 12, no. 2 (2003): 127.
53 B. Peter Rosendorff and Todd Sandler, 'Too Much of a Good Thing? The Proactive Response Dilemma', *Journal of Conflict Resolution* 48, no. 5 (2004): 658.
54 William M. LeoGrande, 'A Splendid Little War: Drawing the Line in El Salvador', *International Security* 6, no. 1 (1981): 31; Elisabeth Jean Wood, *Insurgent Collective Action and Civil War in El Salvador* (Cambridge: Cambridge University Press, 2003), 8, 16.
55 Report of CONADEP (National Commission on the Disappearance of Persons), 'Nunca Más (Never Again)', www.nuncamas.org/index2.htm.
56 Richard Gillespie, *Soldiers of Peron: Argentina's Montoneros* (Oxford: Clarendon Press, 1982), 215–216, 51–52.
57 Charles Tilly, *From Mobilization to Revolution* (Reading: Addison-Wesley Publishing Company, 1978), 100.
58 Jennifer Earl, 'Tanks, Tear Gas, and Taxes: Toward a Theory of Movement Repression', *Sociological Theory* 21, no. 1 (2003): 47–50. Here, this book is referring to the first of Earl's 12 types of repression, which are all based on Tilly's original definition.
59 Hafez and Wiktorowicz, 'Violence as Contention in the Egyptian Islamic Movement', 68.
60 Ibid.
61 Problems of terminology have long plagued the study of 'political warfare'. For instance, writing in 1958, Perusse identified 18 different terms which were used in the literature to describe what he had labelled 'psychological warfare'. Roland I. Perusse, 'Psychological Warfare Reappraised', in *A Psychological Warfare Casebook*, ed. William E. Daugherty and Morris Janowitz (Baltimore: Johns Hopkins Press, 1958), 25–26. This book chose 'political warfare' primarily because it was one of the earliest terms in use.
62 William E. Daugherty and Morris Janowitz, *A Psychological Warfare Casebook* (Baltimore: Johns Hopkins Press, 1958), 2; Christopher Ross, 'Public Diplomacy Comes of Age', *The Washington Quarterly* 25, no. 2 (2002): 75.
63 C. Edda Martinez and Edward A. Suchman, 'Letters from America and the 1948 Elections in Italy', *The Public Opinion Quarterly* 14, no. 1 (1950); Robert T. Holt and Robert W. van de Velde, *Strategic Psychological Operations and American Foreign Policy* (Chicago: Chicago University Press, 1960), 169–205; Christopher Simpson, *Science of Coercion: Communication Research and Psychological Warfare 1945–1960* (Oxford: Oxford University Press, 1994), 48.
64 Yale Richmond, *Cultural Exchange and the Cold War: Raising the Iron Curtain* (University Park: Pennsylvania State University Press, 2003), viii–xiv.
65 Peter G. Peterson, 'Public Diplomacy and the War on Terrorism', *Foreign Affairs* 81, no. 5 (2002): 75.
66 George W. Bush, *National Strategy for Combating Terrorism* (Washington, D.C.: Government Printing Office, 2006), 7–10; National Commission on Terrorist Attacks upon the United States, *The 9/11 Commission Report*, Official Government ed. (Washington, D.C.: U.S. Government Printing Office, 2004), 363, 75–77; Stephen Van Evera, 'Assessing U.S. Strategy in the War on Terror', *The ANNALS of the American Academy of Political and Social Science* 607, no. 1 (2005): 15–20; Ariel Cohen, 'Promoting Freedom and Democracy: Fighting the War of Ideas against Islamic Terrorism', *Comparative Strategy* 22, no. 3 (2003): 211–212; Zeyno Baran, 'Fighting the War of Ideas', *Foreign Affairs* 84, no. 6 (2005): 75–78.
67 William Rosenau, 'Waging the "War of Ideas"', in *The McGraw-Hill Homeland Security Handbook*, ed. David Kamien (New York: McGraw-Hill, 2006), 1132.

68 Kumar Ramakrishna, 'Delegitimizing Global Jihadi Ideology in Southeast Asia', *Contemporary Southeast Asia* 27, no. 3 (2005): 345.
69 William Rosenau, 'Al Qaida Recruitment Trends in Kenya and Tanzania', *Studies in Conflict and Terrorism* 28, no. 1 (2005): 4–6.
70 Ibid.: 5.
71 John Gerring, 'Ideology: A Definitional Analysis', *Political Research Quarterly* 50, no. 4 (1997): 957.
72 Terry Eagleton, *Ideology: An Introduction* (London: Verso, 1991), 1.
73 Baran, 'Fighting the War of Ideas', 68–69; Cohen, 'Promoting Freedom and Democracy', 209.
74 Rosenau, 'Waging the "War of Ideas"', 1134–1136.
75 Willard A. Mullins, 'On the Concept of Ideology in Political Science', *The American Political Science Review* 66, no. 2 (1972): 510; Martin Seliger, *Ideology and Politics* (London: George Allen & Unwin, 1976), 14.
76 Boaz Ganor, *The Counter-Terrorism Puzzle: A Guide for Decision Makers* (New Brunswick and London: Transaction Publishers, 2005), 47.
77 Steven Metz, 'Insurgency and Counterinsurgency in Iraq', *The Washington Quarterly* 27, no. 1 (2003): 33.
78 Julian Paget, *Counter-Insurgency Campaigning* (London: Faber and Faber Limited, 1967), 163–164.
79 Robert Thompson, *Defeating Communist Insurgency: Experiences from Malaya and Vietnam* (London: Chatto & Windus, 1966), 89.
80 Kitson, *Low Intensity Operations*, 95.
81 Daniel Byman, 'Measuring the War on Terrorism: A First Appraisal', *Current History* 102, no. 668 (2003): 413.
82 Gordon H. McCormick, 'Terrorist Decision-Making', *Annual Review of Political Science* 6 (2003): 484.
83 Roger Trinquier, *Modern Warfare: A French View of Counterinsurgency*, trans. Daniel Lee (London and Dunmow: Pall Mall Press, 1964), 26.
84 Anthony Short, *The Communist Insurrection in Malaya 1948–1960* (London: Frederick Muller, 1975), 359–360.
85 Martin S. Alexander and J.F.V. Keiger, 'France and the Algerian War: Strategy, Operations, and Diplomacy', *Journal of Strategic Studies* 25, no. 2 (2002): 6–7; Alistair Horne, *A Savage War of Peace: Algeria 1954–1962* (London: Macmillan, 1977), 198, 219–220; Gilles Martin, 'War in Algeria: The French Experience', *Military Review* 85, no. 4 (2005): 55–56.
86 *Security Legislation Amendment (Terrorism) Act 2002*, (5 July), s. 102.1.
87 *Australian Security Intelligence Organisation Legislation Amendment (Terrorism) Act 2003*, (22 July), s. 34HC.
88 *Anti-Terrorism Act (No. 2) 2005*, (14 December), s. 104–105.
89 Michelle Grattan, 'Wrong Tools to Fight Terrorism', *Sydney Morning Herald*, 10 May 2002, 13.
90 Richard Harris, 'Anti-Democratic Provisions Fall on the Wrong Side of the Law', *The Sydney Morning Herald*, 22 November 2005, 17.
91 Christopher Michaelsen, 'Antiterrorism Legislation in Australia: A Proportionate Response to the Terrorist Threat?', *Studies in Conflict and Terrorism* 28, no. 4 (2005): 334.
92 Marisol Touraine and Yann Galut, cited in: Didier Hassoux, 'La Sécurité Prend Des Libertés', *Libération*, 5 October 2001, 18.
93 Alan Travis, 'Anti-Terror Critics Just Don't Get It, Says Reid', *Guardian*, 10 August 2006, 6.
94 Anastassia Tsoukala, 'Democracy in the Light of Security: British and French Political Discourses on Domestic Counter-Terrorism Policies', *Political Studies* 54, no. 3 (2006): 608. See also: Jessica Wolfendale, 'Terrorism, Security, and the Threat of

Counterterrorism', *Studies in Conflict and Terrorism* 29, no. 7 (2006): 753–754; Richard A. Posner, 'Security Versus Civil Liberties', *The Atlantic Monthly*, December 2001, 46–47.

95 John Howard, 'Counter-Terrorism Laws Strengthened', Office of the Prime Minister of Australia, www.pm.gov.au/News/media_releases/media_Release1551.html.

96 Laura K. Donohue, 'Security and Freedom on the Fulcrum', *Terrorism and Political Violence* 17, no. 1–2 (2005): 70.

97 George W. Bush, 'Press Conference of the President', The White House, www. whitehouse.gov/news/releases/2005/12/20051219–2.html; 'Press Briefing by Attorney General Alberto Gonzales and General Michael Hayden, Principal Deputy Director for National Intelligence', The White House, www.whitehouse.gov/news/releases/2005/12/20051219–1.html.

98 Christopher Hewitt, *The Effectiveness of Anti-Terrorist Policies* (Lanham: University Press of America, 1984), 66–67.

99 Michael Freeman, *Freedom or Security: The Consequences for Democracies Using Emergency Powers to Fight Terror* (Westport and London: Praeger, 2003), 5.

100 Ibid., 12–13, 186.

101 Ibid., 186.

3 *Front de libération du Québec*

1 John Gellner, *Bayonets in the Streets: Urban Guerrilla at Home and Abroad* (Don Mills: Collier-Macmillan, 1974), 83.

2 Jean-C. Bonenfant and Jean-C. Falardeau, 'Cultural and Political Implications of French-Canadian Nationalism', in *French-Canadian Nationalism: An Anthology*, ed. Ramsay Cook (Toronto: Macmillan of Canada, 1969), 20–21; Fernand Ouellet, *Lower Canada 1791–1840: Social Change and Nationalism*, trans. Patricia Claxton (Toronto: McClelland and Stewart, 1980), 87–91, 323–324. Not surprisingly, the origins of French-Canadian nationalism are contested. For instance, Griffin contends that a national consciousness emerged amongst the French-Canadians in the wake of the British Conquest of New France in 1759. Anne Griffin, *Quebec: The Challenge of Independence* (Rutherford, Madison, Teaneck: Fairleigh Dickinson University Press, 1984), 19–30. Ouellet, however, maintains that such concepts as 'nation', 'nationalism', and 'French-Canadian' only entered the French-Canadian lexicon during the first decades of the eighteenth century. Thus, '[t]o date our nationalism back to the French regime, or even to the latter half of the eighteenth century, would be to ascribe to the men of the period a scale of values which they were not yet aware'. Fernand Ouellet, 'The Historical Background of Separatism in Quebec', in *French-Canadian Nationalism: An Anthology*, ed. Ramsay Cook (Toronto: Macmillan of Canada, 1969), 50.

3 Richard Arès provided an excellent example of *l'agriculturisme* when he stated in 1943 that: 'By tradition, vocation as well as necessity, we are a people of peasants. Everything that takes us away from the land diminishes and weakens us as a people and encourages cross-breeding, duplicity and treason'. Cited in: Fernand Dumont and Guy Rocher, 'An Introduction to a Sociology of French Canada', in *French-Canadian Society*, ed. Marcel Rioux and Yves Martin (Toronto: McClelland and Stewart, 1964), 183.

4 Hubert Guindon, *Quebec Society: Tradition, Modernity, and Nationhood*, ed. Roberta Hamilton and John L. McMullan (Toronto, Buffalo, and London: University of Toronto Press, 1988), 51; Susan Mann Trofimenkoff, *The Dream of Nation: A Social and Intellectual History of Quebec* (Toronto: Gage Publishing Limited, 1983), 119.

5 Kenneth McRoberts, *Quebec: Social Change and Political Crisis*, Third ed. (Toronto: McClelland & Stewart, 1988), 85; Ralph Heintzman, 'The Political

Culture of Quebec, 1840–1960', *Canadian Journal of Political Science/Revue canadienne de science politique* 16, no. 1 (1983): 5–6.

6 Michel Brunet, 'Trois Dominantes De La Pensée Canadienne-Française: L'agriculturisme, L'anti-Étatisme Et Le Messianisme', in *La Présence Anglaise Et Les Canadiens* (Montréal: Beauchemin, 1964).

7 Cited in: Michael D. Behiels, *Prelude to Quebec's Quiet Revolution: Liberalism Versus Neo-Nationalism 1945–1960* (Kingston and Montreal: McGill-Queen's University Press, 1985), 48.

8 Ibid., 43–44.

9 Roderic Beaujot and Kevin McQuillan, *Growth and Dualism: The Demographic Development of Canadian Society* (Toronto: Gage Publishing, 1982), 15–16, 89; Yolande Lavoie, *L' Émigration Des Québécois Aux États-Unis De 1840 À 1930* (Montréal: Presses de l'Université de Montréal, 1972), 68.

10 For example, in 1760, the French-Canadian population was estimated to be comprised of 57,000 people. By 1880, this figure had jumped to 1,080,000. Jacques Henripin, *Tendances Et Facteurs De La Fécondité Au Canada* (Ottawa: Bureau Fédéral de la Statistique, 1968), 5.

11 Jacques Henripin, 'From Acceptance of Nature to Control: The Demography of the French Canadians since the Seventeenth Century', *The Canadian Journal of Economics and Political Science* 23, no. 1 (1957): 13.

12 R. K. Vedder and L. E. Gallaway, 'Settlement Patterns of Canadian Emigrants to the United States, 1850–1960', *The Canadian Journal of Economics* 3, no. 3 (1970): 486.

13 Claude Bélanger, 'Ultramontane Nationalism: 1840–1960', Marianolpolis College, www2.marianopolis.edu/quebechistory/events/natpart3.htm.

14 *Report of the Royal Commission on Bilingualism and Biculturalism. Book One: The Official Languages*, (Ottawa: Queen's Printer, 1967), 32.

15 The figures for Ontario were 22.1 per cent in 1931 and 37.7 per cent in 1961; for British Colombia, 50.4 per cent in 1931 and 64.7 per cent in 1961; and for Canada as a whole, 4.7 per cent in 1931 and 9.9 per cent in 1961. In contrast, the figures for Quebec were 0.6 per cent in 1931 and 1.6 per cent in 1961. Ibid., 33.

16 Rudy Fenwick, 'Social Change and Ethnic Nationalism: An Historical Analysis of the Separatist Movement in Quebec', *Comparative Studies in Society and History* 23, no. 2 (1981): 204; Kenneth McRoberts, 'The Sources of Neo-Nationalism in Quebec', in *Quebec since 1945: Selected Readings*, ed. Michael D. Behiels (Toronto, ON: Copp Clark Pitman Limited, 1987), 81; William D. Coleman, *The Independence Movement in Quebec 1945–1980* (Toronto, Buffalo, London: University of Toronto Press, 1984), 219.

17 Fenwick, 'Social Change and Ethnic Nationalism', 201–202.

18 Trofimenkoff, *The Dream of a Nation*, 308.

19 McRoberts, *Quebec*, 136.

20 Fenwick, 'Social Change and Ethnic Nationalism', 203.

21 Richard Hamilton and Maurice Pinard, 'The Quebec Independence Movement', in *National Separatism*, ed. Colin H. Williams (Vancouver and London: University of British Columbia Press, 1982), 211.

22 Ibid., 209.

23 For more information on these parties, see: James William Hagy, 'Quebec Separatists: The First Twelve Years', *Queen's Quarterly* 76, no. 2 (1969); John Saywell, *The Rise of the Parti Québécois 1967–1976* (Toronto and Buffalo: University of Toronto Press, 1977).

24 This figure was derived from Kellett et al'.s database of terrorism incidents in Canada. Anthony Kellett et al., 'Terrorism in Canada 1960–1989', (Ottawa: Ministry of the Solicitor General of Canada, 1991), 226–285, 310–329. In total, Kellett *et al.* list 186 acts of nationalist-separatist 'terrorism' and 57 nationalist thefts and

robberies from 1963 to 1972 (a total of 243 nationalist-separatist violent acts). This book obtained the smaller figure of 212 by only including those instances of violence that could be directly linked to the FLQ (and thus ignoring seemingly isolated and relatively minor acts of nationalist-separatist violence). This book deemed such a linkage to exist if: (1) Kellett *et al.* attributed responsibility of the act to the FLQ; or (2) Fournier, Laurendeau, or Morf assigned the FLQ as the perpetrator of the act. Louis Fournier, *F.L.Q.: The Anatomy of an Underground Movement*, trans. Edward Baxter (Toronto: NC Press Limited, 1984); Marc Laurendeau, *Les Québécois Violents: La Violence Politique 1962–1972*, Augmented and updated edn. (Montréal: Boréal, 1990); Gustave Morf, *Terror in Quebec: Case Studies of the FLQ* (Toronto and Vancouver: Clarke, Irwin & Company Limited, 1970).

25 Brian Jenkins, 'Will Terrorists Go Nuclear?', *ORBIS* 29, no. 3 (1985): 511.

26 The civilians killed were: Wilfrid O'Neil (April 1963), Leslie McWilliams (August 1964), Thérèse Morin (May 1966), Jeanne-D'Arc Saint-Germain (June 1970), and Pierre Laporte (October 1970). The FLQ members killed were: Jean Corbo (July 1966) and Pierre-Louis Bourret (September 1971).

27 David A. Charters, 'The Amateur Revolutionaries: A Reassessment of the FLQ', *Terrorism and Political Violence* 9, no. 1 (1997): 138.

28 Ronald D. Crelinsten, 'The Internal Dynamics of the FLQ During the October Crisis of 1970', in *Inside Terrorist Organizations*, ed. David C. Rapoport (London and Portland: Frank Cass, 2001), 59.

29 Charters, 'The Amateur Revolutionaries', 138.

30 Wayne G. Reilly, 'The Management of Political Violence in Quebec and Northern Ireland: A Comparison', *Terrorism and Political Violence* 6, no. 1 (1994): 50.

31 Carole de Vault and William Johnson, *The Informer: Confessions of an Ex-Terrorist* (Toronto: Fleet Books, 1982); Crelinsten, 'The Internal Dynamics of the FLQ During the October Crisis of 1970'; Fournier, *F.L.Q.*; Laurendeau, *Les Québécois Violents*; Morf, *Terror in Quebec*.

32 Fournier suggests that some members of the UQAM Network, specifically Pierre-Louis Bourret, were responsible for some of these bombings. Fournier, *F.L.Q.*, 192.

33 Pierre Vallières, *White Niggers of America: The Precocious Autobiography of a Quebec 'Terrorist'*, trans. Joan Pinkham (New York and London: Monthly Review Press, 1971), 202.

34 FLQ, 'Message Du FLQ a La Nation', in *La Véritable Histoire Du F.L.Q.*, ed. Claude Savoie (Montréal: Les Éditions du Jour, 1963), 43.

35 Ibid.

36 Ibid.

37 FLQ, 'Le Québec Est Une Colonie', *La Cognée*, no. 1 (1963): 3.

38 Vallières, *White Niggers of America*.

39 FLQ, 'Message Du FLQ a La Nation', 44.

40 Ibid.

41 FLQ, 'Le Québec Est Une Colonie', 4.

42 FLQ, 'Manifesto of the Front De Libération Du Québec', Marianopolis College, www2.marianopolis.edu/quebechistory/docs/october/manifest.htm.

43 FLQ, 'Message Du FLQ a La Nation', 43.

44 Vallières, *White Niggers of America*, 232.

45 Ibid.

46 Ibid., 232–233.

47 Ibid., 218–219, 58.

48 Ibid., 223.

49 This is a reference to the '*l'Affaire Brinks*'. On 29 April 1970, two days before Quebec's general election, the Royal Trust (a trust company with its head office in Montreal) very publicly moved a large quantity of its securities (stocks, bonds, etc.) to its office in Toronto using nine Brinks armoured trucks. The *Parti Québécois* suspected

that the transfer had been staged at the behest of Bourassa's Liberal party to raise public anxiety about the possible consequences of a *Parti Québécois* victory (a dominant Liberal campaign theme).

50 FLQ, 'Manifesto of the Front De Libération Du Québec'.
51 Crelinsten, 'The Internal Dynamics of the FLQ during the October Crisis of 1970', 60.
52 Vallières, *White Niggers of America*, 235.
53 FLQ, *Stratégie Révolutionnaire Et Rôle De L'avant Garde* (Paris 1970), 1.
54 FLQ, 'Révolution Par Le Peuple Pour Le Peuple', in *La Véritable Histoire Du F.L.Q.*, ed. Claude Savoie (Montréal: Les Éditions du Jour, 1963), 27.
55 FLQ, 'Pourquoi Un Parti Révolutionnaire Clandestin?', *La Cognée*, no. 7 (1964): 6, FLQ, 'La Non-Violence Et La Guerre De Libération', *La Cognée*, no. 13 (1964): 9.
56 Vallières, *White Niggers of America*, 269.
57 FLQ, *Stratégie Révolutionnaire Et Rôle De l'avant Garde*, 1–4.
58 David A. Charters, 'The October Crisis: Implications for Canada's Internal Security', in *Terror*, ed. Brian MacDonald (Toronto: The Canadian Institute of Strategic Studies, 1986), 59.
59 Charters, 'The Amateur Revolutionaries', 139–147.
60 FLQ, 'La Non-Violence Et La Guerre De Libération', 7.
61 Ibid.
62 FLQ, 'Communiqué', in *La Véritable Histoire Du F.L.Q.*, ed. Claude Savoie (Montréal: Les Éditions du Jour, 1963), 59.
63 Ibid.
64 FLQ, 'Nous Continuons', *La Cognée*, no. 12 (1964): 1.
65 Vallières, *White Niggers of America*, 260.
66 FLQ, 'Nous Continuons', 1.
67 Vallières, *White Niggers of America*, 202.
68 FLQ, 'Pourquoi Un Parti Révolutionnaire Clandestin?', 4.
69 FLQ, 'La Non-Violence Et La Guerre De Libération', 7.
70 FLQ, 'Manifesto of the Front De Libération Du Québec'.
71 Vallières, *White Niggers of America*, 212.
72 Ibid; FLQ, 'Pourquoi Un Parti Révolutionnaire Clandestin?', 5.
73 Vallières, *White Niggers of America*, 211–212.
74 Charters, 'The Amateur Revolutionaries', 151.
75 Gellner, *Bayonets in the Streets*, 62–63.
76 Vallières, *White Niggers of America*, 211–213.
77 Francis Simard, *Talking It Out: The October Crisis from Inside*, trans. David Homel (Toronto: Guernica, 1987), 117–119.
78 'Constitution Act, 1867', Department of Justice, Canada, www.lois.justice.gc.ca/en/const/c1867_e.html.
79 Peter Janke, *Terrorism and Democracy: Some Contemporary Cases* (Houndsmill, Basingstoke, Hampshire, and London: Macmillan, 1992), 46–47.
80 Though the RCMP is responsible for federal policing matters, it also contracts out its services to various provinces and municipalities.
81 William Kelly and Nora Kelly, *Policing in Canada* (Toronto: Macmillan of Canada, 1976), 51.
82 Ibid., 31, 54.
83 International Institute for Strategic Studies, *Military Balance* (London: The Institute for Strategic Studies, 1969–1970), 20.
84 Dan G. Loomis, *Not Much Glory: Quelling the FLQ* (Toronto: Deneau, 1984), 144.
85 Fournier, *F.L.Q.*, 98.
86 FLQ, 'Demands of the Flq', Marianopolis College, www2.marianopolis.edu/quebechistory/docs/october/demands.htm.
87 Crelinsten, 'The Internal Dynamics of the FLQ during the October Crisis of 1970', 62.

88 Due to a split within the Lanctôt-Rose Network in September 1970 over strategic issues, the Liberation and Chenier Cells maintained distinct decision-making processes before and during the October Crisis. Nevertheless, each cell was in intermittent contact with the other, and generally relied on the same body of 'supporter-*felquistes*' for assistance.

89 Janke, *Terrorism and Democracy*, 51.

90 Stéphane Leman-Langlois and Jean-Paul Brodeur, 'Terrorism Old and New: Counterterrorism in Canada', *Police Practice and Research* 6, no. 2 (2005): 130.

91 Raphael Cohen-Almagor, 'The Terrorists' Best Ally: The Quebec Media Coverage of the FLQ Crisis in October 1970', *Canadian Journal of Communication* 25, no. 2 (2000): 264–265.

92 Crelinsten, 'The Internal Dynamics of the FLQ during the October Crisis of 1970', 63.

93 Michael Freeman, *Freedom or Security: The Consequences for Democracies Using Emergency Powers to Fight Terror* (Westport and London: Praeger, 2003), 127.

94 Ronald D. Crelinsten, 'Power and Meaning: Terrorism as a Struggle over Access to the Communication Structure', in *Contemporary Research on Terrorism*, ed. Paul Wilkinson and Alasdair M. Stewart (Aberdeen: Aberdeen University Press, 1987), 432.

95 'War Measures Act', www2.marianopolis.edu/quebechistory/docs/october/wm-act. htm.

96 George Bain, 'The Making of a Crisis', in *Power Corrupted: The October Crisis and the Repression of Quebec*, ed. Abraham Rotstein (Toronto: New Press, 1971), 11; Denis Smith, *Bleeding Hearts ... Bleeding Country: Canada and the Quebec Crisis* (Edmonton: Hurtig, 1971), 46–50.

97 Charters, 'The Amateur Revolutionaries', 159.

98 Prior to October 1970, the Canadian anti-FLQ campaign was a near-perfect representation of the criminal justice approach to countering non-state violence. That is, the government gave 'responsibility for bearing the "brunt" of the confrontation' to the police (as opposed to the Canadian Armed Forces); and the police conducted their operations and brought charges against suspected *felquistes* within the established legal framework. Peter Chalk, *West European Terrorism and Counter-Terrorism: The Evolving Dynamic* (Basingstoke and London: Macmillan Press Ltd., 1996), 97; Ronald D. Crelinsten and Alex P. Schmid, 'Western Responses to Terrorism: A Twenty-Five Year Balance Sheet', *Terrorism and Political Violence* 4, no. 4 (1992): 307–309.

99 Smith, *Bleeding Hearts ... Bleeding Country*, 34. See also: Jean-François Duchaîne, 'Rapport Sur Les Événements D'octobre 1970', (Québec: Direction générale des publications gouvernementales, 1981), 116–117.

100 'War Measures Act'.

101 Freeman, *Freedom or Security*, 122.

102 'Public Order Regulations', www2.marianopolis.edu/quebechistory/docs/october/ regsoct.htm.

103 Freeman, *Freedom or Security*, 123; Ron Haggart and Aubery E. Golden, *Rumours of War* (Toronto: New Press, 1971), 171.

104 According to Simard (one of Laporte's kidnappers), on the day before he died, Laporte had managed to untie his bonds and, while still blindfolded, throw himself against a window (with a pillow for protection) in a bid to escape. Simard, *Talking It Out*, 47–48. Unfortunately, Laporte's attempt at freedom not only failed, but he also cut himself badly in the process. According to Crelinsten, the Chenier cell refused to take him to hospital for treatment and, on the 17th of October, 'Laporte was killed ... and the circumstances surrounding his death remain unclear to this day'. Crelinsten, 'The Internal Dynamics of the FLQ during the October Crisis of 1970', 64.

105 It is important to note that two members of the Liberation cell – Nigel Hamer and an

anonymous woman who has never been identified – left the hideout where Cross was being held in late October, 1970. Consequently, they both managed to avoid police detection. Indeed, it was not until 1980 that the police arrested Nigel Hamer for his role in the October Crisis.

106 Freeman, *Freedom or Security*, 121.

107 It is important to note that the status of these eight new UQAM recruits is contested. This is primarily due to their connection with Carole de Vault, who was both a member of the UQAM Network and a police informer. Because of this last fact, some observers have accused de Vault of being an *'agent provocateur'*, guilty of creating a 'phony FLQ'. Fournier, *F.L.Q.*, 277. However, de Vault vehemently denies these charges, portraying herself as both a pawn and witness of events. de Vault and Johnson, *The Informer*. Nevertheless, whatever role de Vault may have played, it does appear that the eight new UQAM recruits listed above were unaware of de Vault's connection with the police (indeed, many were arrested for crimes they committed in the name of the FLQ), and joined the movement because they wanted to engender Quebec's independence through the armed struggle. It is for these reasons that this book identifies the eight new UQAM recruits as members of the FLQ.

108 Anthony Kellett, 'Terrorism in Canada, 1960–1992', in *Violence in Canada: Sociopolitical Perspectives*, ed. Jeffrey Ian Ross (Don Mills: Oxford University Press, 1995), 291.

109 McRoberts, *Quebec*, 140.

110 Trofimenkoff, *The Dream*, 309.

111 McRoberts, *Quebec*, 201.

112 Charters, 'The Amateur Revolutionaries', 163.

113 Rheal Seguin, 'Parizeau Broadens Scope of Referendum Struggle', *The Globe and Mail*, 27 September 1995, 4.

114 Loomis, *Not Much Glory*, 48–52.

115 Ibid., 61; Walter Stewart, *Shrug: Trudeau in Power* (Toronto: New Press, 1971), 23.

116 Coleman, *The Independence Movement In Quebec 1945–1980*, 103.

117 On average, Quebec's Anglophones earned $5,918 per year, compared to $3,880 for the province's Francophones. *Report of the Royal Commission on Bilingualism and Biculturalism. Book Three: The Work World*, (Ottawa: Queen's Press, 1967), 21.

118 In 1971, Quebec's Anglophones earned an average income of $8,551 per year, while Quebec's Francophones earned an average income of $6,150 per year. François Vaillancourt, *Differences in Earnings by Language Groups in Quebec, 1970: An Economic Analysis* (Quebec: International Center for Research on Bilingualism, 1980), 43.

119 François Vaillancourt, 'La Situation Démographique Et Socio-Économique Des Francophones De Québec: Une Revue', *Canadian Public Policy – Analyse de politiques* 4 (1979): 547; André Raynauld, 'The Quebec Economy: A General Assessment', in *Quebec Society and Politics: Views from the Inside*, ed. Dale C. Thomson (Toronto, ON: McClelland and Stewart Ltd., 1973), 150–151.

120 McRoberts, *Quebec*, 176.

121 Ibid.

122 Levine provides an excellent in-depth examination of the Saint-Leonard affair. Marc V. Levine, *The Reconquest of Montreal: Language Policy and Social Change in a Bilingual City* (Philadelphia: Temple University Press, 1990), 67–86.

123 *Allophone* is a Canadian term for a person whose native tongue is neither English nor French.

124 Levine, *The Reconquest of Montreal*, 72.

125 Linda Cardinal, 'The Limits of Bilingualism in Canada', *Nationalism and Ethnic Politics* 10, no. 1 (2004): 82.

126 Assemblée nationale du Québec, 'An Act to Promote the French Language in Quebec', in *Lois Du Quebec* (Quebec City: Publications du Québec, 1969), 62.

127   Levine, *The Reconquest of Montreal*, 80.
128   Richard Jones, 'Politics and the Reinforcement of the French Language in Canada and Quebec, 1960–1986', in *Quebec since 1945: Selected Readings*, ed. Michael D. Behiels (Toronto: Copp Clark Pitman Limited, 1987), 230.
129   Though the *Union Nationale's* defeat in April 1970 was due to numerous reasons, the cleavage struck by Bill 63 between the party's moderate and ultra-nationalist wings played an important role. For more information, see: Herbert F. Quinn, *The Union Nationale: Quebec Nationalism from Duplessis to Lévesque*, Second enlarged ed. (Toronto, Buffalo and London: University of Toronto Press, 1979), 255–257.
130   Levine, *The Reconquest of Montreal*, 93.
131   Judy M. Torrance, *Public Violence in Canada, 1867–1982* (Kingston and Montreal: McGill-Queen's University Press, 1986), 22–23.
132   Reg Whitaker, 'Keeping up with the Neighbours? Canadian Responses to 9/11 in Historical and Comparative Context', *Osgoode Hall Law Journal* 41, no. 2 & 3 (2003): 249.
133   Jeffrey Ian Ross, 'The Rise and Fall of Quebecois Separatist Terrorism: A Qualitative Application of Factors from Two Models', *Studies in Conflict and Terrorism* 18 (1995): 292.
134   Jeffrey Ian Ross and Ted Robert Gurr, 'Why Terrorism Subsides: A Comparative Study of Canada and the United States', *Comparative Politics* 21, no. 4 (1989): 413.
135   Charters, 'The October Crisis', 67.
136   Freeman, *Freedom or Security*, 123.
137   Malcolm Levin and Christine Sylvester, *Crisis in Quebec* (Toronto: Ontario Institute for Studies in Education, 1973), 25; Haggart and Golden, *Rumours of War*, 71–76.
138   Commission of Inquiry Concerning Certain Activities of the Royal Canadian Mounted Police, 'Freedom and Security under the Law', (Ottawa: Canadian Government Publishing Centre, 1981), 269.
139   Steve Hewitt, 'Reforming the Canadian Security State: The Royal Canadian Mounted Police Security Service and the "Key Sectors" Program', *Intelligence and National Security* 17, no. 4 (2002): 178–179.
140   Fournier, *F.L.Q.*, 323.
141   Ibid., 328–329.
142   Commission of Inquiry Concerning Certain Activities of the Royal Canadian Mounted Police, 'Freedom and Security under the Law', 270.
143   Léon Dion and Micheline de Sève, 'Quebec: Interest Groups and the Search for an Alternative Political System', *The Annals of the American Academy of Political and Social Science* 413 (1974): 140–141; Graham Fraser, *PQ: René Lévesque & the Parti Québécois in Power* (Toronto: Macmillan of Canada, 1984), 57–58.
144   Saywell, *The Rise of the Parti Québécois 1967–1976*, 58.
145   Fournier, *F.L.Q.*, 312.
146   Ross, 'The Rise and Fall of Quebecois Separatist Terrorism', 293.
147   Charters, 'The October Crisis', 61, Charters, 'The Amateur Revolutionaries', 153.
148   Vallières announced his decision in a number of newspaper articles, which were later published as: Pierre Vallières, *Choose!*, trans. Penelope Williams (Toronto, ON.: New Press, 1972).
149   Cited in: Fournier, *F.L.Q.*, 329.
150   Ross and Gurr, 'Why Terrorism Subsides', 414.
151   Saywell, *The Rise of the Parti Québécois 1967–1976*.
152   Vallières, *Choose!*, 93.
153   Ibid., 94.
154   Ross and Gurr, 'Why Terrorism Subsides', 414.
155   Janke, *Terrorism and Democracy*, 70.
156   Charters, 'The Amateur Revolutionaries', 153.
157   Torrance, *Public Violence in Canada, 1867–1982*, 39.

158 Dion and de Sève, 'Quebec', 141, Reilly, 'The Management of Political Violence', 56.
159 Vallières, *Choose!*, 90–93.
160 Richard Matthew and George Shambaugh, 'The Limits of Terrorism: A Network Perspective', *International Studies Review* 7, no. 4 (2005): 624.
161 Vallières, *Choose!*, 97.
162 Ibid., 102.

4 Movimiento de Liberación Nacional – Tupamaros

1 'The Tupamaros May Do It', *The Economist*, 15 May 1971, 16.
2 Régis Debray, *Strategy for Revolution*, ed. Robin Blackburn (London: J. Cape, 1970), 93.
3 Matt D. Childs, 'An Historical Critique of the Emergence and Evolution of Ernesto Che Guevara's Foco Theory', *Journal of Latin American Studies* 27, no. 3 (1995): 596.
4 Timothy P. Wickham-Crowley, *Guerrillas and Revolution in Latin America: A Comparative Study of Insurgents and Regimes since 1956* (Princeton: Princeton University Press, 1992), 32.
5 Ibid.
6 Eleuterio Fernández Huidobro, cited in: Carlos Núñez, 'Eleuterio Fernández Huidobro', *NACLA Report on the Americas* 20, no. 5 (1986): 47.
7 Ernesto (Che) Guevara, *Guerrilla Warfare* (Middlesex: Penguin, 1969), 13. See also: Jose A. Moreno, 'Che Guevara on Guerrilla Warfare: Doctrine, Practice, and Evaluation', *Comparative studies in society and history* 12, no. 2 (1970): 115–116.
8 Childs, 'An Historical Critique of the Emergence and Evolution of Ernesto Che Guevara's Foco Theory', 594–595, Wickham-Crowley, *Guerrillas and Revolution in Latin America*, 32–33; Maurice Halperin, 'Return to Havana: Portrait of a Loyalist', *Cuban Studies* 23 (1993): 188.
9 Wickham-Crowley, *Guerrillas and Revolution in Latin America*, 32.
10 David Nolan, 'From Foco to Insurrection: Sandinista Strategies of Revolution', *Air University Review*, July–August 1986.
11 This domination came to an end on 31 October 2004, when a coalition of leftist parties (*Encuentro Progresista – Frente Amplio – Nueva Mayoria*) triumphed in the country's presidential elections. Remarkably, the largest faction of this coalition (the *Movimiento de Participación Popular*, or MPP) consisted of former MLN-T members turned politicians. See: 'Vázquez Should Win by a Whisker but Turnout Will Be Decisive', *Latin American Brazil & Southern Cone Report*, 26 October 2004, 12; Larry Rohter, 'Uruguay's Left Makes History by Winning Presidential Ballot', *New York Times*, 1 November 2004, 11.
12 Phillip B. Taylor, 'Interests and Institutional Dysfunction in Uruguay', *The American Political Science Review* 57, no. 1 (1963): 63.
13 Ibid.
14 The exact meaning of *coparticipación* has varied during the history of its usage. For an etymological and in-depth analysis of coparticipation, see: Göran G. Lindahl, *Uruguay's New Path: A Study in Politics During the First Colegiado, 1919–33* (Stockholm: Library and Institute of Ibero-American Studies, 1962), 191–197; Martin Weinstein, *Uruguay: The Politics of Failure* (Westport and London: Greenwood Press, 1975), 50–84.
15 David Rock and Fernando Lopez-Alves, 'State-Building and Political Systems in Nineteenth-Century Argentina and Uruguay', *Past and Present*, no. 167 (2000): 201.
16 Percy Alvin Martin, 'The Career of Jose Batlle Y Ordonez', *The Hispanic American Historical Review* 10, no. 4 (1930): 425–426.

17   Herman E. Daly, 'The Uruguayan Economy: Its Basic Nature and Current Problems', *Journal of Inter-American Studies* 7, no. 3 (1965): 318.
18   For an examination of the development and evolution of Uruguay's welfare system, see: George Pendle, *Uruguay*, Third edn. (London, New York and Toronto: Oxford University Press, 1963), 27–47.
19   In 1956, Uruguay's per capita income was the highest in South America. 'The Measurement of Latin American Real Income in US Dollars', *Economic Bulletin for Latin America* 7, no. 2 (1968). According to Finch, Uruguay was likely to have 'held this position throughout the first half of this [i.e. the twentieth] century'. M.H.J. Finch, *A Political Economy of Uruguay since 1870* (London and Basingstoke: Macmillan Press, 1981), 220.
20   James Kohl and John Litt, *Urban Guerrilla Warfare in Latin America* (Cambridge and London: The MIT Press, 1974), 174.
21   Russell H. Fitzgibbon, 'Uruguay's Agricultural Problems', *Economic Geography* 29, no. 3 (1953): 251.
22   Finch, *A Political Economy of Uruguay since 1870*, 129; Russell H. Brannon, *The Agricultural Development of Uruguay: Problems of Government Policy* (New York, Washington, and London: Frederick A. Praeger Publishers, 1968), 68.
23   Daly, 'The Uruguayan Economy', 325.
24   Finch, *A Political Economy of Uruguay since 1870*, 223.
25   Brannon, *The Agricultural Development of Uruguay*, 57.
26   Phillip B. Taylor, 'Government and Politics of Uruguay', *Tulane Studies in Political Science* 7 (1960): 129.
27   Finch, *A Political Economy of Uruguay since 1870*, 226; According to Brannon, Uruguay's GDP grew by an annual average of 0.0 per cent between 1955 and 1964. Brannon, *The Agricultural Development of Uruguay*, 49.
28   Daly, 'The Uruguayan Economy', 318.
29   Finch, *A Political Economy of Uruguay since 1870*, 223. According to Brannon, Uruguay's per capita income declined by an annual average of 1.4 per cent between 1955 and 1964. Brannon, *The Agricultural Development of Uruguay*, 49.
30   Finch, *A Political Economy of Uruguay since 1870*, 227; Kohl and Litt, *Urban Guerrilla Warfare in Latin America*, 176.
31   World Bank Group, 'World Development Indicators', www.devdata.worldbank.org/dataonline/, Finch, *A Political Economy of Uruguay since 1870*, 229.
32   Fernando Lopez-Alves, 'Political Crises, Strategic Choices, and Terrorism: The Rise and Fall of the Uruguayan Tupamaros', *Terrorism and Political Violence* 1, no. 2 (1989): 211.
33   Weinstein, *Uruguay: The Politics of Failure*, 120; Howard Handelman, 'Labor-Industrial Conflict and the Collapse of Uruguayan Democracy', *Journal of Interamerican Studies and World Affairs* 23, no. 4 (1981): 376.
34   Weinstein, *Uruguay: The Politics of Failure*, 119.
35   Alain Labrousse, *The Tupamaros: Urban Guerrilla in Uruguay*, trans. Dinah Livingstone (Harmondsworth: Penguin Books, 1973), 61.
36   Alexander T. Edelmann, 'The Rise and Demise of Uruguay's Second Plural Executive', *The Journal of Politics* 31, no. 1 (1969): 130–139; Taylor, 'Interests and Institutional Dysfunction in Uruguay', 66–67, Weinstein, *Uruguay: The Politics of Failure*, 114–117.
37   Documentación y Archivo de Lucha Armada DC, 'Cronología Básica 1954–1973', (Montevideo: Facultad de Humanidades, la Universidad de la República, 2006).
38   Astrid Arraras, 'Armed Struggle, Political Learning and Participation in Democracy: The Case of the Tupamaros' (PhD, Princeton University, 1999), 53–54.
39   Lopez-Alves, 'Political Crises, Strategic Choices and Terrorism', 213.
40   Carlos Núñez, *The Tupamaros: Urban Guerrillas of Uruguay* (New York: Times Change Press, 1970).

41 Arturo C. Porzecanski, *Uruguay's Tupamaros: The Urban Guerrilla* (New York, Washington and London: Praeger Publishers, 1973), 5.

42 Arraras, 'Armed Struggle, Political Learning and Participation in Democracy', 57–63.

43 Eleuterio Fernández Huidobro, *Historia De Los Tupamaros* (Montevideo: Ediciones de la Banda Oriental, 1987), 74–75.

44 Arraras, 'Armed Struggle, Political Learning and Participation in Democracy', 67.

45 The name 'Tupamaros' is a derivative of Tupac Amarú, the leader of an indigenous uprising against the Spaniards in colonial Peru in 1780. After defeating Tupac Amarú's forces, the Spanish used the term 'Tupamaros' to label 'all members of rebellious groups' that subsequently emerged in Latin America to challenge colonial authority. Indeed, the forces of José G. Artigas – the hero of Uruguay's independence – were called Tupamaros during their battles with the Spanish in the 1820s. By calling themselves the Tupamaros, the MLN-T was thus attempting to tap into this well of historic and cultural meaning. See: Porzecanski, *Uruguay's Tupamaros*, ix.

46 This figure is derived from: Documentación y Archivo de Lucha Armada DC, 'Cronología Básica 1954–1973'.

47 Fournier describes how the Tupamaros had 'an impact' on the 'ranks of the FLQ'. Louis Fournier, *F.L.Q.: The Anatomy of an Underground Movement*, trans. Edward Baxter (Toronto: NC Press Limited, 1984), 71–72. Similarly, during the late-1960s and early-1970s, a small group of West Berlin radicals established the 'Tupamaros-West Berlin'. This grouping soon evolved into the *Bewegung 2. Juni*. Jeremy Varon, *Bringing the War Home: The Weather Underground, the Red Army Faction, and Revolutionary Violence in the Sixties and Seventies* (Berkeley, Los Angeles and London: University of California Press, 2003), 207–208.

48 Marysa Gerassi, 'Uruguay's Urban Guerrillas', *New Left Review*, no. 62 (1970): 28.

49 Kohl and Litt, *Urban Guerrilla Warfare in Latin America*, 173.

50 Stephen Connolly and Gregory Druehl, 'The Tupamaros: The New Focus in Latin America', *Journal of Contemporary Revolutions* 3 (1971): 59.

51 James A. Miller, 'Urban Terrorism in Uruguay: The Tupamaros', in *Insurgency in the Modern World*, ed. Bard E. O'Neill, William R. Heaton, and Donald J. Alberts (Boulder: Westview Press, 1980), 153.

52 Connolly and Druehl, 'The Tupamaros', 59.

53 Documentación y Archivo de Lucha Armada DC, 'Cronología Básica 1954–1973'.

54 For an exhaustive account of Mitrione's workings with the Uruguayan police and his background, see: A.J. Langguth, *Hidden Terrors* (New York: Pantheon Books, 1978), 223–259.

55 Porzecanski, *Uruguay's Tupamaros*, 32.

56 Miller, 'Urban Terrorism in Uruguay', 161.

57 Porzecanski, *Uruguay's Tupamaros*, 33.

58 Arraras, 'Armed Struggle, Political Learning and Participation in Democracy', 91.

59 Kohl and Litt, *Urban Guerrilla Warfare in Latin America*, 189.

60 Porzecanski, *Uruguay's Tupamaros*, 34.

61 Documentación y Archivo de Lucha Armada DC, 'Cronología Básica 1954–1973'.

62 Porzecanski, *Uruguay's Tupamaros*, 28.

63 Ibid.

64 Arraras, 'Armed Struggle, Political Learning and Participation in Democracy', 117.

65 Ibid., 117, n.19.

66 Ibid., 118.

67 Ibid.

68 Documentación y Archivo de Lucha Armada DC, 'Cronología Básica 1954–1973'.

69 MLN-T, 'Análisis Del MLN Sobre La Situación Nacional Y Continental', in *Los Tupamaros*, ed. Omar Costa (Mexico: Ediciones Era, 1972), 240.

70   MLN-T, 'Interview with Urbano', in *Urban Guerrilla Warfare in Latin America*, ed. James Kohl and James Litt (Cambridge and London: The MIT Press, 1974), 275.

71   MLN-T, 'The Tupamaro Manifesto', in *The Tupamaros: Urban Guerrillas in Uruguay*, ed. Alain Labrousse (Harmondsworth: Penguin Books, 1973), 160.

72   MLN-T, 'Los Tupamaros Ejecutores De La Justicia Popular', in *Los Tupamaros*, ed. Omar Costa (Mexico: Ediciones Era, 1972), 120–121.

73   MLN-T, 'Proclamation of Paysandú', in *Urban Guerrilla Warfare in Latin America*, ed. James Kohl and James Litt (Cambridge and London: The MIT Press, 1974), 297–298.

74   Porzecanski, *Uruguay's Tupamaros*, 3.

75   MLN-T, 'Análisis Del MLN Sobre La Situación Nacional Y Continental', 240.

76   Ibid., 237, MLN-T, 'Facts the Public Should Know', in *The Tupamaros*, ed. Maria Esther Gilio (London: Secker & Warburg, 1972), 118.

77   MLN-T, 'The Tupamaro Manifesto', 159, MLN-T, 'Proclamation of Paysandú', 298.

78   MLN-T, 'Proclamation of Paysandú', 298.

79   MLN-T, 'Interview with Urbano', 275.

80   MLN-T, 'Los Tupamaros Y El Movimiento Estudiantil', in *Los Tupamaros*, ed. Omar Costa (Mexico: Ediciones Era, 1972), 125.

81   MLN-T, 'Today Sr. Pereyra Reverbel Was Arrested by the National Liberation Movement (Tupamaros)', in *The Tupamaros: Urban Guerrillas in Uruguay*, ed. Alain Labrousse (Harmondsworth: Penguin Books, 1973), 66.

82   MLN-T, 'Broadcast on Radio Sarandi, 15 May 1969', in *The Tupamaros: Urban Guerrillas in Uruguay*, ed. Alain Labrousse (Harmondsworth: Penguin Books, 1973), 146.

83   MLN-T, 'Facts the Public Should Know', 118.

84   MLN-T, 'Proclamation of Paysandú', 298.

85   MLN-T, 'Broadcast on Radio Sarandi 15th May 1969', 147.

86   MLN-T, 'Today Sr. Pereyra Reverbel was Arrested by the National Liberation Movement (Tupamaros)', 66.

87   MLN-T, 'Análisis Del MLN Sobre La Situación Nacional Y Continental', 228–229.

88   MLN-T, 'The Tupamaros' Program for Revolutionary Government', in *Urban Guerrilla Warfare in Latin America*, ed. James Kohl and James Litt (Cambridge and London: The MIT Press, 1974), 293–295.

89   MLN-T, 'Facts the Public Should Know', 118, MLN-T, 'Proclamation of Paysandú', 297.

90   Guevara, *Guerrilla Warfare*, 13.

91   Weinstein, *Uruguay: The Politics of Failure*, 92. In contrast, 43 per cent of Cuba's population lived in rural areas when the M-26 first launched its insurrectionary campaign in 1953. See: Javier Corrales, 'Strong Societies, Weak Parties: Regime Change in Cuba and Venezuela in the 1950s and Today', *Latin American Politics and Society* 43, no. 2 (2001): 86.

92   MLN-T, 'Interview with Urbano', 285.

93   MLN-T, 'Thirty Questions to a Tupamaro', in *Urban Guerrilla Warfare in Latin America*, ed. James Kohl and James Litt (Cambridge and London: The MIT Press, 1974), 233.

94   Antonio Mercader and Jorge de Vera, *Tupamaros: Estrategia Y Accion Informe* (Mexico: Editorial Omega, 1971), 20–21.

95   MLN-T, 'Análisis Del MLN Sobre La Situación Nacional Y Continental', 242–243.

96   MLN-T, 'Las Tácticas Que Usa La Guerrilla Urbana', in *Los Tupamaros*, ed. Omar Costa (Mexico: Ediciones Era, 1972), 258.

97   MLN-T, 'Thirty Questions to a Tupamaro', 232–233.

98   Lopez-Alves, 'Political Crises, Strategic Choices, and Terrorism', 213.

99   MLN-T, 'Thirty Questions to a Tupamaro', 228.

100 MLN-T, 'Proclamation of Paysandú', 298.
101 MLN-T, 'Análisis Del MLN Sobre La Situación Nacional Y Continental', 237–238.
102 MLN-T, 'The Tupamaros: An Interview', in *Urban Guerrilla Warfare in Latin America*, ed. James Kohl and James Litt (Cambridge and London: The MIT Press, 1974), 302.
103 MLN-T, 'The Tupamaros' Program for Revolutionary Government', 296.
104 MLN-T, 'Carta Abierta a La Policía', in *Historia De Los Tupamaros*, ed. Eleuterio Fernández Huidobro (Montevideo: Ediciones de la Banda Oriental, 1987), 395–396.
105 MLN-T, 'Interview with Urbano', 276.
106 MLN-T, 'The Tupamaros', 302, MLN-T, 'Interview with Urbano', 276.
107 MLN-T, 'Thirty Questions to a Tupamaro', 227.
108 Ibid.
109 Ibid., 227–228.
110 MLN-T, 'Análisis Del MLN Sobre La Situación Nacional Y Continental', 244.
111 MLN-T, 'Carta Abierta a la Policía', 395, MLN-T, 'Interview with Urbano', 274.
112 Miller, 'Urban Terrorism in Uruguay', 160.
113 Michael Freeman, *Freedom or Security: The Consequences for Democracies Using Emergency Powers to Fight Terror* (Westport and London: Praeger, 2003), 98.
114 Labrousse, *The Tupamaros*, 43.
115 MLN-T, 'Apuntes Sobre Lucha Armada', April 1968, 15.
116 Porzecanski, *Uruguay's Tupamaros*, 35.
117 Arraras, 'Armed Struggle, Political Learning and Participation in Democracy', 160.
118 For background information on Uruguay's political history and structure, see: Taylor, 'Government and Politics of Uruguay'; Weinstein, *Uruguay: The Politics of Failure*.
119 Edelmann, 'The Rise and Demise of Uruguay's Second Plural Executive', 121–122.
120 'Constitución De La República Oriental Del Uruguay', www.georgetown.edu/pdba/Constitutions/Uruguay/uruguay67.html.
121 Thomas E. Weil et al., *Area Handbook for Uruguay* (Washington, D.C.: U.S. Government Printing Office, 1971), 371.
122 Porzecanski, *Uruguay's Tupamaros*, 53.
123 Weil *et al.*, *Area Handbook for Uruguay*, 372.
124 International Institute for Strategic Studies, *Military Balance* (London: The Institute for Strategic Studies, 1969–1970), 61.
125 Ibid; Weil *et al.*, *Area Handbook for Uruguay*, 385.
126 International Institute for Strategic Studies, *Military Balance*, 61.
127 In 1970, there were six members of the FFAA for every 1,000 Uruguayans. The Latin American average was three per 1,000. See: Porzecanski, *Uruguay's Tupamaros*, 65.
128 Edy Kaufman, *Uruguay in Transition: From Civilian to Military Rule* (New Brunswick, NJ.: Transaction Books, 1979), 55.
129 Porzecanski, *Uruguay's Tupamaros*, 66.
130 Weil *et al.*, *Area Handbook for Uruguay*, 389.
131 Robert Moss, *Urban Guerrillas: The New Face of Political Violence* (London: Temple Smith, 1972), 211; Arraras, 'Armed Struggle, Political Learning and Participation in Democracy', 97.
132 Fernández Huidobro, *Historia de Los Tupamoaros*, 237.
133 Documentación y Archivo de Lucha Armada DC, 'Cronología Básica 1954–1973'.
134 Porzecanski, *Uruguay's Tupamaros*, 52.
135 Fernández Huidobro, *Historia de Los Tupamaros*, 340.
136 Moss, *Urban Guerrillas*, 216, Kohl and Litt, *Urban Guerrilla Warfare in Latin America*, 186; Arraras, 'Armed Struggle, Political Learning and Participation in Democracy', 151.
137 MLN-T, 'Interview with Urbano', 286.

138   Fernández Huidobro, *Historia de Los Tupamaros*, 349.
139   MLN-T, 'Interview with Urbano', 287.
140   Fernández Huidobro, *Historia de Los Tupamaros*, 349.
141   Ibid., 350.
142   Arraras, 'Armed Struggle, Political Learning and Participation in Democracy', 131.
143   Weinstein, *Uruguay: The Politics of Failure*, 117.
144   Labrousse, *The Tupamaros*, 10.
145   Uruguay's state-owned power company.
146   Data drawn and compiled from: Documentación y Archivo de Lucha Armada DC, 'Cronología Básica 1954–1973'. The average for 1968 is from August to December. The average for 1971 is from January to August.
147   Michael Radu and Vladimir Tismaneanu, *Latin American Revolutionaries: Groups, Goals, Methods* (Washington, D.C.: Pergamon-Brassey's, 1990), 350.
148   'The Tupamaros May Do It', 16.
149   Documentación y Archivo de Lucha Armada DC, 'Cronología Básica 1954–1973'.
150   Ibid.
151   MLN-T, 'Balance 1969', in *Las Fuerzas Armadas Al Pueblo Oriental*, ed. Junta de Comandantes en Jefe (Montevideo: Republica Oriental del Uruguay, Junta de Comandantes en Jefe, 1978), 568–569.
152   Ibid.
153   Arraras, 'Armed Struggle, Political Learning and Participation in Democracy', 160.
154   Kohl and Litt, *Urban Guerrilla Warfare in Latin America*, 187.
155   Documentación y Archivo de Lucha Armada DC, 'Cronología Básica 1954–1973'.
156   Sergio L. d'Oliveira, 'Uruguay and the Tupamaro Myth', *Military Review* 53, no. 4 (1973): 27.
157   Lopez-Alves, 'Political Crises, Strategic Choices, and Terrorism', 226; MLN-T, 'Balance 1969', 569.
158   Kohl and Litt, *Urban Guerrilla Warfare in Latin America*, 188.
159   Porzecanski, *Uruguay's Tupamaros*, 67.
160   MLN-T, 'Balance 70–71', in *3 Documentos Internos* (Montevideo: MLN-T, 1986), 12.
161   Ibid., 12–13; Documentación y Archivo de Lucha Armada DC, 'Cronología Básica 1954–1973'.
162   Weinstein, *Uruguay: The Politics of Failure*, 128.
163   Ibid., 125–126.
164   Lopez-Alves, 'Political Crises, Strategic Choices, and Terrorism', 230.
165   Carlos Leites, Delega's driver, was also killed.
166   Porzecanski, *Uruguay's Tupamaros*, 68.
167   SERPAJ, *Uruguay Nunca Más: Human Rights Violations, 1972–1985*, trans. Elizabeth Hampsten (Philadelphia: Temple University Press, 1992), 29, *Generals and Tupamaros: The Struggle for Power in Uruguay 1969–1973*, (London and Leeds: Latin America Review of Books, 1974), 41–42.
168   Freeman, *Freedom or Security*, 95.
169   Arraras, 'Armed Struggle, Political Learning and Participation in Democracy', 226.
170   MLN-T, 'Plan De Marzo De 1972: Informe Del Secretariado Ejecutivo Al Comite Central', in *Los Tupamaros*, ed. Omar Costa (Mexico: Ediciones Era, 1972), 406–407.
171   Miller, 'Urban Terrorism in Uruguay', 163.
172   MLN-T, 'The Tupamaros', 304.
173   MLN-T, 'Bases De Discusión Acerca De La Situación Actual De Las FFAA Y El Quehacer', in *Las Fuerzas Armadas Al Pueblo Oriental*, ed. Junta de Comandantes en Jefe (Montevideo: Republica Oriental del Uruguay, Junta de Comandantes en Jefe, 1978), 771.
174   Documentación y Archivo de Lucha Armada DC, 'Cronología Básica 1954–1973'.

175 Arraras, 'Armed Struggle, Political Learning and Participation in Democracy', 226.
176 This propaganda consisted of Tupamaro 'letters' and a journal. See: MLN-T, 'El Tupamaro: Organo Del Movimiento De Liberacion Nacional Tupamaros', 1, no. 1 (1973), MLN-T, 'Correo Tupamaro: Movimiento De Liberacion Nacional Tupamaros Al Pueblo', July 1973.
177 Miller, 'Urban Terrorism in Uruguay', 173; Porzecanski, *Uruguay's Tupamaros*, 70; Freeman, *Freedom or Security*, 99; Lopez-Alves, 'Political Crises, Strategic Choices, and Terrorism', 232.
178 Weinstein, *Uruguay: The Politics of Failure*, 130.
179 Documentación y Archivo de Lucha Armada DC, 'Cronología Básica 1954–1973'.
180 Cited in: Ernesto González Bermejo, *Las Manos En El Fuego* (Montevideo: Ediciones de la Banda Oriental, 1987), 123.
181 Arraras, 'Armed Struggle, Political Learning and Participation in Democracy', 219.
182 Freeman, *Freedom or Security*, 99.
183 Robert Moss, *The War for the Cities* (New York: Coward, McCann & Geoghegan, 1972), 232.
184 USAID, cited in: Wolfgang S Heinz and Hugo Frühling, *Determinants of Gross Human Rights Violations by State and State-Sponsored Actors in Brazil, Uruguay, Chile, and Argentina 1960–1990* (The Hague, Boston and London: Martinus Nijhoff Publishers, 1999), 316.
185 Miller, 'Urban Terrorism in Uruguay', 169.
186 Labrousse, *The Tupamaros*, 103; Langguth, *Hidden Terrors*, 223–259.
187 Weinstein, *Uruguay: The Politics of Failure*, 12; *Generals and Tupamaros*, 118. For first person accounts of police torture, see: Maria Esther Gilio, *The Tupamaros*, trans. Anne Edmondson (London: Secker & Warburg, 1972), 141–172.
188 SERPAJ, *Uruguay Nunca Más*, 79.
189 Ibid. For a comprehensive breakdown of SERPAJ's survey, methodology, and population, see: pp. 321–336.
190 Porzecanski, *Uruguay's Tupamaros*, 68.
191 Ibid.
192 Ibid, SERPAJ, *Uruguay Nunca Más*, 89–104; Freeman, *Freedom or Security*, 94.
193 SERPAJ, *Uruguay Nunca Más*, 82.
194 d'Oliveira, 'Uruguay and the Tupamaro Myth', 32; Freeman, *Freedom or Security*, 94–95.
195 For instance, Strauss, in her seminal article on the subject, notes that, while torture may be of little utility in obtaining information for the purposes of securing a conviction in a court of law, its effectiveness as a means of simply acquiring information is potentially greater, thought ultimately 'unknowable'. This is not to say that torture is effective in obtaining actionable intelligence in all cases; but rather, to acknowledge that '[t]here are times when torture has worked in the past, and there undoubtedly would be successes in the future'. Marcy Strauss, 'Torture', *New York Law School Law Review* 48, no. 1 & 2 (2004): 261–265. For other perspectives, see: Alex J. Bellamy, 'No Pain, No Gain? Torture and Ethics in the War on Terror', *International Affairs* 82, no. 1 (2006): 138–141; Alan M. Dershowitz, *Why Terrorism Works* (New Haven: Yale University Press, 2002), 131–164.
196 Kohl and Litt, *Urban Guerrilla Warfare in Latin America*, 194.
197 *Generals and Tupamaros*, 52.
198 Porzecanski, *Uruguay's Tupamaros*, 21.
199 Arraras, 'Armed Struggle, Political Learning and Participation in Democracy', 226, Documentación y Archivo de Lucha Armada DC, 'Cronología Básica 1954–1973'.
200 *Generals and Tupamaros*, 52.
201 MLN-T, 'Organizavion Y Seguridad', 7 December 1969, 1–2.
202 MLN-T, 'Apuntes Sobre Lucha Armada', 9–11.

203   Lopez-Alves, 'Political Crises, Strategic Choices, and Terrorism', 230, d'Oliveira, 'Uruguay and the Tupamaro Myth', 32.
204   Porzecanski, *Uruguay's Tupamaros*, 69–70.
205   Arraras, 'Armed Struggle, Political Learning and Participation in Democracy', 192.
206   Miller, 'Urban Terrorism in Uruguay', 172.
207   Ibid.
208   For information on the police's unpopularity, see: Labrousse, *The Tupamaros*, 63–64; Lopez-Alves, 'Political Crises, Strategic Choices, and Terrorism', 223; Núñez, *The Tupamaros*, 7–10; Porzecanski, *Uruguay's Tupamaros*, 53–54. For information on public passivity, see: d'Oliveira, 'Uruguay and the Tupamaro Myth', 27. For information on popular respect for the military, see: Aaron S. Klieman, 'Confined to Barracks: Emergencies and the Military in Developing Societies', *Comparative Politics* 12, no. 2 (1980): 151–152; Porzecanski, *Uruguay's Tupamaros*, 66.
209   Christopher Hewitt, 'Terrorism and Public Opinion: A Five Country Comparison', *Terrorism and Political Violence* 2, no. 2 (1990): 145–170.
210   Alexandra Barahona de Brito, *Human Rights and Democratization in Latin America: Uruguay and Chile* (Oxford: Oxford University Press, 1997), 42; Freeman, *Freedom or Security*, 93.
211   'Ley De Seguridad Del Estado Y El Orden Interno', República Oriental del Uruguay, Poder Legislativo, www.parlamento.gub.uy/leyes/ley14068.htm.
212   Martin Weinstein, *Uruguay: Democracy at the Crossroads* (Boulder: Westview, 1988), 46; Barahona de Brito, *Human Rights and Democratization in Latin America*, 42.
213   'Se Aprueba La Ley De Amnistia', República Oriental del Uruguay, Poder Legislativo, www.parlamento.gub.uy/leyes/ley15737.htm.
214   d'Oliveira, 'Uruguay and the Tupamaro Myth', 34–35.
215   Weinstein, *Uruguay: The Politics of Failure*, 128.
216   Barahona de Brito, *Human Rights and Democratization in Latin America*, 42.
217   Ibid.
218   As aforementioned, these dates represent the points at which: (1) the Tupamaros decided to intensify their campaign (i.e. by kidnapping Reverbel); and (2) begin their 'phoney war' with the FFAA.
219   Documentación y Archivo de Lucha Armada DC, 'Cronología Básica 1954–1973'.
220   Ibid.
221   Ibid.
222   Finch, *A Political Economy of Uruguay since 1870*, 226, 43. According to the World Bank Group, Uruguay's GDP grew by 1.9 per cent, 5.9 per cent, and 2.3 per cent in 1968, 1969, and 1970, respectively. The World Bank Group concurs with Finch regarding Uruguay's rate of inflation. World Bank Group, 'World Development Indicators', http://devdata.worldbank.org/dataonline/.
223   Finch, *A Political Economy of Uruguay since 1870*, 262. According to the World Bank Group, Uruguay's GDP contracted by 0.3 per cent and 1.3 per cent in 1971 and 1972, and grew by 0.3 per cent in 1973. World Bank Group, 'World Development Indicators'.
224   Finch, *A Political Economy of Uruguay since 1870*, 262. According to the World Bank Group, Uruguay's GDP grew by 2.9 per cent and 6.1 per cent in 1974 and 1975. World Bank Group, 'World Development Indicators'.
225   Finch, *A Political Economy of Uruguay since 1870*, 253, World Bank Group, 'World Development Indicators'.
226   Finch, *A Political Economy of Uruguay since 1870*, 253.
227   Ibid. Results from 1975 are unavailable.
228   Arraras, 'Armed Struggle, Political Learning and Participation in Democracy', 233. See also: Charles Guy Gillespie, *Negotiating Democracy: Politicians and Generals in Uruguay* (Cambridge: Cambridge University Press, 1991), 57–59.

229 d'Oliveira, 'Uruguay and the Tupamaro Myth', 27, Lopez-Alves, 'Political Crises, Strategic Choices, and Terrorism', 223, Porzecanski, *Uruguay's Tupamaros*, 55.
230 Documentación y Archivo de Lucha Armada DC, 'Cronología Básica 1954–1973'.
231 SERPAJ, *Uruguay Nunca Más*, 29, Porzecanski, *Uruguay's Tupamaros*, 56.
232 Weinstein, *Uruguay: The Politics of Failure*, 128.
233 Porzecanski, *Uruguay's Tupamaros*, 62.
234 Documentación y Archivo de Lucha Armada DC, 'Cronología Básica 1954–1973'.
235 Richard Gott, 'Events since 1971', in *The Tupamaros: Urban Guerrillas in Uruguay*, ed. Alain Labrousse (Harmondsworth: Penguin Books, 1973), 131.
236 Arraras, 'Armed Struggle, Political Learning and Participation in Democracy', 219.
237 Freeman, *Freedom or Security*, 101.
238 Cited in: *Generals and Tupamaros*, 43.
239 See: Ibid., 29.
240 In 1966, the *Frente Izquierda de Liberación* (FIdeL) received 60,541 votes; the *Partido Demócrata Cristiano* (PDC) 31,846; the *Partido Socialista* 10,936; the *Movimiento Cívico Cristiano* (MCC) 3,762; and the *Union Popular* (UP) 2,613. 'Their combined vote was 10.4 per cent of the total'. Edelmann, 'The Rise and Demise of Uruguay's Second Plural Executive', 119–120.
241 Hewitt, 'Terrorism and Public Opinion', 145–170.

5 Provisional Irish Republican Army

1 J. Bowyer Bell, *The IRA 1968–2000: Analysis of a Secret Army* (London and Portland: Frank Cass, 2000), 85.
2 Patrick Bishop and Eamonn Mallie, *The Provisional IRA* (London: Heinemann, 1987), 217.
3 Marie-Therese Fay, Mike Morrissey, and Marie Smyth, *Northern Ireland's Troubles: The Human Costs* (London and Sterling: Pluto Press, 1999), 51.
4 Charles Townshend, *Ireland: The 20th Century* (London, Sydney, Auckland: Arnold, 1998), 76. Estimates of the rebels' total strength range from a low of 700 to a high of 1,600. See: Joseph M. Curran, *The Birth of the Irish Free State 1921–1923* (University: The University of Alabama Press, 1980), 11; Charles Duff, *Six Days to Shake an Empire* (London: J.M. Dent & Sons, 1966), 97.
5 The most incendiary of the British Government actions were: the execution of 16 of the rebels; the deportation of thousands of suspected insurgents to England; and a number of extra-judicial killings that took place during the uprising. For more detail, see: Joost Augusteijn, *From Public Defiance to Guerrilla Warfare: The Experience of Ordinary Volunteers in the Irish War of Independence 1916–1921* (Dublin: Irish Academic Press, 1996), 55; William H. Kautt, *The Anglo-Irish War, 1916–1921: A People's War* (Westport and London: Praeger, 1999), 47–52; Charles Townshend, *Easter 1916: The Irish Rebellion* (London: Penguin Books, 2006), 301–310.
6 Nicholas Whyte, 'The Irish Election of 1918', Northern Ireland Elections, www.ark.ac.uk/elections/h1918.htm.
7 Tim Pat Coogan, *The I.R.A.*, Revised edn. (London: HarperCollins Publishers, 2000), 25–27; Kautt, *The Anglo-Irish War, 1916–1921*, 70–71, Townshend, *Ireland*, 88–89.
8 Michael Hopkinson, *Green against Green: The Irish Civil War* (Dublin: Gill and Macmillan, 1988), 9.
9 Richard English, *Armed Struggle: The History of the IRA* (New York: Oxford University Press, 2003), 31.
10 Coogan, *The I.R.A.*, 29; Townshend, *Ireland*, 116. It is important to note that '[r]eliable casualty figures for the civil war do not exist' and some authors estimate up to 5,000 people were killed. Curran, *The Birth of the Irish Free State 1921–1923*, 276.
11 D. George Boyce, *Nationalism in Ireland*, Third edn. (London and New York: Routledge, 1995), 270–271.

12 David Burnett, 'The Modernisation of Unionism, 1892–1914?', in *Unionism in Modern Ireland: New Perspectives on Politics and Culture*, ed. Richard English and Graham Walker (London: Macmillan Press, 1996), 41.
13 D. George Boyce, 'Weary Patriots: Ireland and the Making of Unionism', in *Defenders of the Union: A Survey of British and Irish Unionism since 1801*, ed. D. George Boyce and Alan O'Day (London and New York: Routledge, 2001), 26; Thomas Hennessey, *A History of Northern Ireland 1920–1996* (New York: St. Martin's Press, 1997), 2–3; Joseph Ruane and Jennifer Todd, *The Dynamics of Conflict in Northern Ireland: Power, Conflict, and Emancipation* (Cambridge: Cambridge University Press, 1996), 88–89.
14 Alvin Jackson, 'Irish Unionism, 1870–1922', in *Defenders of the Union: A Survey of British and Irish Unionism since 1801*, ed. D. George Boyce and Alan O'Day (London and New York: Routledge, 2001), 115; J.C. Beckett, 'Northern Ireland', *Journal of Contemporary History* 6, no. 1 (1971): 124.
15 Burnett, 'The Modernisation of Unionism, 1892–1914?', 41.
16 Ibid, Hennessey, *A History of Northern Ireland 1920–1996*, 4; Alan O'Day, 'Defending the Union: Parliamentary Options, 1869 and 1886', in *Defenders of the Union: A Survey of British and Irish Unionism since 1801*, ed. D. George Boyce and Alan O'Day (London and New York: Routledge, 2001), 105–107.
17 Ian McBride, 'Ulster and the British Problem', in *Unionism in Modern Ireland: New Perspectives on Politics and Culture*, ed. Richard English and Graham Walker (London: Macmillan Press, 1996), 6–7; Beckett, 'Northern Ireland', 123.
18 'Anglo-Irish Treaty, 6 December 1921', The National Archive of Ireland, www.nationalarchives.ie/topics/anglo_irish/dfaexhib2.html.
19 Feargal Cochrane, *Unionist Politics and the Politics of Unionism since the Anglo-Irish Agreement* (Cork: Cork University Press, 1997), 38.
20 Beckett, 'Northern Ireland', 128–129; Brendan O'Leary and John McGarry, *The Politics of Antagonism: Understanding Northern Ireland*, Second edn. (London and Atlantic Highlands: The Athlone Press, 1996), 135–139; Townshend, *Ireland*, 189.
21 Townshend, *Ireland*, 189.
22 de Valera was officially President of the Executive Council from 1932 to 1937, and Taoiseach from 1937 to 1948. Both positions are the equivalent of a Prime Minister.
23 'Bunreacht Na Héireann – Constitution of Ireland, 1937', Conflict Archive on the Internet (CAIN), www.cain.ulst.ac.uk/issues/politics/docs/coi37a.htm.
24 O'Leary and McGarry, *The Politics of Antagonism*, 136.
25 Paul Dixon, *Northern Ireland: The Politics of War and Peace* (Houndsmill and New York: Palgrave, 2001), 52; O'Leary and McGarry, *The Politics*, 139.
26 Beckett, 'Northern Ireland', 129.
27 O'Leary and McGarry, *The Politics of Antagonism*, 120; Townshend, *Ireland*, 189–190.
28 'Disturbances in Northern Ireland: Report of the Commission Appointed by the Governor of Northern Ireland', (Belfast: Her Majesty's Stationery Office, 1969), para. 134.
29 Dixon, *Northern Ireland*, 51.
30 Ruane and Todd, *The Dynamics of Conflict in Northern Ireland*, 120.
31 Ibid., 122.
32 Hennessey, *A History of Northern Ireland 1920–1996*, 46.
33 Ruane and Todd, *The Dynamics of Conflict in Northern Ireland*, 124–126; Townshend, *Ireland*, 199–201.
34 Ibid., 126–127; Hennessey, *A History of Northern Ireland 1920–1996*, 126–138.
35 After the DHAC and NICRA had announced their plans to march on 5 October 1968, the Apprentice Boys of Derry, a unionist group, declared that they would be marching on the same day, at the same time, along the same route. This was a favoured tactic by unionists to frustrate civil rights marches, since the authorities were required to ban marches if there was a reasonable prospect of intra-communal violence.

36 For an account of the events associated with the 5 October 1968 march, see: 'Distur-bances in Northern Ireland', para. 37–55; Niall Ó Dochartaigh, *From Civil Rights to Armalites: Derry and the Birth of the Irish Troubles* (Cork: Cork University Press, 1997), 20–21.

37 Ó Dochartaigh, *From Civil Rights to Armalites*, 119–130.

38 Peter Taylor, *Provos: The IRA and Sinn Fein* (London: Bloomsbury, 1997), 53; Ruane and Todd, *The Dynamics of Conflict in Northern Ireland*, 129.

39 J. Bowyer Bell, *The Secret Army: The IRA*, Third edn. (New Brunswick and London: Transaction Publishers, 1997), 48–53; Coogan, *The I.R.A.*, 44–45; English, *Armed Struggle*, 42–43.

40 J. McGarrity (pseudonym), cited in: M.L.R. Smith, *Fighting for Ireland? The Mili-tary Strategy of the Irish Republican Movement* (London and New York: Routledge, 1995), 67.

41 Ibid., 68–71; Coogan, *The I.R.A.*, 297–329; Bell, *The Secret Army*, 289–309.

42 Bishop and Mallie, *The Provisional IRA*, 32; Tony Geraghty, *The Irish War: The Hidden Conflict between the IRA and British Intelligence* (Baltimore and London: The Johns Hopkins University Press, 2000), 3.

43 English, *Armed Struggle*, 94; Kevin J. Kelley, *The Longest War: Northern Ireland and the IRA*, New ed. (London: Zed Books, 1988), 126–127.

44 English, *Armed Struggle*, 84.

45 Kelley, *The Longest War*, 121–122.

46 Ed Moloney, *A Secret History of the IRA* (New York and London: W.W. Norton & Company, 2002), 68.

47 English, *Armed Struggle*, 106.

48 It is important to note that, although the Belfast Agreement is commonly used as an end-date of The Troubles, violence persisted in Northern Ireland after April 1998. Indeed, one of the bloodiest attacks in the six counties occurred on 15 August 1998, when a Real Irish Republican Army (RIRA) bomb killed 29 people. Rather than being seen as the end of violence in Northern Ireland, the Belfast Agreement should be conceptualised as the point at which the Northern Ireland conflict transformed. That is, from an extended period of organised, insurgent conflict, to a period of war-lordism and (generally) low-level sectarian attacks. Neil Jarman, 'From War to Peace? Changing Patterns of Violence in Northern Ireland, 1990–2003', *Terrorism and Political Violence* 16, no. 3 (2004).

49 PSNI, 'Casualties as a Result of Paramilitary-Style Attacks, 1973–2005', Statistics Branch, www.psni.police.uk/persons_injured_cy-21.doc; Malcolm Sutton, 'An Index of Deaths from the Conflict in Ireland', Conflict Archive on the Internet (CAIN), www.cain.ulst.ac.uk/sutton/index.html.

50 Bernadette C. Hayes and Ian McAllister, 'Sowing Dragon's Teeth: Public Support for Political Violence and Paramilitarism in Northern Ireland', *Political Studies* 49 (2001): 901.

51 Extracts from the IRA's 1923 constitution that outlined the organisation's structure can be found at: Coogan, *The I.R.A.*, 42–44.

52 Bell, *The IRA*, 126.

53 Bishop and Mallie, *The Provisional IRA*, 21.

54 Taylor, *Provos*, 17.

55 PIRA, 'No Opportunity Will Be Lost: Army Council's Easter Message', *An Phoblacht* 1, no. 3 (1970): 1.

56 Tone, 1798, cited in: Frank Charles MacDermot, *Theobald Wolfe Tone: A Biograph-ical Study* (London: Macmillan, 1939), 296. Tone is generally considered as one of the 'fathers' of Republicanism, and was heavily promoted by both the IRA and PIRA.

57 For an overview of the colonial argument in Republican thinking, see: Smith, *Fight-ing for Ireland?*, 6–9.

58 PIRA, 'Our Aims and Methods', *An Phoblacht* 1, no. 2 (1970): 8.

59 Ibid.

60 PIRA, 'Dole Queus [*Sic*], Guns, Unemployment, Talks and Handouts', *An Phoblacht* 1, no. 6 (1971): 7.

61 Smith, *Fighting for Ireland?*, 7. See also: Joanne Wright, *Terrorist Propaganda: The Red Army Faction and the Provisional IRA, 1968–86* (Basingstoke and London: Macmillan, 1991), 53–54; Garrett O'Boyle, 'Theories of Justification and Political Violence: Examples from Four Groups', *Terrorism and Political Violence* 14, no. 2 (2002): 30.

62 As Kelley states, the 'nationalist people of Northern Ireland did not usually welcome the sight of a British army uniform, especially in their own neighbourhoods. Now, however, the soldiers were viewed less as agents of an occupying power, than as a comparatively benign alternative to the R.U.C. and B-Specials'. Kelley, *The Longest War*, 121.

63 PIRA, 'Army of Occupation', *Republican News* 1, no. 7 (1971): 7.

64 PIRA, 'Another Victim of British Rule', *Republican News* 1, no. 3 (1970): 3. See also: PIRA, '"Para" Security', *An Phoblacht* 6, no. 37 (1975): 1, PIRA, 'British Army Murders', *An Phoblacht* 5, no. 11 (1974): 8.

65 PIRA, 'Terror in Belfast', *Republican News* 1, no. 8 (1971): 1. The PIRA also frequently referred to the British Army's alleged open and derogatory attitude towards 'paddys'. For instance, see: PIRA, '"I Hate Paddys"', *Republican News* 1, no. 8 (1971): 10.

66 For example, see: PIRA, 'Revolt in the North', *An Phoblacht* 1, no. 9 (1971): 1, PIRA, 'The North Raped', *Republican News* 2, no. 3 (1971): 1,12, PIRA, 'We Repeat – Don't Fraternise!', *Republican News* 1, no. 11 (1971): 1.

67 PIRA, 'Civil Rights', *An Phoblacht* 1, no. 1 (1970): 2, PIRA, 'Fermanagh 1970 … And How It Was Maintained', *An Phoblacht* 1, no. 5 (1970): 5, PIRA, 'The IRA – Justified', *An Phoblacht* 3, no. 6 (1972): 7.

68 PIRA, 'British Murder Gangs Step-up Campaign', *Republican News* 2, no. 72 (1973).

69 PIRA, 1974, cited in: Smith, *Fighting for Ireland?*, 118.

70 O'Boyle, 'Theories of Justification and Political Violence', 30.

71 Bishop and Mallie, *The Provisional IRA*, 166.

72 English, *Armed Struggle*, 84, Sean Cronin, *Irish Nationalism: A History of Its Roots and Ideology* (Dublin: The Academy Press, 1980), 202.

73 Wright, *Terrorist Propaganda*, 61–65.

74 PIRA, 'The Price of Freedom', *Republican News* 2, no. 11 (1971): 4, PIRA, 'Our Aims and Methods', 8.

75 PIRA, 'And What Shall I Do Now?', *Republican News* 1, no. 9 (1971): 12.

76 Andrew Garfield, 'PIRA Lessons Learned: A Model of Terrorist Leadership Succession', *Low Intensity Conflict & Law Enforcement* 11, no. 2/3 (2002): 278.

77 Taylor, *Provos*, 77.

78 Sean MacStiofain, *Memoirs of a Revolutionary* (Edinburgh: Gordon Cremonesi, 1975), 146.

79 PIRA, 'Will Defend Irish People: The IRA Answers Belfast CCDC', *An Phoblacht* 1, no. 11 (1970): 8.

80 Smith, *Fighting for Ireland?*, 97.

81 For more information on 'shock and awe', see: Harlan K. Ullman and James P. Wade, *Shock and Awe: Achieving Rapid Dominance* (Washington, D.C.: National Defense University Press, 1996).

82 Smith, *Fighting for Ireland?*, 97.

83 PIRA, 'The IRA – Justified', 7.

84 PIRA, 'The Question of Physical Force', *Republican News* 2, no. 71 (1973): 5.

85 PIRA, 'The IRA – Justified', 6.

86 Ibid.
87 Wright, *Terrorist Propaganda*, 55.
88 Smith, *Fighting for Ireland?*, 15.
89 Cronin, *Irish Nationalism*, 1.
90 Maria McGuire, *To Take up Arms: A Year in the Provisional IRA* (London: Macmillan, 1973), 74–75.
91 PIRA, 'The Question of Physical Force', 5.
92 PIRA, 'The IRA – Justified', 6.
93 Ibid.
94 PIRA, 'Guerrilla War a Legitimate Political Tactic', *An Phoblacht* 5, no. 27 (1974): 7.
95 Ibid.
96 PIRA, 'Victory in Sight', *Republican News* 2, no. 11 (1971): 12.
97 PIRA, '1972: The Year of Victory', *Republican News* 2, no. 18 (1972): 1.
98 PIRA, 'The Final Phase', *An Phoblacht* 5, no. 15 (1974): 1.
99 PIRA, 1977, cited in: Smith, *Fighting for Ireland?*, 135.
100 Rogelio Alonso, 'The Modernization in Irish Republican Thinking toward the Utility of Violence', *Studies in Conflict and Terrorism* 24, no. 2 (2001): 132.
101 PIRA, 'British Terrorists Murder Six Catholics: Hierarchy Condemns the IRA', *Republican News* 2, no. 10 (1971): 1.
102 PIRA, 'Our View', *Republican News* 2, no. 4 (1971): 1. Edward Heath was the Prime Minister of the United Kingdom from 1970 to 1974. James Wilson was the Prime Minster of the United Kingdom from 1964 to 1970 and from 1974 to 1976.
103 PIRA, 'Get Off the Fence', *Republican News* 1, no. 8 (1971): 10.
104 Frank Burton, *The Politics of Legitimacy: Struggles in a Belfast Community* (London, Henley and Boston: Routledge and Kegan Paul, 1978), 90–91; Wright, *Terrorist Propaganda*, 52; O'Boyle, 'Theories of Justification and Political Violence', 30.
105 It is important to note the difficulties associated with ascertaining Sinn Féin's level of popular support at the 1918 general election. Although the party won 69.5 per cent of Ireland's seats in Westminster, it only received 46.9 per cent of the total vote. However, this latter percentage likely undervalues Sinn Féin's actual public support in 1918, given that the party won 25 of its 73 seats unopposed (thus depressing its vote). According to Whyte, if one assumes that Sinn Féin would have received a similar proportion of votes in its unopposed electorates as it received in its contested electorates, then the party would have likely won 53 per cent of the total vote. See: Whyte, 'The Irish Election of 1918'.
106 Leslie Macfarlance, 'The Right to Self-Determination in Ireland and the Justification of IRA Violence', *Terrorism and Political Violence* 2, no. 1 (1990): 38–39.
107 Moloney, *A Secret History of the IRA*, 80.
108 Cited in: Robert W. White, *Provisional Irish Republicans: An Oral and Interpretive History* (Westport and London: Greenwood Press, 1993), 38.
109 Bell, *The IRA*, 80–83.
110 English, *Armed Struggle*, 120–124; Moloney, *A Secret History of the IRA*, 80; White, *Provisional Irish Republicans*, 89–93.
111 White, *Provisional Irish Republicans*, 103.
112 Ibid., 104–108.
113 Taylor, *Provos*, 71.
114 White, *Provisional Irish Republicans*, 106.
115 Ibid., 107–108.
116 Sydney Elliott and W.D. Flackes, *Conflict in Northern Ireland: An Encyclopedia* (Santa Barbara, Denver and Oxford: ABC-CLIO, 1999), 606.
117 Ibid., 607.
118 The Northern Ireland Assembly was suspended on 14 October 2002 after the arrest

of three Sinn Féin party members. It was formally dissolved on 28 April 2003 with an election in November 2003. The Northern Ireland Act 2006 created a non-legislative fixed-term Assembly. Its remit was to prepare for devolved government and a fully restored Assembly. Devolution was restored on 8 May 2007.

119 Elliott and Flackes, *Conflict in Northern Ireland*, 648.

120 Peter R. Neumann, *Britain's Long War: British Strategy in the Northern Ireland Conflict, 1969–98* (Houndmills and New York: Palgrave Macmillan, 2003), 190.

121 For a list of the tour of duties of all British Army units that served in Northern Ireland during the 1970s, see: Michael Dewar, *The British Army in Northern Ireland* (London: Arms and Armour Press, 1985), 255–264.

122 Peter Taylor, *Brits: The War against the IRA* (London: Bloomsbury, 2002), 190.

123 Cynthia H. Enloe, 'Police and Military in Ulster: Peacekeeping or Peace-Subverting Forces?', *Journal of Peace Research* 15, no. 3 (1978): 250.

124 Chris Ryder, *The RUC 1922–1997: A Force under Fire*, Revised ed. (London: Mandarin, 1997), 115–116. Callaghan was acting on the recommendations of Lord Hunt, whose report on the RUC was published in October 1969.

125 Neumann, *Britain's Long War*, 109; Enloe, 'Police and Military in Ulster', 251–253.

126 Neumann, *Britain's Long War*, 81–82; Desmond Hamill, *Pig in the Middle: The Army in Northern Ireland 1969–1984* (London: Methuen London, 1985), 154, 217.

127 For more information on the establishment of the USC, see: Michael Farrell, *Arming the Protestants: The Formation of the Ulster Special Constabulary and the Royal Ulster Constabulary 1920–27* (London and Sydney: Pluto Press, 1983), 30–54; Arthur Hezlet, *The 'B' Specials: A History of the Ulster Special Constabulary* (London: Tom Stacey, 1973), 1–26.

128 Elliott and Flackes, *Conflict in Northern Ireland*, 656.

129 Ryder, *The RUC 1922–1997*, 57.

130 Bell, *The Secret Army*, 302–303.

131 Kelley, *The Longest War*, 153.

132 R.J. Spjut, 'Internment and Detention without Trial in Northern Ireland 1971–1975: Ministerial Policy and Practice', *Modern Law Review* 49 (1986): 716; John E. Finn, *Constitutions in Crisis: Political Violence and the Rule of Law* (New York and Oxford: Oxford University Press, 1991), 69.

133 W.D. Flackes, *Northern Ireland: A Political Directory 1968–79* (New York: St. Martin's Press, 1980), 99; English, *Armed Struggle*, 139, Bishop and Mallie, *The Provisional IRA*, 144.

134 Spjut, 'Internment and Detention without Trial in Northern Ireland 1971–1975', 740.

135 As Bell notes, the PIRA 'did not feel the need for membership rolls'; and former-Volunteers generally exhibit a reluctance to talk in detail about the organisation's recruitment. Bell, *The IRA*, 130.

136 An anonymous member of the IRA, cited by: Moloney, *A Secret History of the IRA*, 90.

137 Gerry Adams, *The Politics of Irish Freedom* (Dingle: Brandon Books, 1986), 55. Bell supports Adams' observation, noting that 'IRA recruiting soared' in the aftermath of the 'Rape of the Falls'. See: Bell, *The Secret Army*, 377.

138 English, *Armed Struggle*, 140; Smith, *Fighting for Ireland?*, 101.

139 Taylor, *Provos*, 126–127. In the immediate aftermath of the killings, the British Government established an inquiry under the Lord Chief Justice, Lord Widgery, to investigate the events of 30 January 1972. His report, published 11 weeks after 'Bloody Sunday', essentially upheld the British Army's assertion that the Parachute Regiment had been fired on first, and that the soldiers were shooting primarily at armed paramilitaries.

140 Bell, *The IRA*, 77, Bell, *The Secret Army*, 374; Dewar, *The British Army in Northern*

Ireland, 47. Though, it is important to note that both English and Kelley estimate the PIRA's strength at 1,000 strong in mid-1970. See: Kelley, *The Longest War*, 13; English, *Armed Struggle*, 114.

141 Bell, *The Secret Army*, 364; Moloney, *A Secret History of the IRA*, 103; Smith, *Fighting for Ireland?*, 92.

142 Keith Jeffery, 'The British Army and Ireland since 1922', in *A Military History of Ireland*, ed. Thomas Bartlett and Keith Jeffery (Cambridge: Cambridge University Press, 1996), 452.

143 Sutton, 'An Index of Deaths from the Conflict in Ireland'.

144 According to Smith, 'The year 1972 was the simultaneous zenith and nadir of the IRA's campaign. It was at this time that the IRA reached its potentially most powerful position in the conflict'. See: M.L.R. Smith, 'Fin De Siecle, 1972: The Provisional IRA's Strategy and the Beginning of the Eight-Thousand-Day Stalemate', in *Political Violence in Northern Ireland: Conflict and Conflict Resolution*, ed. Alan O'Day (Westport: Praeger, 1997), 30.

145 Sutton, 'An Index of Deaths from the Conflict in Ireland'; Hennessey, *A History of Northern Ireland 1920–1996*, 212.

146 Smith, 'Fin De Siecle, 1972', 28.

147 Neumann, *Britain's Long War*, 51–52, 78–80.

148 Smith, *Fighting for Ireland?*, 110.

149 Neumann, *Britain's Long War*, 79.

150 Ibid.

151 Kelley, *The Longest War*, 184.

152 Bishop and Mallie, *The Provisional IRA*, 181.

153 Bell, *The IRA*, 84.

154 Bell, *The Secret Army*, 394; Charles Drake, 'The Provisional IRA: Reorganisation and the Long War', in *Terrorism's Laboratory: The Case of Northern Ireland*, ed. Alan O'Day (Aldershot: Dartmouth, 1995), 89; Smith, *Fighting for Ireland?*, 133; Taylor, *Provos*, 173–175; Kelley, *The Longest War*, 235.

155 Bishop and Mallie, *The Provisional IRA*, 218.

156 Ibid.

157 Cited in: Taylor, *Provos*, 213.

158 Over both periods, the PIRA lost an average of three Volunteers every two months. See: Sutton, 'An Index of Deaths from the Conflict in Ireland'.

159 Taylor, *Brits*, 153.

160 Moloney, *A Secret History of the IRA*, 128.

161 Bishop and Mallie, *The Provisional IRA*, 192.

162 Ibid., 188.

163 Cited in: Taylor, *Brits*, 172.

164 Flackes, *Northern Ireland*, 117.

165 Cited in: Laurence McKeown, *Out of Time: Irish Republican Prisoners, Long Kesh 1972–2000* (Belfast: Beyond the Pale, 2001), 53.

166 Drake, 'The Provisional IRA', 89.

167 Tommy McKearney, cited in: Taylor, *Provos*, 213.

168 Kelley, *The Longest War*, 285.

169 PSNI, 'Security-Related Incidents, 1969–2005', Statistics Branch, www.psni.police.uk/security_related_incidents_cy-18.doc.

170 Sutton, 'An Index of Deaths from the Conflict in Ireland'.

171 Moloney, *A Secret History of the IRA*, 149.

172 Ibid.

173 Ibid., 150; Smith, *Fighting for Ireland?*, 148; English, *Armed Struggle*, 216–218.

174 Smith, *Fighting for Ireland?*, 154.

175 PIRA, 'Extracts of the "Staff Report"', in *The I.R.A.*, ed. Tim Pat Coogan (London: HarperCollins Publishers, 2000), 467.

176 Jimmy Drumm, 1977, cited in: Gerry Adams, *Before the Dawn: An Autobiography* (London: Heinemann, 1996), 265.

177 PIRA, 'Extracts of the "Staff Report"', 467.

178 Smith, *Fighting for Ireland?*, 145.

179 James M. Glover, 'Appendix Xviii – Northern Ireland: Future Terrorist Trends (2 November 1978)', in *Irish Nationalism: A History of Its Roots and Ideology*, ed. Sean Cronin (Dublin: The Academy Press, 1980), 342.

180 Charles Drake, 'The Provisional IRA: A Case Study', *Terrorism and Political Violence* 3, no. 1 (1991): 54; Bell, *The IRA*, 90–93; Wayne G. Reilly, 'The Management of Political Violence in Quebec and Northern Ireland: A Comparison', *Terrorism and Political Violence* 6, no. 1 (1994): 57.

181 Estimates of the PIRA's strength since the late-1970s vary, but generally fall around the 300 range. The remainder of this note will provide a selection of estimates; stating the author's name, the relevant time period, and the approximate number of volunteers. References will be outlined after the estimates. Glover, 1978, 310; Smith, late-1970s, 300; Sluka, early-1980s, 250–300; Thomas, 1985, 300; English, mid-1980s, 'between 200 and 300'; Drake, mid-1980s to mid-1990s, 'between 200 and 600'; Wright, late-1980s, 100–200; Freeman, 1990s, 300. See: Drake, 'The Provisional IRA', 94; English, *Armed Struggle*, 344; Glover, 'Future Terrorist Trends', 343–344; Smith, *Fighting for Ireland?*, 145; Wright, *Terrorist Propaganda*, 221; Michael Freeman, *Freedom or Security: The Consequences for Democracies Using Emergency Powers to Fight Terror* (Westport and London: Praeger, 2003), 64; Jeffrey A. Sluka, *Hearts and Minds, Water and Fish: Support for the IRA and INLA in a Northern Ireland Ghetto* (Greenwich, CT: JAI Press, 1989), 63; Jo Thomas, 'The Agony of Ulster', *New York Times*, 10 March 1985, 6.

182 Bell, *The IRA*, 85.

183 Bishop and Mallie, *The Provisional IRA*, 254.

184 Smith, *Fighting for Ireland?*, 145.

185 Kelley, *The Longest War*, 262.

186 Bishop and Mallie, *The Provisional IRA*, 217; English, *Armed Struggle*, 212; Taylor, *Provos*, 198–199; Moloney, *A Secret History of the IRA*, 150.

187 Smith, *Fighting for Ireland?*, 145.

188 Taylor, *Provos*, 210.

189 PIRA, 'Extracts of the "'Staff Report"'', 465–467.

190 Ibid., 467.

191 Bradley W.C. Bamford, 'The Role and Effectiveness of Intelligence in Northern Ireland', *Intelligence and National Security* 20, no. 4 (2005): 586; David A. Charters, 'Intelligence and Psychological Warfare Operations in Northern Ireland', *RUSI Journal* 122, no. 3 (1977): 23; Keith Jeffery, 'Security Policy in Northern Ireland: Some Reflections on the Management of Violent Conflict', *Terrorism and Political Violence* 2, no. 1 (1990): 26–27.

192 Jeffery, 'Security Policy in Northern Ireland', 26.

193 Charters, 'Intelligence and Psychological Warfare Operations in Northern Ireland', 23.

194 Geraghty, *The Irish War*, 13; Hamill, *Pig in the Middle*, 51–52; Jeffery, 'Security Policy in Northern Ireland', 27.

195 Jeffery, 'Security Policy in Northern Ireland', 26.

196 Ibid; Hamill, *Pig in the Middle*, 52; Geraghty, *The Irish War*, 136.

197 Charters, 'Intelligence and Psychological Warfare Operations in Northern Ireland', 23; Bamford, 'The Role and Effectiveness of Intelligence in Northern Ireland', 586.

198 Martin Dillon, *The Dirty War: Covert Strategies and Tactics Used in Political Conflicts* (New York: Routledge, 1990), 26–42.

199 Taylor, *Brits*, 132.

200 Neumann, *Britain's Long War*, 78.

201 Michael Addison, *Violent Politics: Strategies of Internal Conflict* (Basingstoke and New York: Palgrave, 2002), 99.

202 Adams, *Before the Dawn*, 211.

203 Bishop and Mallie, *The Provisional IRA*, 187; Hamill, *Pig in the Middle*, 121, 33.

204 Taylor, *Brits*, 144; Steven Greer, *Supergrasses: A Study in Anti-Terrorist Law Enforcement in Northern Ireland* (Oxford: Clarendon Press, 1995), 34.

205 Geraghty, *The Irish War*, 139–140.

206 Taylor, *Brits*, 144.

207 Bamford, 'The Role and Effectiveness of Intelligence in Northern Ireland', 591.

208 Coogan, *The I.R.A.*, 465.

209 Drake, 'The Provisional IRA', 91; Kelley, *The Longest War*, 283–284.

210 Smith, *Fighting for Ireland?*, 133.

211 For more information, see: Amnesty International, 'Northern Ireland: Report of an Amnesty International Mission to Northern Ireland', (London: Amnesty International, 1978); Ryder, *The RUC*, 187–225; Peter Taylor, *Beating the Terrorists? Interrogation in Omagh, Gough and Castlereagh* (Harmondsworth: Penguin, 1980).

212 Taylor, *Brits*, 201.

213 PIRA, 'Extracts of the "Staff Report"', 465.

214 Cited in: Moloney, *A Secret History of the IRA*, 154–155. According to Hogan and Taylor, 'it was not an infrequent event for a PIRA Volunteer ... to implicate up to 12 men, and in one case 35'. John Hogan and Max Taylor, 'The Provisional Irish Republican Army: Command and Functional Structure', *Terrorism and Political Violence* 9, no. 3 (1997): 21.

215 PIRA, 'Extracts of the "Staff Report"', 466.

216 Ibid.

217 Drake, 'The Provisional IRA', 91.

218 Bishop and Mallie, *The Provisional IRA*, 256.

219 Drake, 'The Provisional IRA', 91.

220 Taylor, *Provos*, 211.

221 Bamford, 'The Role and Effectiveness of Intelligence in Northern Ireland', 591; Bishop and Mallie, *The Provisional IRA*, 256; Hamill, *Pig in the Middle*, 235–236; Hogan and Taylor, 'The Provisional Irish Republican Army', 21; Smith, *Fighting for Ireland?*, 145; Kelley, *The Longest War*, 285.

222 Coogan, *The I.R.A.*, 551.

223 PIRA, 'Extracts of the "Staff Report"', 465.

224 PIRA, 'Extracts from the "Green Book"', in *The I.R.A.*, ed. Tim Pat Coogan (London: HarperCollins Publishers, 2000), 545.

225 Ibid., 546–547.

226 Ibid.

227 Ibid., 560–567.

228 Kiran Sarma, 'Informers and the Battle against Republican Terrorism: A Review of 30 Years of Conflict', *Police Practice and Research* 6, no. 2 (2005): 173.

229 PIRA, 'Extracts from the "Green Book"', 560–567.

230 Moloney, *A Secret History of the IRA*, 155, English, *Armed Struggle*, 213.

231 Sarma, 'Informers and the Battle against Republican Terrorism', 172.

232 Kelley, *The Longest War*, 285.

233 Sarma, 'Informers and the Battle against Republican Terrorism', 172–173.

234 Laura K. Donohue, 'Regulating Northern Ireland: The Special Powers Acts, 1922–1972', *The Historical Journal* 41, no. 4 (1998): 1090–1091.

235 'Civil Authorities (Special Powers) Act (Northern Ireland), 1922', Conflict Archive on the Internet (CAIN), www.cain.ulst.ac.uk/hmso/spa1922.htm.

236 A key document in this regard is the Diplock Report, which the British Government commissioned in October 1972 to consider 'what arrangements for the administration of justice in Northern Ireland could be made in order to deal more effectively

with terrorist organisations … otherwise than by Internment'. 'Report of the Commission to Consider Legal Procedures to Deal with Terrorist Activities in Northern Ireland (Diplock Report)', (London: Her Majesty's Stationery Office, 1972), para. 1. The recommendations of the Diplock Report eventually formed the basis of the Emergency Provisions Act.

237   Laura K. Donohue, 'Civil Liberties, Terrorism, and Liberal Democracy: Lessons from the United Kingdom', in *BCSIA Discussion Paper 2000–05* (John F. Kennedy School of Government, Harvard University, 2000), 4; Gerard Hogan and Clive Walker, *Political Violence and the Law in Ireland* (Manchester and New York: Manchester University Press, 1989), 27.

238   Freeman, *Freedom or Security*, 59; Finn, *Constitutions in Crisis*, 88–89, 99–109.

239   Clive Walker, *The Prevention of Terrorism in British Law* (Manchester: Manchester University Press, 1986), 23.

240   Freeman, *Freedom or Security*, 59; Finn, *Constitutions in Crisis*, 119–125; 'Prevention of Terrorism (Temporary Provisions) Act', Conflict Archive on the Internet (CAIN), www.cain.ulst.ac.uk/hmso/pta1974.htm.

241   Spjut, 'Internment and Detention without Trial in Northern Ireland', 716.

242   Moloney, *A Secret History of the IRA*, 112; Smith, *Fighting for Ireland?*, 104.

243   Michael J. Cunningham, *British Government Policy in Northern Ireland, 1969–2000* (Manchester: Manchester University Press, 2001), 79; Neumann, *Britain's Long War*, 71.

244   Fionnuala McKenna, 'Referendum ("Border Poll") (Ni), Thursday 8 March 1973', Conflict Archive on the Internet (CAIN), www.cain.ulst.ac.uk/issues/politics/election/ref1973.htm.

245   Ruane and Todd, *The Dynamics of Conflict in Northern Ireland*, 158.

246   Both this figure and the subsequent are in 1992 prices.

247   Ruane and Todd, *The Dynamics of Conflict in Northern Ireland*, 158–159; Fionnuala McKenna and Martin Melaugh, 'Table NI-Eco-02: Subvention (£ Million) to Northern Ireland from the United Kingdom, 1966–67 to 1992–93', Conflict Archive on the Internet (CAIN), www.cain.ulst.ac.uk/ni/economy.htm#02.

248   Ruane and Todd, *The Dynamics of Conflict in Northern Ireland*, 158–159; McKenna and Melaugh, 'Table NI-Eco-02'.

249   Sluka, *Hearts and Minds, Water and Fish*, 171.

250   Ibid., 172.

251   Spjut, 'Internment and Detention without Trial in Northern Ireland', 731.

252   For instance, the Diplock Report stated that the reintroduction of Internment in August 1971 'led to the arrest and detention of a number of persons against whom suspicion was founded on inadequate and inaccurate information'. 'Diplock Report', para. 15.

253   David R. Lowry, 'Internment: Detention without Trial in Northern Ireland', *Human Rights* 5, no. 3 (1976): 293; Spjut, 'Internment and Detention without Trial in Northern Ireland', 719.

254   Hogan and Walker, *Political Violence and the Law in Ireland*, 94.

255   Spjut, 'Internment and Detention without Trial in Northern Ireland', 722.

256   Lowry, 'Internment', 305.

257   White, *Provisional Irish Republicans*, 65, 171.

258   English, *Armed Struggle*, 123.

259   Burton, *The Politics of Legitimacy*, 85–88.

260   Sluka, *Hearts and Minds, Water and Fish*, 172.

261   Christopher Hewitt, 'Terrorism and Public Opinion: A Five Country Comparison', *Terrorism and Political Violence* 2, no. 2 (1990): 159–160.

262   Kelley, *The Longest War*, 199; Smith, *Fighting for Ireland?*, 136.

263   Bell, *The Secret Army*, 428–430; Bishop and Mallie, *The Provisional IRA*, 228–230; Brendan Lynn, 'Tactic or Principle? The Evolution of Republican Thinking on Abstentionism in Ireland, 1970–1998', *Irish Political Studies* 17, no. 2 (2002): 77.

264 The three children were killed (and their mother, Anne Maguire, seriously injured) on 10 August 1976 after they were hit by an out-of-control car; the driver of which (Danny Lennon, a member of the PIRA) had moments earlier been shot and killed by a British Army patrol in pursuit.

265 Bishop and Mallie, *The Provisional IRA*, 229.

266 Bell, *The Secret Army*, 429; Bishop and Mallie, *The Provisional IRA*, 229; Kelley, *The Longest War*, 254; Lynn, 'Tactic or Principle?', 77.

267 Smith, *Fighting for Ireland?*, 147.

6 Conclusion

1 Astrid Arraras, 'Armed Struggle, Political Learning and Participation in Democracy: The Case of the Tupamaros' (PhD, Princeton University, 1999), 219.

2 Patrick Bishop and Eamonn Mallie, *The Provisional IRA* (London: Heinemann, 1987), 254.

3 R.J. Spjut, 'Internment and Detention without Trial in Northern Ireland 1971–1975: Ministerial Policy and Practice', *Modern Law Review* 49 (1986): 731.

4 For information on the relationship between repression and protest participation, see: Jennifer Earl, 'Introduction: Repression and the Social Control of Protest', *Mobilization: An International Quarterly* 11, no. 2 (2006): 134–135; Mark Irving Lichbach, 'Deterrence or Escalation? The Puzzle of Aggregate Studies of Repression and Dissent', *The Journal of Conflict Resolution* 31, no. 2 (1987).

5 Peter R. Neumann, 'Europe's Jihadist Dilemma', *Survival* 48, no. 2 (2006).

6 Xavier Raufer, 'Al Qaeda: A Different Diagnosis', *Studies in Conflict and Terrorism* 26 (2003): 393–395; Jason Burke, *Al-Qaeda: Casting a Shadow of Terror* (London, New York: I.B. Tauris, 2003), 12–17; R.T. Naylor, *Wages of Crime: Black Markets, Illegal Finance, and the Underworld Economy*, Revised edn. (Ithaca: Cornell University Press, 2004), 290.

7 Marc Sageman, *Understanding Terror Networks* (Philadelphia: University of Pennsylvania Press, 2004), 107–109.

8 Daniel Benjamin and Steven Simon, *The Next Attack: The Failure of the War on Terror and a Strategy for Getting It Right* (New York: Owls Books, 2006), 23–25; Dafna Linzer and Walter Pincus, 'Intelligence Chief Pessimistic in Assessing Worldwide Threats', *Washington Post*, 12 January 2007, 12; Mark Mazzetti, 'New Generation of Qaeda Chiefs Is Seen on Rise', *New York Times*, 2 April 2007, 1.

9 Vittorio Bufacchi and Jean Maria Arrigo, 'Torture, Terrorism and the State: A Refutation of the Ticking-Bomb Argument', *Journal of Applied Philosophy* 23, no. 3 (2006): 361.

10 Mary Habeck, *Knowing the Enemy: Jihadist Ideology and the War on Terror* (New Haven: Yale University Press, 2006), 161–178.

References

Abuza, Zachary. 'Balik-Terrorism: The Return of the Abu Sayyaf'. Carlisle: Strategic Studies Institute, 2005.

Adams, Gerry. *Before the Dawn: An Autobiography*. London: Heinemann, 1996.

——. The Politics of Irish Freedom. Dingle: Brandon Books, 1986.

Addison, Michael. *Violent Politics: Strategies of Internal Conflict*. Basingstoke and New York: Palgrave, 2002.

Alexander, Martin S. and J.F.V. Keiger. 'France and the Algerian War: Strategy, Operations, and Diplomacy'. *Journal of Strategic Studies* 25, no. 2 (2002): 1–32.

Alonso, Rogelio. 'The Modernization in Irish Republican Thinking toward the Utility of Violence'. *Studies in Conflict and Terrorism* 24, no. 2 (2001): 131–144.

Amnesty International. 'Northern Ireland: Report of an Amnesty International Mission to Northern Ireland'. London: Amnesty International, 1978.

'Anglo-Irish Treaty, 6 December 1921'. The National Archive of Ireland, www.national archives.ie/topics/anglo_irish/dfaexhib2.html.

Anti-Terrorism Act (No. 2) 2005. 14 December.

Aquinas, Saint Thomas. *Summa Theologica*. Vol. 3. New York: Benziger Brothers, 1981.

Arraras, Astrid. 'Armed Struggle, Political Learning and Participation in Democracy: The Case of the Tupamaros'. PhD, Princeton University, 1999.

Assemblée nationale du Québec. 'An Act to Promote the French Language in Quebec'. In *Lois Du Quebec*, 61–63. Quebec City: Publications du Québec, 1969.

Atran, Scott. 'Mishandling Suicide Terrorism'. *The Washington Quarterly* 27, no. 3 (2004): 67–90.

Augusteijn, Joost. *From Public Defiance to Guerrilla Warfare: The Experience of Ordinary Volunteers in the Irish War of Independence 1916–1921*. Dublin: Irish Academic Press, 1996.

Aust, Stefan. *The Baader-Meinhof Group: The inside Story of a Phenomenon*. Translated by Anthea Bell. London: The Bodley Head, 1987.

Australian Security Intelligence Organisation Legislation Amendment (Terrorism) Act 2003. 22 July.

Bäck, Allan. 'Thinking Clearly About Violence'. *Philosophical Studies* 117, no. 1–2 (2004): 219–230.

Bain, George. 'The Making of a Crisis'. In *Power Corrupted: The October Crisis and the Repression of Quebec*, edited by Abraham Rotstein. Toronto: New Press, 1971.

Bamford, Bradley W.C. 'The Role and Effectiveness of Intelligence in Northern Ireland'. *Intelligence and National Security* 20, no. 4 (2005): 581–607.

Barahona de Brito, Alexandra. *Human Rights and Democratization in Latin America: Uruguay and Chile*. Oxford: Oxford University Press, 1997.

Baran, Zeyno. 'Fighting the War of Ideas'. *Foreign Affairs* 84, no. 6 (2005): 68–78.

Barkan, Steven E. and Lynne L. Snowden. *Collective Violence*. Boston: Allyn and Bacon, 2001.

Beaujot, Roderic, and Kevin McQuillan. *Growth and Dualism: The Demographic Development of Canadian Society*. Toronto: Gage Publishing, 1982.

Beckett, Ian F.W. *Modern Insurgencies and Counter-Insurgencies: Guerrillas and Their Opponents since 1750*. London and New York: Routledge, 2001.

Beckett, J.C. 'Northern Ireland'. *Journal of Contemporary History* 6, no. 1 (1971): 121–134.

Behiels, Michael D. *Prelude to Quebec's Quiet Revolution: Liberalism Versus Neo-Nationalism 1945–1960*. Kingston and Montreal: McGill-Queen's University Press, 1985.

Bélanger, Claude. 'Ultramontane Nationalism: 1840–1960'. Marianolpolis College, www2.marianopolis.edu/quebechistory/events/natpart3.htm.

Bell, J. Bowyer. *The IRA 1968–2000: Analysis of a Secret Army*. London and Portland: Frank Cass, 2000.

——. *The Secret Army: The IRA*. Third edn. New Brunswick and London: Transaction Publishers, 1997.

Bellamy, Alex J. 'No Pain, No Gain? Torture and Ethics in the War on Terror'. *International Affairs* 82, no. 1 (2006): 121–148.

Bender, Bryan. 'US Military Worried over Change in Iraq Attacks'. *The Boston Globe*, 24 April 2005, 1.

Benford, Robert D. 'You Could Be the Hundredth Monkey: Collective Action Frames and Vocabularies of Motive within the Nuclear Disarmament Movement'. *Sociological Quarterly* 34, no. 2 (1993): 195–216.

Benford, Robert D. and David A. Snow. 'Framing Processes and Social Movements: An Overview and Assessment'. *Annual Review of Sociology* no. 26 (2000): 611–639.

Benjamin, Daniel and Steven Simon. *The Next Attack: The Failure of the War on Terror and a Strategy for Getting It Right*. New York: Owls Books, 2006.

Biddle, Stephen D. 'American Grand Strategy after 9/11: An Assessment'. Carlisle: Strategic Studies Institute, 2005.

bin Laden, Osama. 'Fatwa against Americans, February 23, 1998'. In *Osama Bin Laden: America's Enemy in His Own Words*, edited by Randall B. Hamud, 60–63. San Diego: Nadeem Publishing, 2005.

Bishop, Patrick and Eamonn Mallie. *The Provisional IRA*. London: Heinemann, 1987.

Blaufarb, Douglas S. *The Counterinsurgency Era: U.S. Doctrine and Performance, 1950 to the Present*. New York: Free Press, 1977.

Bonenfant, Jean-C. and Jean-C. Falardeau. 'Cultural and Political Implications of French-Canadian Nationalism'. In *French-Canadian Nationalism: An Anthology*, edited by Ramsay Cook. Toronto: Macmillan of Canada, 1969.

Boyce, D. George. *Nationalism in Ireland*. Third edn. London and New York: Routledge, 1995.

——. 'Weary Patriots: Ireland and the Making of Unionism'. In *Defenders of the Union: A Survey of British and Irish Unionism since 1801*, edited by D. George Boyce and Alan O'Day, 15–38. London and New York: Routledge, 2001.

Brannon, Russell H. *The Agricultural Development of Uruguay: Problems of Government Policy*. New York, Washington, and London: Frederick A. Praeger Publishers, 1968.

Brockes, Jeremy P., Anoop Kumar, and Cristiana P. Velloso. 'Regeneration as an Evolutionary Variable'. *Journal of Anatomy* 199, no. 1–2 (2001): 3–11.

Bruce, Steve. *The Red Hand: Protestant Paramilitaries in Northern Ireland*. Oxford: Oxford University Press, 1992.

Brunet, Michel. 'Trois Dominantes De La Pensée Canadienne-Française: L'agriculturisme, L'anti-Étatisme Et Le Messianisme'. In *La Présence Anglaise Et Les Canadiens*, 113–166. Montréal: Beauchemin, 1964.

Brush, Stephen G. 'Dynamics of Theory Change in the Social Sciences: Relative Deprivation and Collective Violence'. *The Journal of Conflict Resolution* 40, no. 4 (1996): 523–545.

Bufacchi, Vittorio and Jean Maria Arrigo. 'Torture, Terrorism and the State: A Refutation of the Ticking-Bomb Argument'. *Journal of Applied Philosophy* 23, no. 3 (2006): 355–373.

'Bunreacht Na Héireann – Constitution of Ireland, 1937'. Conflict Archive on the Internet (CAIN), www.cain.ulst.ac.uk/issues/politics/docs/coi37a.htm.

Burke, Jason. *Al-Qaeda: Casting a Shadow of Terror*. London, New York: I.B. Tauris, 2003.

Burnett, David. 'The Modernisation of Unionism, 1892–1914?' In *Unionism in Modern Ireland: New Perspectives on Politics and Culture*, edited by Richard English and Graham Walker, 41–62. London: Macmillan Press, 1996.

Burton, Frank. *The Politics of Legitimacy: Struggles in a Belfast Community*. London, Henley and Boston: Routledge and Kegan Paul, 1978.

Bush, George W. *National Strategy for Combating Terrorism*. Washington, D.C.: Government Printing Office, 2006.

——. 'Press Conference of the President'. The White House, www.whitehouse.gov/news/releases/2005/12/20051219–2.html.

Byman, Daniel. 'Measuring the War on Terrorism: A First Appraisal'. *Current History* 102, no. 668 (2003): 411–416.

Cardinal, Linda. 'The Limits of Bilingualism in Canada'. *Nationalism and Ethnic Politics* 10, no. 1 (2004): 79–103.

Chalk, Peter. *West European Terrorism and Counter-Terrorism: The Evolving Dynamic*. Basingstoke and London: Macmillan Press Ltd., 1996.

Charters, David A. 'The Amateur Revolutionaries: A Reassessment of the FLQ'. *Terrorism and Political Violence* 9, no. 1 (1997): 133–169.

——. 'Intelligence and Psychological Warfare Operations in Northern Ireland'. *RUSI Journal* 122, no. 3 (1977): 22–27.

——. 'The October Crisis: Implications for Canada's Internal Security'. In *Terror*, edited by Brian MacDonald, 55–72. Toronto: The Canadian Institute of Strategic Studies, 1986.

Childs, Matt D. 'An Historical Critique of the Emergence and Evolution of Ernesto Che Guevara's Foco Theory'. *Journal of Latin American Studies* 27, no. 3 (1995): 593–624.

'Civil Authorities (Special Powers) Act (Northern Ireland), 1922'. Conflict Archive on the Internet (CAIN), www.cain.ulst.ac.uk/hmso/spa1922.htm.

Cochrane, Feargal. *Unionist Politics and the Politics of Unionism since the Anglo-Irish Agreement*. Cork: Cork University Press, 1997.

Cohen-Almagor, Raphael. 'The Terrorists' Best Ally: The Quebec Media Coverage of the FLQ Crisis in October 1970'. *Canadian Journal of Communication* 25, no. 2 (2000): 251–284.

Cohen, Ariel. 'Promoting Freedom and Democracy: Fighting the War of Ideas against Islamic Terrorism'. *Comparative Strategy* 22, no. 3 (2003): 207–221.

Coleman, William D. *The Independence Movement in Quebec 1945–1980.* Toronto, Buffalo, London: University of Toronto Press, 1984.

Commission of Inquiry Concerning Certain Activities of the Royal Canadian Mounted Police. 'Freedom and Security under the Law'. Ottawa: Canadian Government Publishing Centre, 1981.

Commonwealth of Australia. *Transnational Terrorism: The Threat to Australia.* Canberra 2004.

Connolly, Stephen and Gregory Druehl. 'The Tupamaros: The New Focus in Latin America'. *Journal of Contemporary Revolutions* 3, (1971): 59–68.

'Constitución De La República Oriental Del Uruguay'. www.georgetown.edu/pdba/ Constitutions/Uruguay/uruguay67.html.

'Constitution Act, 1867'. Department of Justice, Canada, www.lois.justice.gc.ca/en/const/ c1867_e.html.

Conteh-Morgan, Earl. *Collective Political Violence: An Introduction to the Theories and Cases of Violent Conflicts.* London and New York: Routledge, 2004.

Coogan, Tim Pat. *The I.R.A.* Revised edn. London: HarperCollins Publishers, 2000.

Corrales, Javier. 'Strong Societies, Weak Parties: Regime Change in Cuba and Venezuela in the 1950s and Today'. *Latin American Politics and Society* 43, no. 2 (2001): 81–113.

Coyle, R.G. 'A System Description of Counter Insurgency Warfare'. *Policy Sciences* 18, no. 1 (1985): 55–78.

Cragin, Kim and Peter Chalk. *Terrorism & Development: Using Social and Economic Development to Inhibit a Resurgence of Terrorism.* Santa Monica: RAND, 2003.

Crelinsten, Ronald D. 'The Internal Dynamics of the FLQ During the October Crisis of 1970'. In *Inside Terrorist Organizations*, edited by David C. Rapoport, 59–89. London and Portland: Frank Cass, 2001.

———. 'Power and Meaning: Terrorism as a Struggle over Access to the Communication Structure'. In *Contemporary Research on Terrorism*, edited by Paul Wilkinson and Alasdair M. Stewart, 419–450. Aberdeen: Aberdeen University Press, 1987.

Crelinsten, Ronald D. and Alex P. Schmid. 'Western Responses to Terrorism: A Twenty-Five Year Balance Sheet'. *Terrorism and Political Violence* 4, no. 4 (1992): 307–340.

Crenshaw, Martha. 'The Causes of Terrorism'. *Comparative Politics* 13, no. 4 (1981): 379–399.

———. 'Thoughts on Relating Terrorism to Historical Contexts'. In *Terrorism in Context*, edited by Martha Crenshaw, 3–26. University Park: The Pennsylvania State University Press, 1995.

Cronin, Sean. *Irish Nationalism: A History of Its Roots and Ideology.* Dublin: The Academy Press, 1980.

Cunningham, Michael J. *British Government Policy in Northern Ireland, 1969–2000.* Manchester: Manchester University Press, 2001.

Curran, Joseph M. *The Birth of the Irish Free State 1921–1923.* University: The University of Alabama Press, 1980.

d'Oliveira, Sergio L. 'Uruguay and the Tupamaro Myth'. *Military Review* 53, no. 4 (1973): 25–36.

Daly, Herman E. 'The Uruguayan Economy: Its Basic Nature and Current Problems'. *Journal of Inter-American Studies* 7, no. 3 (1965): 316–330.

Danner, Mark. 'Taking Stock of the Forever War'. *New York Times Magazine*, 11 September 2005, 45–60.

Dartnell, Michael Y. *Action Directe: Ultra-Left Terrorism in France, 1979–1987*. London: Frank Cass, 1995.

Daugherty, William E., and Morris Janowitz. *A Psychological Warfare Casebook*. Baltimore: Johns Hopkins Press, 1958.

de Vault, Carole and William Johnson. *The Informer: Confessions of an Ex-Terrorist*. Toronto: Fleet Books, 1982.

Debray, Régis. *Strategy for Revolution*. Edited by Robin Blackburn. London: J. Cape, 1970.

della Porta, Donatella. *Social Movements, Political Violence, and the State: A Comparative Analysis of Italy and Germany*. Cambridge and New York: Cambridge University Press, 1995.

Dershowitz, Alan M. *Why Terrorism Works*. New Haven: Yale University Press, 2002.

Dewar, Michael. *The British Army in Northern Ireland*. London: Arms and Armour Press, 1985.

Dillon, Martin. *The Dirty War: Covert Strategies and Tactics Used in Political Conflicts*. New York: Routledge, 1990.

Dion, Léon and Micheline de Sève. 'Quebec: Interest Groups and the Search for an Alternative Political System'. *The Annals of the American Academy of Political and Social Science* 413, (1974): 124–144.

'Disturbances in Northern Ireland: Report of the Commission Appointed by the Governor of Northern Ireland'. Belfast: Her Majesty's Stationery Office, 1969.

Dixon, Paul. *Northern Ireland: The Politics of War and Peace*. Houndsmill and New York: Palgrave, 2001.

Documentación y Archivo de Lucha Armada DC. 'Cronología Básica 1954–1973'. Montevideo: Facultad de Humanidades, la Universidad de la República, 2006.

Donohue, Laura K. 'Civil Liberties, Terrorism, and Liberal Democracy: Lessons from the United Kingdom'. In *BCSIA Discussion Paper 2000–05*: John F. Kennedy School of Government, Harvard University, 2000.

——. 'Regulating Northern Ireland: The Special Powers Acts, 1922–1972'. *The Historical Journal* 41, no. 4 (1998): 1089–1120.

——. 'Security and Freedom on the Fulcrum'. *Terrorism and Political Violence* 17, no. 1–2 (2005): 69–87.

Drake, Charles. 'The Provisional IRA: A Case Study'. *Terrorism and Political Violence* 3, no. 1 (1991): 43–60.

——. 'The Provisional IRA: Reorganisation and the Long War'. In *Terrorism's Laboratory: The Case of Northern Ireland*, edited by Alan O'Day, 87–114. Aldershot: Dartmouth, 1995.

Duchaîne, Jean-François. 'Rapport Sur Les Événements D'octobre 1970'. Québec: Direction générale des publications gouvernementales, 1981.

Duff, Charles. *Six Days to Shake an Empire*. London: J.M. Dent & Sons, 1966.

Dumont, Fernand and Guy Rocher. 'An Introduction to a Sociology of French Canada'. In *French-Canadian Society*, edited by Marcel Rioux and Yves Martin, 178–200. Toronto: McClelland and Stewart, 1964.

Eagleton, Terry. *Ideology: An Introduction*. London: Verso, 1991.

Earl, Jennifer. 'Introduction: Repression and the Social Control of Protest'. *Mobilization: An International Quarterly* 11, no. 2 (2006): 129–143.

——. 'Tanks, Tear Gas, and Taxes: Toward a Theory of Movement Repression'. *Sociological Theory* 21, no. 1 (2003): 44–68.

Edelmann, Alexander T. 'The Rise and Demise of Uruguay's Second Plural Executive'. *The Journal of Politics* 31, no. 1 (1969): 119–139.

Elliott, Sydney and W.D. Flackes. *Conflict in Northern Ireland: An Encyclopedia*. Santa Barbara, Denver and Oxford: ABC-CLIO, 1999.

English, Richard. *Armed Struggle: The History of the IRA*. New York: Oxford University Press, 2003.

Enloe, Cynthia H. 'Police and Military in Ulster: Peacekeeping or Peace-Subverting Forces?' *Journal of Peace Research* 15, no. 3 (1978): 243–258.

Evans, Gareth. 'Where Are We in the War on Terrorism?' *Australian Book Review no. 261* (2004): 13–16.

Fallows, James. 'Bush's Lost Year'. *The Atlantic Monthly*, October 2004, 68–81.

Farrell, Michael. *Arming the Protestants: The Formation of the Ulster Special Constabulary and the Royal Ulster Constabulary 1920–1927*. London and Sydney: Pluto Press, 1983.

Fay, Marie-Therese, Mike Morrissey, and Marie Smyth. *Northern Ireland's Troubles: The Human Costs*. London and Sterling: Pluto Press, 1999.

Fenwick, Rudy. 'Social Change and Ethnic Nationalism: An Historical Analysis of the Separatist Movement in Quebec'. *Comparative Studies in Society and History* 23, no. 2 (1981): 196–216.

Fernández Huidobro, Eleuterio. *Historia De Los Tupamaros*. Montevideo: Ediciones de la Banda Oriental, 1987.

Finch, M.H.J. *A Political Economy of Uruguay since 1870*. London and Basingstoke: Macmillan Press, 1981.

Finn, John E. *Constitutions in Crisis: Political Violence and the Rule of Law*. New York and Oxford: Oxford University Press, 1991.

Fitzgibbon, Russell H. 'Uruguay's Agricultural Problems'. *Economic Geography* 29, no. 3 (1953): 251–262.

Flackes, W.D. *Northern Ireland: A Political Directory 1968–79*. New York: St. Martin's Press, 1980.

FLQ. 'Communiqué'. In La Véritable Histoire Du F.L.Q., edited by Claude Savoie, 59–61. Montréal: Les Éditions du Jour, 1963.

———. 'Demands of the Flq'. Marianopolis College, www2.marianopolis.edu/quebechistory/docs/october/demands.htm.

———. 'La Non-Violence Et La Guerre De Libération'. *La Cognée no. 13* (1964): 7–9.

———. 'Le Québec Est Une Colonie'. *La Cognée no. 1* (1963): 3–4.

———. 'Manifesto of the Front De Libération Du Québec'. Marianopolis College, www2.marianopolis.edu/quebechistory/docs/october/manifest.htm.

———. 'Message Du FLQ a La Nation'. In *La Véritable Histoire Du F.L.Q.*, edited by Claude Savoie, 43–46. Montréal: Les Éditions du Jour, 1963.

———. 'Nous Continuons'. *La Cognée no. 12* (1964): 1–2.

———. 'Pourquoi Un Parti Révolutionnaire Clandestin?' *La Cognée no. 7* (1964): 4–6.

———. 'Révolution Par Le Peuple Pour Le Peuple'. In *La Véritable Histoire Du F.L.Q.*, edited by Claude Savoie, 27–28. Montréal: Les Éditions du Jour, 1963.

———. *Stratégie Révolutionnaire Et Rôle De L'avant Garde*. Paris 1970.

Foreign Affairs Committee. 'Tenth Report of Session 2002–03, Foreign Policy Aspects of the War against Terrorism'. London: House of Commons, 2003.

Fournier, Louis. *F.L.Q.: The Anatomy of an Underground Movement*. Translated by Edward Baxter. Toronto: NC Press Limited, 1984.

Fraser, Graham. *PQ: René Lévesque & the Parti Québécois in Power*. Toronto: Macmillan of Canada, 1984.

Freeman, Michael. *Freedom or Security: The Consequences for Democracies Using Emergency Powers to Fight Terror*. Westport and London: Praeger, 2003.

Gamson, William A. *Talking Politics*. Cambridge: Cambridge University Press, 1992.

Ganor, Boaz. *The Counter-Terrorism Puzzle: A Guide for Decision Makers*. New Brunswick and London: Transaction Publishers, 2005.

Garfield, Andrew. 'PIRA Lessons Learned: A Model of Terrorist Leadership Succession'. *Low Intensity Conflict & Law Enforcement* 11, no. 2/3 (2002): 271–284.

Gellner, Ernest. *Nations and Nationalism*. Ithaca: Cornell University Press, 1983.

Gellner, John. *Bayonets in the Streets: Urban Guerrilla at Home and Abroad*. Don Mills: Collier-Macmillan, 1974.

Generals and Tupamaros: The Struggle for Power in Uruguay 1969–1973. London and Leeds: Latin America Review of Books, 1974.

Geoghegan, Vincent. 'Socialism'. In *Political Ideologies: An Introduction*, edited by Robert Eccleshall, Alan Finlayson, Vincent Geoghegan, Michael Kenny, Moya Lloyd, Iain MacKenzie and Rick Wilford, 73–96. New York: Routledge, 2003.

Geraghty, Tony. *The Irish War: The Hidden Conflict between the IRA and British Intelligence*. Baltimore and London: The Johns Hopkins University Press, 2000.

Gerassi, Marysa. 'Uruguay's Urban Guerrillas'. *New Left Review* no. 62 (1970): 22–29.

Gerring, John. 'Ideology: A Definitional Analysis'. I 50, *Political Research Quarterly* no. 4 (1997): 957–994.

Gilio, Maria Esther. *The Tupamaros*. Translated by Anne Edmondson. London: Secker & Warbug, 1972.

Gill, K.P.S. 'Endgame in Punjab: 1988–1993'. *Faultlines: Writings on Conflict & Resolution* 1, no. 1 (1999): 1–70.

Gillespie, Charles Guy. *Negotiating Democracy: Politicians and Generals in Uruguay*. Cambridge: Cambridge University Press, 1991.

Gillespie, Richard. 'Political Violence in Argentina: Guerrillas, Terrorists, and Carapintadas'. In *Terrorism in Context*, edited by Martha Crenshaw, 211–248. University Park: The Pennsylvania State University Press, 1995.

———. *Soldiers of Peron: Argentina's Montoneros*. Oxford: Clarendon Press, 1982.

Glover, James M. 'Appendix xviii – Northern Ireland: Future Terrorist Trends (2 November 1978)'. In *Irish Nationalism: A History of Its Roots and Ideology*, edited by Sean Cronin, 339–357. Dublin: The Academy Press, 1980.

Goffman, Erving. *Frame Analysis: An Essay on the Organization of Experience*. Harmondsworth: Penguin Books, 1974.

González Bermejo, Ernesto. *Las Manos En El Fuego*. Montevideo: Ediciones de la Banda Oriental, 1987.

Goss, Richard J. 'The Natural History (and Mystery) of Regeneration'. In *A History of Regeneration Research: Milestones in the Evolution of a Science*, edited by Charles E. Dinsmore, 7–24. Cambridge: Cambridge University Press, 1991.

———. *Principles of Regeneration*. New York and London: Academic Press, 1969.

Gott, Richard. 'Events since 1971'. In *The Tupamaros: Urban Guerrillas in Uruguay*, edited by Alain Labrousse, 126–132. Harmondsworth: Penguin Books, 1973.

Graham, Bradley. 'Rumsfeld Questions Anti-Terrorism Efforts'. *Washington Post*, 23 October 2003, 1A.

Grattan, Michelle. 'Wrong Tools to Fight Terrorism'. *Sydney Morning Herald*, 10 May 2002, 13.

Greer, Steven. *Supergrasses: A Study in Anti-Terrorist Law Enforcement in Northern Ireland*. Oxford: Clarendon Press, 1995.

Griffin, Anne. *Quebec: The Challenge of Independence*. Rutherford, Madison, Teaneck: Fairleigh Dickinson University Press, 1984.

Guevara, Ernesto (Che). *Guerrilla Warfare*. Middlesex: Penguin, 1969.

Guindon, Hubert. *Quebec Society: Tradition, Modernity, and Nationhood*. Edited by Roberta Hamilton and John L. McMullan. Toronto, Buffalo, and London: University of Toronto Press, 1988.

Gurr, Ted Robert. *Why Men Rebel*. Princeton: Princeton University Press, 1970.

Habeck, Mary. *Knowing the Enemy: Jihadist Ideology and the War on Terror*. New Haven: Yale University Press, 2006.

Hafez, Mohammed M. and Quintan Wiktorowicz. 'Violence as Contention in the Egyptian Islamic Movement'. In *Islamic Activism: A Social Movement Theory Approach*, edited by Quintan Wiktorowicz, 61–88. Bloomington: Indiana University Press, 2004.

Haggart, Ron and Aubery E. Golden. *Rumours of War*. Toronto: New Press, 1971.

Hagy, James William. 'Quebec Separatists: The First Twelve Years'. *Queen's Quarterly* 76, no. 2 (1969): 229–238.

Halperin, Maurice. 'Return to Havana: Portrait of a Loyalist'. *Cuban Studies* 23, (1993): 187–193.

Hamill, Desmond. *Pig in the Middle: The Army in Northern Ireland 1969–1984*. London: Methuen London, 1985.

Hamilton, Richard and Maurice Pinard. 'The Quebec Independence Movement'. In *National Separatism*, edited by Colin H. Williams, 203–233. Vancouver and London: University of British Columbia Press, 1982.

Handelman, Howard. 'Labor-Industrial Conflict and the Collapse of Uruguayan Democracy'. *Journal of Interamerican Studies and World Affairs* 23, no. 4 (1981): 371–394.

Harmon, Christopher C. *Terrorism Today*. London and Portland: Frank Cass, 2000.

Harris, Richard. 'Anti-Democratic Provisions Fall on the Wrong Side of the Law'. *Sydney Morning Herald*, 22 November 2005, 17.

Hassoux, Didier. 'La Sécurité Prend Des Libertés'. Libération, 5 October 2001, 18.

Hayes, Bernadette C., and Ian McAllister. 'Sowing Dragon's Teeth: Public Support for Political Violence and Paramilitarism in Northern Ireland'. *Political Studies* 49, (2001): 901–922.

Hazarika, Sanjoy. 'Sikh's Mood: Insulted, Hurt and out for Revenge'. *New York Times*, 6 July 1984, 2.

Heintzman, Ralph. 'The Political Culture of Quebec, 1840–1960'. *Canadian Journal of Political Science/Revue canadienne de science politique* 16, no. 1 (1983): 3–59.

Heinz, Wolfgang S. and Hugo Frühling. *Determinants of Gross Human Rights Violations by State and State-Sponsored Actors in Brazil, Uruguay, Chile, and Argentina 1960–1990*. The Hague, Boston and London: Martinus Nijhoff Publishers, 1999.

Hennessey, Thomas. *A History of Northern Ireland 1920–1996*. New York: St. Martin's Press, 1997.

Henripin, Jacques. 'From Acceptance of Nature to Control: The Demography of the French Canadians since the Seventeenth Century'. *The Canadian Journal of Economics and Political Science* 23, no. 1 (1957): 10–19.

———. *Tendances Et Facteurs De La Fécondité Au Canada*. Ottawa: Bureau Fédéral de la Statistique, 1968.

Hewitt, Christopher. *The Effectiveness of Anti-Terrorist Policies*. Lanham: University Press of America, 1984.

———. 'Terrorism and Public Opinion: A Five Country Comparison'. *Terrorism and Political Violence* 2, no. 2 (1990): 145–170.

Hewitt, Steve. 'Reforming the Canadian Security State: The Royal Canadian Mounted

Police Security Service and the "Key Sectors" Program'. *Intelligence and National Security* 17, no. 4 (2002): 165–184.

Heywood, Andrew. *Political Ideologies: An Introduction*. Third edn. Basingstoke: Palgrave Macmillan, 2003.

Hezlet, Arthur. *The 'B' Specials: A History of the Ulster Special Constabulary*. London: Tom Stacey, 1973.

Hirschman, Charles, Samuel Preston, and Vu Manh Loi. 'Vietnamese Casualties During the American War: A New Estimate'. *Population and Development Review* 21, no. 4 (1995): 783–812.

Hoffman, Bruce. *Inside Terrorism*. New York: Columbia University Press, 1998.

Hogan, Gerard and Clive Walker. *Political Violence and the Law in Ireland*. Manchester and New York: Manchester University Press, 1989.

Hogan, John and Max Taylor. 'The Provisional Irish Republican Army: Command and Functional Structure'. *Terrorism and Political Violence* 9, no. 3 (1997): 1–32.

Holt, Robert T. and Robert W. van de Velde. *Strategic Psychological Operations and American Foreign Policy*. Chicago: Chicago University Press, 1960.

Hopkinson, Michael. *Green against Green: The Irish Civil War*. Dublin: Gill and Macmillan, 1988.

Horchem, Hans Josef. 'Terrorism and Government Response: The German Experience'. *The Jerusalem Journal of International Relations* 4, no. 3 (1980): 43–55.

Horne, Alistair. *A Savage War of Peace: Algeria* 1954–1962. London: Macmillan, 1977.

Howard, John. 'Counter-Terrorism Laws Strengthened'. Office of the Prime Minister of Australia, www.pm.gov.au/News/media_releases/media_Release1551.html.

Hunt, Richard A. 'Strategies at War: Pacification and Attrition in Vietnam'. In *Lessons from an Unconventional War: Reassessing U.S. Strategies for Future Conflicts*, edited by Richard A. Hunt and Richard Shultz, 23–47. New York: Pergamon Press, 1982.

International Institute for Strategic Studies. *Military Balance*. London: The Institute for Strategic Studies, 1969–1970.

Jackson, Alvin. 'Irish Unionism, 1870–1922'. In *Defenders of the Union: A Survey of British and Irish Unionism since 1801*, edited by D. George Boyce and Alan O'Day, 115–136. London and New York: Routledge, 2001.

Jackson, Robert. *The Malayan Emergency: The Commonwealth's Wars 1948–1966*. London and New York: Routledge, 1991.

Janke, Peter. *Terrorism and Democracy: Some Contemporary Cases*. Houndsmill, Basingstoke, Hampshire, and London: Macmillan, 1992.

Jarman, Neil. 'From War to Peace? Changing Patterns of Violence in Northern Ireland, 1990–2003'. *Terrorism and Political Violence* 16, no. 3 (2004): 420–438.

Jeffery, Keith. 'The British Army and Ireland since 1922'. In *A Military History of Ireland*, edited by Thomas Bartlett and Keith Jeffery, 431–458. Cambridge: Cambridge University Press, 1996.

——. 'Security Policy in Northern Ireland: Some Reflections on the Management of Violent Conflict'. *Terrorism and Political Violence* 2, no. 1 (1990): 21–34.

Jenkins, Brian. 'Will Terrorists Go Nuclear?' *ORBIS* 29, no. 3 (1985): 507–516.

Jenkins, Brian Michael. *Countering Al Qaeda: An Appreciation of the Situation and Suggestions for Strategy*. Santa Monica: RAND, 2002.

——. *The Study of Terrorism: Definitional Problems*. Santa Monica: RAND, 1980.

Johnson, Chalmers. 'Civilian Loyalties and Guerrilla Conflict'. *World Politics* 14, no. 4 (1962): 646–661.

Johnson, Lyndon B. *The Vantage Point: Perspectives of the Presidency*, 1963–1969. New York: Holt, Rinehart and Winston, 1971.

Jones, Richard. 'Politics and the Reinforcement of the French Language in Canada and Quebec, 1960–1986'. In *Quebec since 1945: Selected Readings*, edited by Michael D. Behiels, 223–240. Toronto: Copp Clark Pitman Limited, 1987.

Jones, Sidney. 'The Changing Nature of Jemaah Islamiyah'. *Australian Journal of International Affairs* 59, no. 2 (2005): 169–178.

Judge, Paramjit S. Religion, *Identity and Nationhood: The Sikh Militant Movement*. Jaipur: Rawat Publications, 2005.

Kaufman, Edy. *Uruguay in Transition: From Civilian to Military Rule*. New Brunswick, NJ.: Transaction Books, 1979.

Kautt, William H. *The Anglo-Irish War, 1916–1921: A People's War*. Westport and London: Praeger, 1999.

Kellett, Anthony. 'Terrorism in Canada, 1960–1992'. In *Violence in Canada: Sociopolitical Perspectives*, edited by Jeffrey Ian Ross, 286–312. Don Mills: Oxford University Press, 1995.

Kellett, Anthony, Bruce Beanlands, James Deacon, Heather Jeffrey, and Chantal Lapalme. 'Terrorism in Canada 1960–1989'. Ottawa: Ministry of the Solicitor General of Canada, 1991.

Kelley, Kevin J. *The Longest War: Northern Ireland and the IRA*. New edn. London: Zed Books, 1988.

Kelly, William and Nora Kelly. *Policing in Canada*. Toronto: Macmillan of Canada, 1976.

Kilcullen, David J. 'Countering Global Insurgency'. *The Journal of Strategic Studies* 28, no. 4 (2005): 597–617.

Kitson, Frank. *Low Intensity Operations: Subversion, Insurgency, Peacekeeping*. London: Faber, 1973.

Klandermans, Bert. *The Social Psychology of Protest*. Oxford and Cambridge MA.: Blackwell Publishers, 1997.

Klandermans, Bert, Marlene Roefs, and Rohan Olivier. 'Grievance Formation in a Country in Transition: South Africa, 1994–1998'. *Social Psychology Quarterly* 64, no. 1 (2001): 41–54.

Klieman, Aaron S. 'Confined to Barracks: Emergencies and the Military in Developing Societies'. *Comparative Politics* 12, no. 2 (1980): 143–163.

Kohl, James and John Litt. *Urban Guerrilla Warfare in Latin America*. Cambridge and London: The MIT Press, 1974.

Labrousse, Alain. *The Tupamaros: Urban Guerrilla in Uruguay*. Translated by Dinah Livingstone. Harmondsworth: Penguin Books, 1973.

Langguth, A.J. *Hidden Terrors*. New York: Pantheon Books, 1978.

Laqueur, Walter. *A History of Terrorism*. New Brunswick and London: Transaction Publishers, 2002.

Laurendeau, Marc. *Les Québécois Violents: La Violence Politique 1962–1972*. Augmented and updated ed. Montréal: Boréal, 1990.

Lavoie, Yolande. *L'Émigration Des Québécois Aux États-Unis De 1840 À 1930*. Montréal: Presses de l'Université de Montréal, 1972.

Leites, Nathan and Charles Wolf. *Rebellion and Authority: An Analytical Essay on Insurgent Conflicts*. Chicago: Markham Publishing Company, 1970.

Leman-Langlois, Stéphane and Jean-Paul Brodeur. 'Terrorism Old and New: Counterterrorism in Canada'. *Police Practice and Research* 6, no. 2 (2005): 121–140.

LeoGrande, William M. 'A Splendid Little War: Drawing the Line in El Salvador'. *International Security* 6, no. 1 (1981): 27–52.

Levin, Malcolm and Christine Sylvester. *Crisis in Quebec*. Toronto: Ontario Institute for Studies in Education, 1973.

Levine, Marc V. *The Reconquest of Montreal: Language Policy and Social Change in a Bilingual City*. Philadelphia: Temple University Press, 1990.

Lewis, Paul H. *Guerrillas and Generals: The Dirty War in Argentina*. Westport: Praeger, 2002.

'Ley De Seguridad Del Estado Y El Orden Interno'. República Oriental del Uruguay, Poder Legislativo, www.parlamento.gub.uy/leyes/ley14068.htm.

Lichbach, Mark Irving. 'Deterrence or Escalation? The Puzzle of Aggregate Studies of Repression and Dissent'. *The Journal of Conflict Resolution* 31, no. 2 (1987): 266–297.

Lijphart, Arend. 'The Comparable-Cases Strategy in Comparative Research'. *Comparative Political Studies* 8, no. 2 (1975): 158–177.

——. 'Comparative Politics and the Comparative Method'. *The American Political Science Review* 65, no. 3 (1971): 682–693.

Lindahl, Göran G. *Uruguay's New Path: A Study in Politics During the First Colegiado, 1919–33*. Stockholm: Library and Institute of Ibero-American Studies, 1962.

Linzer, Dafna and Walter Pincus. 'Intelligence Chief Pessimistic in Assessing Worldwide Threats'. *Washington Post*, 12 January 2007, 12.

Long, Austin. *On 'Other War': Lessons from Five Decades of RAND Counterinsurgency Research*. Santa Monica: RAND, 2006.

Loomis, Dan G. *Not Much Glory: Quelling the FLQ*. Toronto: Deneau, 1984.

Lopez-Alves, Fernando. 'Political Crises, Strategic Choices, and Terrorism: The Rise and Fall of the Uruguayan Tupamaros'. *Terrorism and Political Violence* 1, no. 2 (1989): 202–241.

Lowry, David R. 'Internment: Detention without Trial in Northern Ireland'. *Human Rights* 5, no. 3 (1976): 261–331.

Lynn, Brendan. 'Tactic or Principle? The Evolution of Republican Thinking on Abstentionism in Ireland, 1970–1998'. *Irish Political Studies* 17, no. 2 (2002): 74–94.

McBride, Ian. 'Ulster and the British Problem'. In *Unionism in Modern Ireland: New Perspectives on Politics and Culture*, edited by Richard English and Graham Walker, 1–18. London: Macmillan Press, 1996.

McCormick, Gordon H. 'Terrorist Decision-Making'. *Annual Review of Political Science* 6, (2003): 473–507.

MacDermot, Frank Charles. *Theobald Wolfe Tone: A Biographical Study*. London: Macmillan, 1939.

McFadden, Eric M. 'Contemporary Counterinsurgency Operations: History as a Guide to Assist in the Development of the Joint Interagency Task Force'. *Comparative Strategy* 24, no. 4 (2005): 361–378.

Macfarlance, Leslie. 'The Right to Self-Determination in Ireland and the Justification of IRA Violence'. *Terrorism and Political Violence* 2, no. 1 (1990): 35–53.

McGuire, Maria. *To Take up Arms: A Year in the Provisional IRA*. London: Macmillan, 1973.

McKenna, Fionnuala. 'Referendum ("Border Poll") (Ni), Thursday 8 March 1973'. *Conflict Archive on the Internet (CAIN)*, www.cain.ulst.ac.uk/issues/politics/election/ref1973.htm.

McKenna, Fionnuala and Martin Melaugh. 'Table NI-Eco-02: Subvention (£ Million) to Northern Ireland from the United Kingdom, 1966–67 to 1992–93'. *Conflict Archive on the Internet (CAIN)*, www.ulst.ac.uk/ni/economy.htm#02.

McKeown, Laurence. *Out of Time: Irish Republican Prisoners, Long Kesh 1972–2000*. Belfast: Beyond the Pale, 2001.

McRoberts, Kenneth. *Quebec: Social Change and Political Crisis*. Third edn. Toronto: McClelland & Stewart, 1988.

——. 'The Sources of Neo-Nationalism in Quebec'. In *Quebec since 1945: Selected Readings*, edited by Michael D. Behiels, 80–107. Toronto, ON.: Copp Clark Pitman Limited, 1987.

MacStiofain, Sean. *Memoirs of a Revolutionary*. Edinburgh: Gordon Cremonesi, 1975.

Malkasian, Carter. *A History of Modern Wars of Attrition*. Westport: Praeger, 2002.

Marchak, Patricia. *God's Assassins: State Terrorism in Argentina in the 1970s*. Montreal: McGill-Queen's University Press, 1999.

Marks, Thomas A. *Maoist Insurgency since Vietnam*. New York: Frank Cass, 1996.

Martin, Gilles. 'War in Algeria: The French Experience'. *Military Review* 85, no. 4 (2005): 51–57.

Martin, Percy Alvin. 'The Career of Jose Batlle Y Ordonez'. *The Hispanic American Historical Review* 10, no. 4 (1930): 413–428.

Martinez, C. Edda and Edward A. Suchman. 'Letters from America and the 1948 Elections in Italy'. *The Public Opinion Quarterly* 14, no. 1 (1950): 111–125.

Mason, T. David. 'Insurgency, Counterinsurgency, and the Rational Peasant'. *Public Choice* 86, no. 1–2 (1996): 63–83.

Matthew, Richard and George Shambaugh. 'The Limits of Terrorism: A Network Perspective'. *International Studies Review* 7, no. 4 (2005): 617–627.

Mayer, Margit. 'The German October of 1977'. *New German Critique* no. 13 (1978): 155–163.

Mazzetti, Mark. 'New Generation of Qaeda Chiefs Is Seen on Rise'. *New York Times*, 2 April 2007, 1.

'The Measurement of Latin American Real Income in US Dollars'. *Economic Bulletin for Latin America* 7, no. 2 (1968).

Merari, Ariel. 'Terrorism as a Strategy of Insurgency'. *Terrorism and Political Violence* 5, no. 4 (1993): 213–251.

Mercader, Antonio, and Jorge de Vera. *Tupamaros: Estrategia Y Accion Informe*. Mexico: Editorial Omega, 1971.

Merkl, Peter H. 'West German Left-Wing Terrorism'. In *Terrorism in Context*, edited by Martha Crenshaw, 160–210. University Park, PA: Pennsylvania State University Press, 1995.

Merom, Gil. *How Democracies Lose Small Wars: State, Society, and the Failures of France in Algeria, Israel in Lebanon, and the United States in Vietnam*. Cambridge: Cambridge University Press, 2003.

Metz, Steven. *The Future of Insurgency*. Carlisle: Strategic Studies Institute, 1993.

——. 'Insurgency and Counterinsurgency in Iraq'. *The Washington Quarterly* 27, no. 1 (2003): 25–36.

Metz, Steven and Raymond Millen. *Insurgency and Counterinsurgency in the 21st Century: Reconceptualizing Threat and Response*. Carlisle: Strategic Studies Institute, 2004.

Michaelsen, Christopher. 'Antiterrorism Legislation in Australia: A Proportionate Response to the Terrorist Threat?' *Studies in Conflict and Terrorism* 28, no. 4 (2005): 321–339.

Miller, James A. 'Urban Terrorism in Uruguay: The Tupamaros'. In *Insurgency in the Modern World*, edited by Bard E. O'Neill, William R. Heaton and Donald J. Alberts, 137–188. Boulder: Westview Press, 1980.

MLN-T. 'Análisis Del MLN Sobre La Situación Nacional Y Continental'. In *Los Tupamaros*, edited by Omar Costa, 228–250. Mexico: Ediciones Era, 1972.

——. 'Apuntes Sobre Lucha Armada'. April 1968, Mimeograph.

——. 'Balance 70–71'. In *3 Documentos Internos*, 12–15. Montevideo: MLN-T, 1986.

——. 'Balance 1969'. In *Las Fuerzas Armadas Al Pueblo Oriental*, edited by Junta de Comandantes en Jefe, 561–570. Montevideo: Republica Oriental del Uruguay, Junta de Comandantes en Jefe, 1978.

——. 'Bases De Discusión Acerca De La Situación Actual De Las FFAA Y El Quehacer'. In *Las Fuerzas Armadas Al Pueblo Oriental*, edited by Junta de Comandantes en Jefe, 770–772. Montevideo: Republica Oriental del Uruguay, Junta de Comandantes en Jefe, 1978.

——. 'Broadcast on Radio Sarandi, 15 May 1969'. In *The Tupamaros: Urban Guerrillas in Uruguay*, edited by Alain Labrousse, 146–149. Harmondsworth: Penguin Books, 1973.

——. 'Carta Abierta a La Policía'. In *Historia De Los Tupamaros*, edited by Eleuterio Fernández Huidobro, 394–396. Montevideo: Ediciones de la Banda Oriental, 1987.

——. 'Correo Tupamaro: Movimiento De Liberacion Nacional Tupamaros Al Pueblo'. July 1973.

——. 'El Tupamaro: Organo Del Movimiento De Liberacion Nacional Tupamaros'. 1, no. 1 (1973).

——. 'Facts the Public Should Know'. In *The Tupamaros*, edited by Maria Esther Gilio, 117–119. London: Secker & Warburg, 1972.

——. 'Interview with Urbano'. In *Urban Guerrilla Warfare in Latin America*, edited by James Kohl and James Litt, 266–292. Cambridge and London: The MIT Press, 1974.

——. 'Las Tácticas Que USA La Guerrilla Urbana'. In *Los Tupamaros*, edited by Omar Costa, 251–262. Mexico: Ediciones Era, 1972.

——. 'Los Tupamaros Ejecutores De La Justicia Popular'. In *Los Tupamaros*, edited by Omar Costa, 120–122. Mexico: Ediciones Era, 1972.

——. 'Los Tupamaros Y El Movimiento Estudiantil'. In *Los Tupamaros*, edited by Omar Costa, 125–126. Mexico: Ediciones Era, 1972.

——. 'Organizavion Y Seguridad'. 7 December 1969, Mimeograph.

——. 'Plan De Marzo De 1972: Informe Del Secretariado Ejecutivo Al Comite Central'. In *Los Tupamaros*, edited by Omar Costa, 403–411. Mexico: Ediciones Era, 1972.

——. 'Proclamation of Paysandú'. In *Urban Guerrilla Warfare in Latin America*, edited by James Kohl and James Litt, 297–299. Cambridge and London: The MIT Press, 1974.

——. 'Thirty Questions to a Tupamaro'. In *Urban Guerrilla Warfare in Latin America*, edited by James Kohl and James Litt, 227–236. Cambridge and London: The MIT Press, 1974.

——. 'Today Sr. Pereyra Reverbel Was Arrested by the National Liberation Movement (Tupamaros)'. In *The Tupamaros: Urban Guerrillas in Uruguay*, edited by Alain Labrousse, 66–67. Harmondsworth: Penguin Books, 1973.

——. 'The Tupamaro Manifesto'. In *The Tupamaros: Urban Guerrillas in Uruguay*, edited by Alain Labrousse, 157–162. Harmondsworth: Penguin Books, 1973.

——. 'The Tupamaros' Program for Revolutionary Government'. In *Urban Guerrilla Warfare in Latin America*, edited by James Kohl and James Litt, 293–296. Cambridge and London: The MIT Press, 1974.

——. 'The Tupamaros: An Interview'. In *Urban Guerrilla Warfare in Latin America*, edited by James Kohl and James Litt, 300–307. Cambridge and London: The MIT Press, 1974.

Moloney, Ed. *A Secret History of the IRA*. New York and London: W.W. Norton & Company, 2002.

Moniz, Dave and Tom Squitieri. 'Rumsfeld Memo Prompts Praise and Told-You-So's'. *USA Today*, 23 October 2003, 6A.

Moreno, Jose A. 'Che Guevara on Guerrilla Warfare: Doctrine, Practice, and Evaluation'. *Comparative Studies in Society and History* 12, no. 2 (1970): 114–133.

Morf, Gustave. *Terror in Quebec: Case Studies of the FLQ*. Toronto and Vancouver: Clarke, Irwin & Company Limited, 1970.

Moss, Robert. *Urban Guerrillas: The New Face of Political Violence*. London: Temple Smith, 1972.

——. *The War for the Cities*. New York: Coward, McCann & Geoghegan, 1972.

Mueller, John E. 'The Search for the "Breaking Point" in Vietnam'. *International Studies Quarterly* 24, no. 4 (1980): 497–519.

Mullins, Willard A. 'On the Concept of Ideology in Political Science'. *The American Political Science Review* 66, no. 2 (1972): 498–510.

Munro, Catharine. 'Amrozi Says Bomb Was to Get White People out of Bali'. *Australian Associated Press*, 13 June 2003.

Narayanan, V.N. *Tryst with Terror: Punjab's Turbulent Decade*. New Dehli: Ajanta Publications, 1996.

National Commission on Terrorist Attacks upon the United States. The 9/11 Commission Report. Official Government edn. Washington, D.C.: U.S. Government Printing Office, 2004.

National Intelligence Council. 'Declassified Key Judgments of the National Intelligence Estimate "Trends in Global Terrorism: Implications for the United States" Dated April 2006'. Washington, D.C., 2006.

——. 'National Intelligence Estimate: The Terrorist Threat to the US Homeland'. Washington, D.C., 2007.

Naylor, R.T. *Wages of Crime: Black Markets, Illegal Finance, and the Underworld Economy*. Revised ed. Ithaca: Cornell University Press, 2004.

Neumann, Peter R. *Britain's Long War: British Strategy in the Northern Ireland Conflict, 1969–98*. Houndmills and New York: Palgrave Macmillan, 2003.

——. 'Europe's Jihadist Dilemma'. *Survival* 48, no. 2 (2006): 71–84.

Nevin, John A. 'Retaliating against Terrorists'. *Behavior and Social Issues* 12, no. 2 (2003): 109–128.

Nolan, David. 'From Foco to Insurrection: Sandinista Strategies of Revolution'. *Air University Review*, July–August 1986.

Núñez, Carlos. 'Eleuterio Fernández Huidobro'. *NACLA Report on the Americas* 20, no. 5 (1986): 43–50.

——. *The Tupamaros: Urban Guerrillas of Uruguay*. New York: Times Change Press, 1970.

O'Boyle, Garrett. 'Theories of Justification and Political Violence: Examples from Four Groups'. *Terrorism and Political Violence* 14, no. 2 (2002): 23–46.

O'Day, Alan. 'Defending the Union: Parliamentary Options, 1869 and 1886'. In *Defenders of the Union: A Survey of British and Irish Unionism since 1801*, edited by D. George Boyce and Alan O'Day, 90–111. London and New York: Routledge, 2001.

O'Leary, Brendan and John McGarry. *The Politics of Antagonism: Understanding Northern Ireland*. Second edn. London and Atlantic Highlands: The Athlone Press, 1996.

O'Neill, Bard E. *Insurgency and Terrorism: Inside Modern Revolutionary Warfare*. Washington, D.C.: Brassey's Incorporated, 1990.

Ó Dochartaigh, Niall. *From Civil Rights to Armalites: Derry and the Birth of the Irish Troubles*. Cork: Cork University Press, 1997.

Opp, Karl-Dieter and Wolfgang Roehl. 'Repression, Micromobilization, and Political Protest'. *Social Forces* 69, no. 2 (1990): 521–547.

Ouellet, Fernand. 'The Historical Background of Separatism in Quebec'. In *French-Canadian Nationalism: An Anthology*, edited by Ramsay Cook, 49–71. Toronto: Macmillan of Canada, 1969.

——. *Lower Canada 1791–1840: Social Change and Nationalism*. Translated by Patricia Claxton. Toronto: McClelland and Stewart, 1980.

Paget, Julian. *Counter-Insurgency Campaigning*. London: Faber and Faber Limited, 1967.

Patterson, Henry. *The Politics of Illusion: Republicanism and Socialism in Modern Ireland*. London: Hutchinson Radius, 1989.

Pendle, George. *Uruguay*. Third edn. London, New York and Toronto: Oxford University Press, 1963.

Perusse, Roland I. 'Psychological Warfare Reappraised'. In *A Psychological Warfare Casebook*, edited by William E. Daugherty and Morris Janowitz, 25–35. Baltimore: Johns Hopkins Press, 1958.

Peterson, Peter G. 'Public Diplomacy and the War on Terrorism'. *Foreign Affairs* 81, no. 5 (2002): 74–94.

PIRA. '1972: The Year of Victory'. *Republican News* 2, no. 18 (1972): 1.

——. 'And What Shall I Do Now?' *Republican News* 1, no. 9 (1971): 12.

——. 'Another Victim of British Rule'. *Republican News* 1, no. 3 (1970): 3.

——. 'Army of Occupation'. *Republican News* 1, no. 7 (1971): 7.

——. 'British Army Murders'. *An Phoblacht* 5, no. 11 (1974): 8.

——. 'British Murder Gangs Step-up Campaign'. *Republican News* 2, no. 72 (1973): 1.

——. 'British Terrorists Murder Six Catholics: Hierarchy Condemns the IRA'. *Republican News* 2, no. 10 (1971): 1.

——. 'Civil Rights'. *An Phoblacht* 1, no. 1 (1970): 2.

——. 'Dole Queus [Sic], Guns, Unemployment, Talks and Handouts'. *An Phoblacht* 1, no. 6 (1971): 7.

——. 'Extracts from the "Green Book"'. In *The I.R.A.*, edited by Tim Pat Coogan, 545–571. London: HarperCollins Publishers, 2000.

——. 'Extracts of the "Staff Report"'. In *The I.R.A.*, edited by Tim Pat Coogan, 465–467. London: HarperCollins Publishers, 2000.

——. 'Fermanagh 1970 ... And How It Was Maintained'. *An Phoblacht* 1, no. 5 (1970): 5, 7.

——. 'The Final Phase'. *An Phoblacht* 5, no. 15 (1974): 1.

——. 'Get Off the Fence'. *Republican News* 1, no. 8 (1971): 10.

——. 'Guerrilla War a Legitimate Political Tactic'. *An Phoblacht* 5, no. 27 (1974): 7.

——. '"I Hate Paddys"'. *Republican News* 1, no. 8 (1971): 10.

——. 'The IRA – Justified'. *An Phoblacht* 3, no. 6 (1972): 6–7.

——. 'No Opportunity Will Be Lost: Army Council's Easter Message'. *An Phoblacht* 1, no. 3 (1970): 1.

——. 'The North Raped'. *Republican News* 2, no. 3 (1971): 1, 12.

——. 'Our Aims and Methods'. *An Phoblacht* 1, no. 2 (1970): 8.

——. 'Our View'. *Republican News* 2, no. 4 (1971): 1, 4.

——. '"Para" Security'. *An Phoblacht* 6, no. 37 (1975): 1.

——. 'The Price of Freedom'. *Republican News* 2, no. 11 (1971): 4.

——. 'The Question of Physical Force'. *Republican News* 2, no. 71 (1973): 5.

——. 'Revolt in the North'. *An Phoblacht* 1, no. 9 (1971): 1.

——. 'Terror in Belfast'. *Republican News* 1, no. 8 (1971): 1.

——. 'Victory in Sight'. *Republican News* 2, no. 11 (1971): 12.

——. 'We Repeat – Don't Fraternise!' *Republican News* 1, no. 11 (1971): 1.

——. 'Will Defend Irish People: The IRA Answers Belfast CCDC'. *An Phoblacht* 1, no. 11 (1970): 8.

Pisano, Vittorfranco S. 'The Red Brigades: A Challenge to Italian Democracy'. *Conflict Studies* no. 120 (1980).

Pluchinsky, Dennis A. 'An Organizational and Operational Analysis of Germany's Red Army Faction Terrorist Group (1972–91)'. In *European Terrorism: Today & Tomorrow*, edited by Yonah Alexander and Dennis A. Pluchinsky, 43–92. McLean, VA: Brassey's (US), Inc., 1992.

Polity IV Project. 'Polity IV Annual Time-Series Dataset'. *Integrated Network for Societal Conflict Research*, www.cidcm.umd.edu/inscr/polity/index.htm.

Porzecanski, Arturo C. *Uruguay's Tupamaros: The Urban Guerrilla*. New York, Washington and London: Praeger Publishers, 1973.

Posner, Richard A. 'Security Versus Civil Liberties'. *The Atlantic Monthly*, December 2001, 46–47.

'Press Briefing by Attorney General Alberto Gonzales and General Michael Hayden, Principal Deputy Director for National Intelligence'. The White House, www.whitehouse. gov/news/releases/2005/12/20051219–1.html.

'Prevention of Terrorism (Temporary Provisions) Act'. *Conflict Archive on the Internet (CAIN)*, www.cain.ulst.ac.uk/hmso/pta1974.htm.

PSNI. 'Casualties as a Result of Paramilitary-Style Attacks, 1973–2005'. Statistics Branch, www.psni.police.uk/persons_injured_cy-21.doc.

——. 'Number of persons charged with terrorist and serious public order offences, 1972–2005'. Statistics Branch, www.psni.police.uk/persons_charged_cy-19.doc.

——. 'Security-Related Incidents, 1969–2005'. Statistics Branch, www.psni.police.uk/security_related_incidents_cy-18.doc.

——. 'Public Order Regulations'. www2.marianopolis.edu/quebechistory/docs/october/regsoct.htm.

Quinn, Herbert F. *The Union Nationale: Quebec Nationalism from Duplessis to Lévesque*. Second enlarged edn. Toronto, Buffalo and London: University of Toronto Press, 1979.

Radu, Michael and Vladimir Tismaneanu. *Latin American Revolutionaries: Groups, Goals, Methods*. Washington, D.C.: Pergamon-Brassey's, 1990.

Ramakrishna, Kumar. 'Delegitimizing Global Jihadi Ideology in Southeast Asia'. *Contemporary Southeast Asia* 27, no. 3 (2005): 343–369.

Raufer, Xavier. 'Al Qaeda: A Different Diagnosis'. *Studies in Conflict and Terrorism* 26, (2003): 391–398.

Raynauld, André. 'The Quebec Economy: A General Assessment'. In *Quebec Society and Politics: Views from the Inside*, edited by Dale C. Thomson, 139–154. Toronto, ON: McClelland and Stewart Ltd., 1973.

Record, Jeffrey. *The Wrong War: Why We Lost in Vietnam*. Annapolis: Naval Institute Press, 1998.

Reilly, Wayne G. 'The Management of Political Violence in Quebec and Northern Ireland: A Comparison'. *Terrorism and Political Violence* 6, no. 1 (1994): 44–61.

Report of CONADEP (National Commission on the Disappearance of Persons). 'Nunca Más (Never Again)'. www.nuncamas.org/index2.htm.

'Report of the Commission to Consider Legal Procedures to Deal with Terrorist Activities in Northern Ireland (Diplock Report)'. London: Her Majesty's Stationery Office, 1972.

Report of the Royal Commission on Bilingualism and Biculturalism. Book One: The Official Languages. Ottawa: Queen's Printer, 1967.

Report of the Royal Commission on Bilingualism and Biculturalism. Book Three: The Work World. Ottawa: Queen's Press, 1967.

Richmond, Yale. *Cultural Exchange and the Cold War: Raising the Iron Curtain*. University Park: Pennsylvania State University Press, 2003.

Rock, David and Fernando Lopez-Alves. 'State-Building and Political Systems in Nineteenth-Century Argentina and Uruguay'. *Past and Present* no. 167 (2000): 176–202.

Rohter, Larry. 'Uruguay's Left Makes History by Winning Presidential Ballot'. *New York Times*, 1 November 2004, 11.

Rojahn, Christoph. 'Left-Wing Terrorism in Germany: The Aftermath of Ideological Violence'. *Conflict Studies* no. 313 (1998): 1–25.

Rosenau, William. 'Al Qaida Recruitment Trends in Kenya and Tanzania'. *Studies in Conflict and Terrorism* 28, no. 1 (2005): 1–10.

——. 'Waging the "War of Ideas"'. In *The McGraw-Hill Homeland Security Handbook*, edited by David Kamien, 1131–1148. New York: McGraw-Hill, 2006.

Rosendorff, B. Peter and Todd Sandler. 'Too Much of a Good Thing? The Proactive Response Dilemma'. *Journal of Conflict Resolution* 48, no. 5 (2004): 657–671.

Ross, Christopher. 'Public Diplomacy Comes of Age'. *The Washington Quarterly* 25, no. 2 (2002): 75–83.

Ross, Jeffrey Ian. 'The Rise and Fall of Quebecois Separatist Terrorism: A Qualitative Application of Factors from Two Models'. *Studies in Conflict and Terrorism* 18, (1995): 285–297.

——. 'Structural Causes of Oppositional Political Terrorism: Towards a Causal Model'. *Journal of Peace Research* 30, no. 3 (1993): 317–329.

Ross, Jeffrey Ian and Ted Robert Gurr. 'Why Terrorism Subsides: A Comparative Study of Canada and the United States'. *Comparative Politics* 21, no. 4 (1989): 405–426.

Ruane, Joseph and Jennifer Todd. *The Dynamics of Conflict in Northern Ireland: Power, Conflict, and Emancipation*. Cambridge: Cambridge University Press, 1996.

Rubin, Harriet. 'Terrorism, Trauma, and the Search for Redemption'. *Fast Company* no. 52 (2001): 158–168.

Rumsfeld, Donald H. 'Global War on Terrorism'. GlobalSecurity.org, www.globalsecurity.org/military/library/policy/dod/d20031016sdmemo.pdf.

——. 'Town Hall Meeting: Remarks as Delivered by Secretary of Defense Donald H. Rumsfeld, Soto Cano Air Base, Honduras'. www.defenselink.mil/speeches/2003/sp20030920-secdef2075.html.

Ryder, Chris. The RUC 1922–1997: *A Force under Fire*. Revised edn. London: Mandarin, 1997.

Sageman, Marc. *Understanding Terror Networks*. Philadelphia: University of Pennsylvania Press, 2004.

Sarma, Kiran. 'Informers and the Battle against Republican Terrorism: A Review of 30 Years of Conflict'. *Police Practice and Research* 6, no. 2 (2005): 165–180.

Saywell, John. *The Rise of the Parti Québécois 1967–1976*. Toronto and Buffalo: University of Toronto Press, 1977.

Schmidt, Anthony J. *Cellular Biology of Vertebrate Regeneration and Repair*. Chicago and London: The University of Chicago Press, 1968.

'Se Aprueba La Ley De Amnistia'. República Oriental del Uruguay, Poder Legislativo, www.parlamento.gub.uy/leyes/ley15737.htm.

Security Legislation Amendment (Terrorism) Act 2002. 5 July.

Seguin, Rheal. 'Parizeau Broadens Scope of Referendum Struggle'. *The Globe and Mail*, 27 September 1995, 4.

Seliger, Martin. *Ideology and Politics*. London: George Allen & Unwin, 1976.

SERPAJ. *Uruguay Nunca Más: Human Rights Violations, 1972–1985*. Translated by Elizabeth Hampsten. Philadelphia: Temple University Press, 1992.

Shafer, D. Michael. 'The Unlearned Lessons of Counterinsurgency'. *Political Science Quarterly* 103, no. 1 (1988): 57–80.

Shanker, Thom. 'Rumsfeld Sees Need to Realign Military Fight against Terror'. *New York Times*, 23 October 2003, 12.

Short, Anthony. *The Communist Insurrection in Malaya 1948–1960*. London: Frederick Muller, 1975.

Shultz, Richard. 'Breaking the Will of the Enemy During the Vietnam War: The Operationalization of the Cost-Benefit Model of Counterinsurgency Warfare'. *Journal of Peace Research* 15, no. 2 (1978): 109–129.

———. 'Coercive Force and Military Strategy: Deterrence Logic and the Cost–Benefit Model of Counterinsurgency Warfare'. *The Western Political Quarterly* 32, no. 4 (1979): 444–466.

Simard, Francis. *Talking It Out: The October Crisis from Inside*. Translated by David Homel. Toronto: Guernica, 1987.

Simpson, Christopher. *Science of Coercion: Communication Research and Psychological Warfare 1945–1960*. Oxford: Oxford University Press, 1994.

Singh, Gurharpal. 'India's Akali–BJP Alliance: The 1997 Legislative Assembly Elections'. *Asian Survey* 38, no. 4 (1998): 398–409.

———. 'Punjab since 1984: Disorder, Order, and Legitimacy'. *Asian Survey* 36, no. 4 (1996): 410–421.

———. 'Understanding the "Punjab Problem"'. *Asian Survey* 27, no. 12 (1987): 1268–1277.

Singh, Gurpreet. *Terrorism: Punjab's Recurring Nightmare*. New Dehli: Sehgal Book Distributors, 1996.

Sluka, Jeffrey A. *Hearts and Minds, Water and Fish: Support for the IRA and INLA in a Northern Ireland Ghetto*. Greenwich, CT: JAI Press, 1989.

Smith, Denis. *Bleeding Hearts ... Bleeding Country: Canada and the Quebec Crisis*. Edmonton: Hurtig, 1971.

Smith, M.L.R. *Fighting for Ireland? The Military Strategy of the Irish Republican Movement*. London and New York: Routledge, 1995.

———. 'Fin De Siecle, 1972: The Provisional IRA's Strategy and the Beginning of the Eight-Thousand-Day Stalemate'. In *Political Violence in Northern Ireland: Conflict and Conflict Resolution*, edited by Alan O'Day, 15–32. Westport: Praeger, 1997.

Snow, David A. and Robert D. Benford. 'Ideology, Frame Resonance, and Participant Mobilization'. In *International Social Movement Research: A Research Annual*, edited by Bert Klandermans, Hanspeter Kriesi and Sidney Tarrow, 197–217. Greenwich and London: JAI Press, 1988.

South Asia Terrorism Portal. 'Annual Casualties in Terrorist Related Violence'. www.satp.org/satporgtp/countries/india/states/punjab/data_sheets/annual_casualties.htm.

Spjut, R.J. 'Internment and Detention without Trial in Northern Ireland 1971–1975: Ministerial Policy and Practice'. *Modern Law Review* 49, (1986): 712–740.

Steinberg, James B. 'Counterterrorism: A New Organizing Principle for American National Security?' *The Brookings Review* 20, no. 3 (2002): 4–7.

Stern, Jessica. *Terror in the Name of God: Why Religious Militants Kill*. New York: HarperCollins, 2003.

Stewart, Walter. *Shrug: Trudeau in Power*. Toronto: New Press, 1971.

Strauss, Marcy. 'Torture'. *New York Law School Law Review* 48, no. 1 & 2 (2004): 201–274.

Stubbs, Richard. *Hearts and Minds in Guerrilla Warfare: The Malayan Emergency 1948–1960*. Singapore: Eastern Universities Press, 2004.

Sutton, Malcolm. 'An Index of Deaths from the Conflict in Ireland'. *Conflict Archive on the Internet (CAIN)*, www.cain.ulst.ac.uk/sutton/index.html.

Tarrow, Sidney. *Power in Movement: Social Movements, Collective Action and Politics*. Cambridge: Cambridge University Press, 1994.

Taylor, Peter. *Beating the Terrorists? Interrogation in Omagh, Gough and Castlereagh*. Harmondsworth: Penguin, 1980.

——. *Brits: The War against the IRA*. London: Bloomsbury, 2002.

——. *Provos: The IRA and Sinn Fein*. London: Bloomsbury, 1997.

Taylor, Phillip B. 'Government and Politics of Uruguay'. *Tulane Studies in Political Science* 7, (1960).

——. 'Interests and Institutional Dysfunction in Uruguay'. *The American Political Science Review* 57, no. 1 (1963): 62–74.

Thomas, Jo. 'The Agony of Ulster'. *New York Times*, 10 March 1985, 6.

Thompson, Robert. *Defeating Communist Insurgency: Experiences from Malaya and Vietnam*. London: Chatto & Windus, 1966.

Tilly, Charles. *From Mobilization to Revolution*. Reading: Addison-Wesley Publishing Company, 1978.

Torrance, Judy M. *Public Violence in Canada, 1867–1982*. Kingston and Montreal: McGill-Queen's University Press, 1986.

Townshend, Charles. *Easter 1916: The Irish Rebellion*. London: Penguin Books, 2006.

——. *Ireland: The 20th Century*. London, Sydney, Auckland: Arnold, 1998.

Travis, Alan. 'Anti-Terror Critics Just Don't Get It, Says Reid'. *Guardian*, 10 August 2006, 6.

Trinquier, Roger. *Modern Warfare: A French View of Counterinsurgency*. Translated by Daniel Lee. London and Dunmow: Pall Mall Press, 1964.

Trofimenkoff, Susan Mann. *The Dream of Nation: A Social and Intellectual History of Quebec*. Toronto: Gage Publishing Limited, 1983.

Tsoukala, Anastassia. 'Democracy in the Light of Security: British and French Political Discourses on Domestic Counter-Terrorism Policies'. *Political Studies* 54, no. 3 (2006): 607–627.

'The Tupamaros May Do It'. *The Economist*, 15 May 1971, 16.

'U.S. Ground Strategy and Force Deployments, 1965–1968; Section 3'. In *The Pentagon Papers: The Defense Department History of United States Decisionmaking on Vietnam*, 385–447. Boston: Beacon Press, 1971.

Ullman, Harlan K. and James P. Wade. *Shock and Awe: Achieving Rapid Dominance*. Washington, D.C.: National Defense Universty Press, 1996.

Vaillancourt, François. *Differences in Earnings by Language Groups in Quebec, 1970:*

An Economic Analysis. Quebec: International Center for Research on Bilingualism, 1980.

——. 'La Situation Démographique Et Socio-Économique Des Francophones De Québec: Une Revue'. *Canadian Public Policy – Analyse de politiques* 4, (1979): 542–552.

Vallières, Pierre. *Choose!* Translated by Penelope Williams. Toronto, ON: New Press, 1972.

——. *White Niggers of America: The Precocious Autobiography of a Quebec 'Terrorist'.* Translated by Joan Pinkham. New York and London: Monthly Review Press, 1971.

Van Evera, Stephen. 'Assessing U.S. Strategy in the War on Terror'. *The ANNALS of the American Academy of Political and Social Science* 607, no. 1 (2005): 10–26.

Varon, Jeremy. *Bringing the War Home: The Weather Underground, the Red Army Faction, and Revolutionary Violence in the Sixties and Seventies.* Berkeley, Los Angeles and London: University of California Press, 2003.

'Vázquez Should Win by a Whisker but Turnout Will Be Decisive'. *Latin American Brazil & Southern Cone Report*, 26 October 2004.

Vedder, R K. and L.E. Gallaway. 'Settlement Patterns of Canadian Emigrants to the United States, 1850–1960'. *The Canadian Journal of Economics* 3, no. 3 (1970): 476–486.

Walker, Clive. *The Prevention of Terrorism in British Law.* Manchester: Manchester University Press, 1986.

Wallace, Paul. 'Political Violence and Terrorism in India: The Crisis of Identity'. In *Terrorism in Context*, edited by Martha Crenshaw, 352–409. University Park: The Pennsylvania State University Press, 1995.

'War Measures Act'. www2.marianopolis.edu/quebechistory/docs/october/wm-act.htm.

Wardlaw, Grant. *Political Terrorism: Theory, Tactics and Counter-Measures.* Cambridge: Cambridge University Press, 1989.

Weil, Thomas E., Jan Kippers Black, Kenneth W. Martindale, David S. McMorris, Sally Engle Merry, and Frederick P. Munson. *Area Handbook for Uruguay.* Washington, D.C.: U.S. Government Printing Office, 1971.

Weinberg, Leonard, Ami Pedahzur, and Sivan Hirsch-Hoefler. 'The Challenges of Conceptualizing Terrorism'. *Terrorism and Political Violence* 16, no. 4 (2004): 777–794.

Weinstein, Martin. *Uruguay: Democracy at the Crossroads.* Boulder: Westview, 1988.

——. *Uruguay: The Politics of Failure.* Westport and London: Greenwood Press, 1975.

Weisman, Steven R. 'In Punjab, the Young Are Particularly Restless'. *New York Times*, 29 June 1986, 3.

Westmoreland, William C. *A Soldier Reports.* New York: Doubleday & Company, 1976.

Whitaker, Reg. 'Keeping up with the Neighbours? Canadian Responses to 9/11 in Historical and Comparative Context'. *Osgoode Hall Law Journal* 41, no. 2 & 3 (2003): 241–264.

White, Robert W. *Provisional Irish Republicans: An Oral and Interpretive History.* Westport and London: Greenwood Press, 1993.

Whyte, Nicholas. 'The Irish Election of 1918'. Northern Ireland Elections, www.ark.ac.uk/elections/h1918.htm.

Wickham-Crowley, Timothy P. *Guerrillas and Revolution in Latin America: A Comparative Study of Insurgents and Regimes since 1956.* Princeton: Princeton University Press, 1992.

Wolfendale, Jessica. 'Terrorism, Security, and the Threat of Counterterrorism'. *Studies in Conflict and Terrorism* 29, no. 7 (2006): 753–770.

Wood, Elisabeth Jean. *Insurgent Collective Action and Civil War in El Salvador*. Cambridge: Cambridge University Press, 2003.

World Bank Group. 'World Development Indicators'. www.devdata.worldbank.org/dataonline.

Wright, Joanne. *Terrorist Propaganda: The Red Army Faction and the Provisional IRA, 1968–86*. Basingstoke and London: Macmillan, 1991.

Index

For Product Safety Concerns and Information please contact our EU
representative GPSR@taylorandfrancis.com
Taylor & Francis Verlag GmbH, Kaufingerstraße 24, 80331 München, Germany

www.ingramcontent.com/pod-product-compliance
Lightning Source LLC
Chambersburg PA
CBHW050709280326
41926CB00088B/2902